Dwelling in Conflict

Dwelling in Conflict

Negev Landscapes and the Boundaries of Belonging

Emily McKee

Stanford University Press
Stanford, California

Stanford University Press
Stanford, California

Printed in the United States of America on acid-free, archival-quality paper

Library of Congress Cataloging-in-Publication Data

McKee, Emily (Ph. D.), author.
  Dwelling in conflict : land, belonging and exclusion in the Negev / Emily McKee.
    pages cm
  Includes bibliographical references and index.
    ISBN 978-0-8047-9760-3 (cloth : alk. paper) — ISBN 978-0-8047-9830-3 (pbk. : alk. paper) — ISBN 978-0-8047-9832-7 (electronic)
    1. Land tenure—Israel—Negev. 2. Land use, Rural—Israel—Negev. 3. Jews—Colonization—Israel—Negev. 4. Bedouins—Civil rights—Israel—Negev. 5. Social conflict—Israel—Negev. 6. Negev (Israel)—Ethnic relations. I. Title.
    HD850.Z8N446 2016
    333.3095694'9--dc23

Typeset by Bruce Lundquist in 10/14 Minion

Contents

Illustrations

Preface

SITTING ON A PATCH OF GRASS IN GIVAT RAM, JERUSALEM, IN 2007, I had a meeting that launched two years of fieldwork and initiated the network of social connections that I trace throughout this book. Ra'ed Al-Mickawi had just taken over directorship of a small environmental justice NGO called Bustan l'Shalom ("Orchard for Peace," usually shortened to "Bustan") three months earlier. We sat together that afternoon in the chilly December sun to discuss Bustan's work and my research. I was starting an ethnographic study comparing practices of environmental activism in Israel. I hoped to use environmentalism as an alternative lens for examining the attachments to land so commonly cited as the cornerstone of the region's Arab-Jewish conflict.

Bustan consisted of half a dozen Jewish and Bedouin Arab staff members and a network of occasional volunteers. They worked with residents of the Negev, the desert region in Israel's south, to promote socially and environmentally sustainable lifestyles, and they advocated outside the region for policy changes that would address the Negev's land conflict in socially and environmentally responsible ways. Ra'ed leaned forward and spoke with energy as he described the intertwined ecological and political goals of Bustan's projects in community gardening, sustainability classes, and installation of solar-powered medical equipment for ill children in Bedouin Arab villages without electricity. Realizing that my research interests fit well with Bustan's mission of environmental justice, Ra'ed invited me to join the group to conduct my research.

Five days later, I moved into Bustan's Green Center, an apartment in the city of Beersheba that served as the organization's headquarters, volunteer housing, and demonstration site for sustainable living. I arrived by bus late at night with two suitcases, and Anna, the Green Center coordinator, welcomed me and showed me my room. The next day, I began exploring my surroundings, meeting other Bustan staff members and volunteers, walking through Beersheba in search of the produce market, and learning my way around the Green Center's herb garden.

Two days after my arrival in Beersheba, I was cooking and cleaning with Leah, a volunteer living at the Green Center, when we got a phone call from Ra'ed. Tonight his friend, a filmmaker, had a public showing of his new film about Bedouins in an unrecognized village. Would we like to come along? We both readily agreed, dumped our half-eaten dinners into Tupperware containers, and went outside to meet Ra'ed in a taxi. On the other side of town, Ra'ed led us to the entrance of an old bomb shelter. A light glowed from inside, and posters on the door advertised the place in Hebrew, Arabic, and English as the "Multaka-Mifgash," home of a local nongovernmental organization called the Negev Coexistence Forum. We entered the shelter, climbing downstairs to find a large room with rows of plastic chairs and a projector. Through a doorway across the room, people mingled, drinking mint tea and crunching on wafer cookies while they waited for the movie to start.

Everyone soon took their seats, and we watched the story of a three-generation family unfold. The movie opened with text explaining that 76,000 Bedouin Israeli citizens live in forty-six villages not recognized by the state. Though most of these villages existed before the State of Israel was founded, a 1965 Israeli law declared them all to be illegal. In 2000, the text continued, the government offered residents of one village, Wadi al-Na'am, a deal to leave their village home and move to a government-planned town. The el-Masoudin family is deciding what to do. The text ended, and the movie unfolded to show us daily life in a rural home without electricity or hot water that lay just 14 kilometers away from us. We met a mother who wanted the educational opportunities promised in the planned town, a young son who wished for the running water and electricity there, and a grandfather who wanted to continue farming and playing with his grandson in the olive trees he planted decades ago.

Following the movie, the filmmaker and the council head of a different unrecognized village spoke and answered questions from the audience, a mixed group of Jewish and Bedouin Arab Israelis speaking in Hebrew. Most people asking questions were aware of the difficult living conditions in unrecognized villages and the land disputes that shape their unrecognized status. However, an intimate glimpse into the home life of a family in one of these villages and the chance for Jewish and Arab residents of this segregated region to speak candidly with each other were unusual. Residents took the opportunity to discuss how families were dealing with internal disagreements about relocating to government-planned towns, why many Jewish Israelis viewed Bedouins as lawbreakers and how Bedouins responded to the label, and how best to open constructive discussions among the wider Israeli public about the unrecognized villages.

The evening gave me a glimpse into the investigative value of crossing social boundaries and attending to everyday dwelling. The Negev was new to me that December, and it was through field visits with Bustan members, meetings with their partners, and visits to the homes of their volunteers that I began learning the social and ecological landscapes of this desert region. Within my first week in the Negev, I visited a middle school whose principal wanted to develop an eco-arts program with Bustan, attended the public film viewing, participated in a workshop at the Green Center in which a group of women from a Bedouin Arab town learned how to make herbal salves, sat in a meeting with one of Bustan's "Negev Unplugged" tour guides as he trained a new staff member to lead these environmental justice tours, traveled with Ra'ed to a farm near Jerusalem to discuss a possible collaboration in distributing heritage seeds, and joined Bustan's monthly staff meeting to plan projects. In the process, I met Bedouin Arab residents of both government-planned towns and "unrecognized" villages and Jewish residents of Beersheba and smaller towns. I spoke with Muslims and Jews and atheists, with illiterate and well-educated people. All these activities taught me about Bustan's approach to socioenvironmental activism.

Equally importantly, the activities introduced me to a variety of social milieus unusual outside of Arab-Jewish coexistence activism. The Negev is deeply divided not only along lines of Bedouin Arabs and Jews, but also along differences of religiosity, class, and political orientation. With Bustan, as I continued traveling for meetings and events and eventually took over coordination of an environmental education class, it became clear to me that I was crossing physical and sociopolitical boundaries that typically divide the Negev into a segregated landscape. Divisions consisted of physical barriers, like walls and highways; practices, like the use of different languages, and changes in bodily comportment; and policies that directed government funds toward some groups more than others and eased legalization of land use for some while restricting it for others.

Boundary crossing became central to my fieldwork approach, since it allowed me to investigate divisions more dynamically. My research shifted from being about environmental*ism* to being a study of land relations more broadly, with environmentalism as one aspect. After spending six months with Bustan, I made plans to continue research while living in two of the region's most segregated spaces, a government-planned Bedouin township and a Jewish *moshav* (farming village). By both embedding myself in segregated parts of the Negev and moving between these places, I could see more clearly how landscapes were being divided and claimed.

This book works backwards, in a sense. I dove into research first with a group focused on challenging boundaries, and only later did I turn my attention to how these boundaries are hardened. This book, however, begins by identifying the boundary lines that define and fortify land conflict in the Negev through land-use planning, history telling, and law making. It explains how these demarcations rest on a set of nested oppositions between Jew and Arab, culture and nature, and progress and tradition. Then the book uses case studies to explore how Negev residents dwell within, and sometimes challenge, these supposedly strict oppositions. Though I return to the story of Bustan only in the final chapter, it is significant that this small NGO at the margins of Israel's sociopolitical spectrum was my entry point to the Negev. A view from the edges helped me see boundary lines more clearly—both the omnipresence of contemporary segregation and the possibility of softening those lines.

Acknowledgments

MANY PEOPLE HAVE HELPED ME CREATE THIS BOOK, and I am deeply grateful to them all. First and foremost, I thank the residents of the Negev who welcomed me and taught me about their homes and their lives. My gratitude goes to the staff and volunteers at Bustan who first welcomed me to the Negev, enthusiastically working with me as colleagues, roommates, friends, and research participants. I appreciate the honesty and warm welcome that many residents in "'Ayn al-'Azm" and "Dganim" shared with me, particularly the four families who made their homes my home and the staff and attendees at Moadon ha-Kashishim. Residents and environmental and social activists in the many other Negev locales I visited were also generous participants in this research. From hot meals and many cups of tea to captivating stories and insightful commentary, they made this research possible. Beyond the confines of this study, they have taught me lasting lessons through their hospitality and graciousness, even when living through trying times.

I would also like to thank colleagues in Israel who shared their knowledge, time, and address books, and sometimes even their homes, including Fran Markowitz, Shlomi Arnon, Dan Rabinowitz, Kassem Alshafiee, Yaakov Garb, David Epstein, Laithi Gnaim, Jeremy Benstein, Nadim Kassem, Aref Abu-Rabia, Alon Tal, and Erez Tzfadia. The staff at the David Tuviyahu Archives of the Negev facilitated my archival work there. For the financial support that made this research possible, I am grateful to the Woodrow Wilson Foundation, the National Science Foundation, the United States-Israel Educational Foundation, and the Institute of International Education. The Anthropology Department, the Rackham Graduate School, the Frankel Center, and the International Institute at the University of Michigan each also provided funding for fieldwork and analysis.

At the University of Michigan I gained intellectual tools and camaraderie that propelled this research, due both to the inspiring work of my mentors and colleagues in the Anthropology Department and to the strong interdisciplinary ties and challenging conversations in which I was fortunate to participate across the university. For their keen guidance and Middle East scholarship that has informed my thinking in important ways, I am grateful to Marcia Inhorn, Andrew Shryock, and Ruth Tsoffar. I was particularly fortunate to find in Stuart Kirsch a scholar whose analytical rigor and ethical stances are both worthy of emulation. His wise and enthusiastic counsel profoundly influenced my research design and early analysis. I continue striving to live up to all of their standards. I would also like to thank the members of an extended writing workshop, Jessica Robbins, Kelly Fayard, Henrike Florusbosch, Anna Genina, Sumi Cho, Erin Mahaffey, Xochitl Ruiz, and Anneeth Hundle. Gillian Feeley-Harnik, who led the workshop, invested great care and insight into comments on rough and tentative chapter drafts. Before I ever reached Michigan, it was Deborah Gewertz and Marybeth MacPhee who fostered my early inklings of anthropological interest at Amherst College, and I am grateful to them, as well.

Several other institutions have helped to make this book possible by providing financial backing and placing me in vibrant academic communities that have fueled the writing process. Yale University's Council on Middle East Studies and Brandeis University's Schusterman Center for Israel Studies, colleagues from each of these area studies centers, and the anthropology departments at both universities created welcoming and intellectually stimulating environments. I especially appreciate Marcia Inhorn's and Ilan Troen's support during these appointments. In my new institutional home at Northern Illinois University, I have found a dynamic Anthropology Department and interdisciplinary Institute for the Study of the Environment, Sustainability, and Energy. My thanks go to colleagues and students at NIU for thought-provoking conversations connecting this research with broader issues in anthropology and environmental studies.

Many keen eyes and critical minds have examined early chapter drafts and the conference papers that fed into this book. Throughout years of intrepid support, and now reaching across three time zones, Mikaela Rogozen-Soltar and Kathryn Graber have been my pillars in writing. As both scholars and friends, they have been a source of discerning critique and unfailing encouragement, and I look forward to many more years of our academic cooperative. Through chapter exchanges and conference chats, I have also benefited greatly from my intellectual conversations with Karen Rignall and Michael Hathaway. I am grateful to the participants and discussants at conferences where I tested out some of the ideas that made their way into this book, particularly Peter Brosius, Tracey Heatherington, Mandana Limbert, Tad Mutersbaugh, and Alison Alkon. More recently, I have benefited from the perceptive interdisciplinary perspectives of Mark Schuller, Laura Heideman, and Andy Bruno. Suggestions from two anonymous reviewers found by Stanford University Press (SUP) greatly strengthened the manuscript, as well. I am thankful to Steve Charlton for his cartographic skills, and to Tom Pingel for his guidance in the map making. Kate Wahl, at SUP, has been generous with her editorial advice and always responsive to my inquiries.

Finally, this work has always lived with me at home. For more than five years now, Tim Horsley has been the most supportive partner for whom I could have hoped. Weathering the highs and lows of this writing process, he has been a constant source of reinforcement, both intellectually and emotionally. My parents, Ray and Brenda, have always fed my curiosity, even when it has taken me far away on international explorations. Their confidence in me, as well as the love and encouragement of Sean, Lori, and Emma, have been great sources of strength.

A Note on Language

FIELDWORK FOR THIS STUDY was conducted in Hebrew, Arabic, and English. Hebrew or Arabic terminology is generally transcribed using characters easily understandable to English readers, rather than using extensive diacritics. The letters *ayin, chet,* and *qaf,* for example, are approximated to the English characters *'a, kh,* and *q,* respectively. When referring to Bedouin colloquial Arabic terms, I transliterate the colloquial, rather than the Modern Standard Arabic pronunciation. Unless otherwise noted, all translations in the text are my own.

Choosing conventions for labeling people and places in a context of sociopolitical conflict is notoriously sensitive. An array of labels exists to identify approximately the same group of people: "Bedouins," "Bedouin Arabs," "Israel's Arab citizens," and "Bedouin Palestinians," to name a few. Group belonging and the proper terms for demarcating insiders from outsiders are key elements of contestation in the conflicts I study. Do Negev Arab residents have more meaningful connections with Jewish Israelis or with Palestinians of the West Bank and Gaza? Are Bedouins a distinct cultural group, or is this label an artifact the Israeli government uses to weaken Arab unity? Because these are not idle academic questions of definition, I choose my terminology carefully. "Bedouin Arab" encompasses the multiple senses of belonging most commonly expressed by the Negev residents with whom I spoke, so I prefer this term. However, when referring to others' perspectives in the text, I use their terminology. The label "Jewish Israelis" distinguishes other residents of my research site from the global ethnoreligious group of "Jews." Though this label is less contested, there are those who find it restrictive, for instance those self-identifying as "Arab Jews," who call for recognition of a common Arab identity that is not negated by Jewishness. Social identity labels are ethnographically useful because they convey common understandings about group boundaries in Israel. Unfortunately, the labeling also risks reifying these group boundaries and sidelining alternative notions of identity and relatedness.

Place naming is also fraught with historical and contemporary power relations. When discussing a place within the narrative of a particular group, I use the name commonly attributed by that group, such as "Naqab" among Arabic speakers and "Negev" among Hebrew speakers. Otherwise, I use common English names (in this case, "Negev"), where these are available.

To guard my research participants' anonymity, personal names in the text are pseudonyms, as are names of the two small communities that feature prominently in this book: 'Ayn al-'Azm for the Bedouin township and Dganim for the Jewish *moshav*. Community pseudonyms are not always sufficient to protect residents from unwanted scrutiny, though (Scheper-Hughes 2000). Thus, while I include enough detail about these places and their residents to accurately explore the socioenvironmental dynamics shaping land relations and views of land conflict, I sometimes alter identifying information to safeguard the privacy of those who taught and talked with me. Two exceptions to the use of pseudonyms include public figures (for example, governmental officials and NGO representatives) and the names of Bedouin unrecognized villages. Bustan's leaders requested that the organization's real name be used. When referring to members' activities in public contexts, I use real names, while for private conversations I use pseudonyms. When writing of unrecognized villages that are pursuing recognition from the Israeli government and public, I do not wish to repeat the social erasure against which they struggle.

Finally, the text distinguishes between verbatim and reconstructed statements. Any text set in quotation marks represents a verbatim transcript of a statement. When reported speech is based on field notes rather than a full transcript, it is not placed in quotation marks.

Abbreviations

AJEEC	Arab-Jewish Center for Equality, Empowerment and Cooperation
Bimkom	BIMKOM—Planners for Planning Rights
Bustan	Bustan l'Shalom/Bustan al-Salaam
IDF	Israel Defense Forces
ILA	Israel Land Administration
JA	Jewish Agency
JNF	Jewish National Fund (Keren Kayemet l'Yisrael; KKL)
NDA	Negev Development Authority
RCUV	Regional Council of Unrecognized Villages (in the Negev)
SPNI	Society for the Protection of Nature in Israel

Dwelling in Conflict

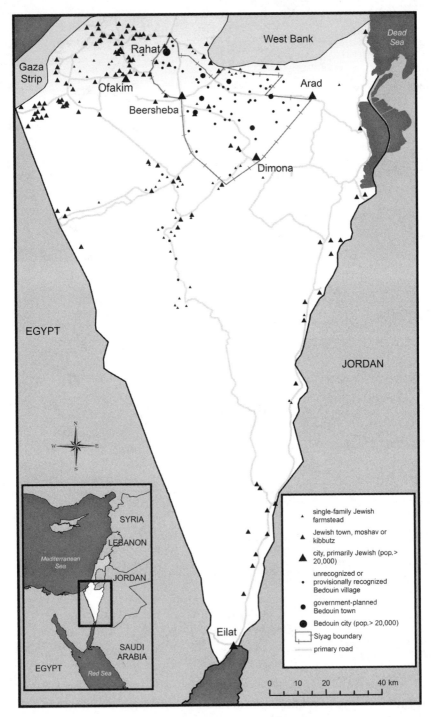

The Negev/Naqab is the desert region (area shown in white) that comprises the entire south of Israel. No precise demarcation exists, but shading at the map's top shows the approximate northern border of the region, as defined by average annual precipitation (less than 300mm in the white area). It is bordered to the west by Egypt's Sinai Peninsula and to the east by the Arabah/Arava Valley and the border with Jordan.

Introduction

THE PROBLEM OF LAND CONFLICT IN THE NAQAB is bigger than in the West Bank, Sliman told me. We stood together one spring day in 2009 on a rooftop looking north across the hills of the northern Naqab/Negev, the arid southern half of Israel.[1] The West Bank Separation Barrier, a complex of concrete wall, barbed wire, and patrol roads, was on the horizon. Soon, Sliman continued, the Palestinian Authority will take real governmental control throughout the West Bank, and there will not be a problem of land conflict there. But here, he said, directing my gaze to the land below us and to the south, he saw no hope for resolution. There are Bedouin in almost every place, he said, but these lands are also "designated as something else" now.

Sliman's pronouncement about the West Bank may have been unrealistically optimistic. But his pessimistic view of the Naqab compared with the West Bank, widely known for its virulent conflict, conveys the pernicious tensions he sensed in Naqab land relations. And this Naqab–West Bank pronouncement was not naïvely made. The building we looked from was part of Kibbutz Lahav, a community for Jewish Israelis, but Sliman knew these lands as al-Huwaylga, home to his Bedouin tribe before 1948. His family was displaced, and he returned to this place only as a worker. Sliman had Israeli citizenship, but many extended family members, who fled in 1948 across what became the armistice line between Israel and the West Bank, or "the Green Line," did not. Sliman identified himself as a Bedouin, and also felt ties, like many Naqab Bedouins, to a wider Palestinian community. He frequently crossed back and forth over the Green Line and worked as a guide in the Bedouin cultural museum in Kibbutz Lahav. He knew the region well and was voicing concerns I heard during many other conversations since first arriving in the Negev two years earlier.

Sliman and I were overlooking just a portion of the Negev's disputed lands that day. The areas where we saw clusters of Bedouin Arabs' homes were designated in Israeli state records as national forest lands, sites for building Jewish communities, or agricultural zones. Similarly overlapping landscapes spread across much of the northern Negev. State officials declare these Bedouin hamlets and villages to be illegal settlements on state-owned lands and order residents—between 65,000 and 100,000 by widely varying estimates—to move to one of several government-planned townships.[2] However, Bedouin Arab residents, who are also Israeli citizens, complain of poor conditions in the townships and view these state declarations of ownership as illegitimate because they ignore families' historical residence in villages, many of which predate the establishment of Israel. An impasse festers, forming layers of resentment and sometimes erupting into violence. Some Bedouin residents continue to inhabit and expand the villages labeled as "illegal," and government demolition crews continue to destroy houses and crops in these villages.

This impasse has life-changing consequences for all the Negev's residents, with reverberating economic and emotional effects well beyond the region. Land tied up in legal disputes cannot be protected or developed with long-term plans. This uncertain status makes ecological sustainability difficult to achieve (Orenstein, Tal, and Miller 2013). Economic opportunities in the Negev lag behind other areas of Israel. Unemployment rates are higher for the Negev's residents than Israel's national average, and Bedouin Arabs' jobless rates are typically two to three times the rates of Jews in the region (Swirski and Hasson 2006). Many Jewish residents and municipalities complain of their inability to implement urban development plans because Bedouins live "illegally" in areas designated for expansion (Yahel 2006). Meanwhile, the families living on these disputed lands face house demolitions and the denial of social services available to other Israeli citizens.[3] Because they do not exist on official maps and development plans, Bedouin Arab communities often find waste sites, highways, and military facilities built nearby or within their midst. Their unofficial status, on the other hand, means that power grids, running water, and bomb shelters are not provided by the state (Amara, Abu-Saad, and Yiftachel 2013).[4] Such disparities fuel the frustration and alienation of a generation of Palestinian citizens throughout Israel (Rabinowitz and Abu Baker 2005), and events in the Negev now feature in the grievances and publicity materials of human and civil rights groups working throughout the region, on both sides of the Green Line.[5]

Amid the cacophony of opinions circulating about Negev land conflict, no single perspective exists among Bedouin residents. Some seek greater integration within Israeli society, while others push for distinctive cultural rights and more autonomy. Some live in unrecognized villages and demand full recognition of land tenure rights, while others seek better government-planned townships. Bedouin Arabs may express fond affinity for Israeli society, as did one former farmer in his sixties who told me about being homesick when he heard Hebrew while traveling in Turkey. Similarly, there is no single Jewish Israeli perspective. Some Jewish Israelis value Bedouin Arabs' connection to Negev lands, support their claims to land rights, and even dedicate themselves to full-time nonprofit work toward this goal; while others criticize these individuals as traitors to the Jewish people. Further, Jews of some ethnic backgrounds have experienced discrimination at the hands of other Jews.

Despite this heterogeneity and these crosscutting affiliations, land disputes in the Negev are most commonly spoken of—in media coverage, personal accounts, and scholarship—as a standoff between well-defined and naturally distinct groups of Bedouin Arabs and Jews. Many Jewish Israelis express anxiety about the loyalties of Bedouin Arabs, wondering whether ties of religion, ethnicity, or nationality across state borders will override their shared Israeli citizenship. Bedouin Arabs are well aware of these suspicions and struggle to negotiate ambivalent affiliations with Israeli society and Palestinian or pan-Arab identities. Like other Palestinian citizens of Israel, they are not fully incorporated members of the nation-state because of its definition as Jewish (Rabinowitz and Abu Baker 2005). Worries periodically circulate in public discussions and newspaper articles about a looming "Bedouin Intifada" driven by mounting frustration over structural violence and second-class citizenship status (Barzilai 2004; Kabha 2007). *Intifada*, meaning "awakening" or "popular uprising" in Arabic, more commonly refers to uprisings in the Occupied Palestinian Territories during 1987–1993 (First Intifada) and 2000–2005 (Second Intifada), and applying this word to Bedouin citizens highlights anxieties about their loyalty to Israel.

During my research, I asked many people, both Jewish and Bedouin Arab, how this problem should be solved. It's not possible, many replied. In another ten years, a resident named Sarah, of a Bedouin township, told me as we sat together in the shade of her courtyard, "there will be more people with less land. . . . The same situation, but worse." Similarly, Ofra, a resident of a Jewish village, stated as we sat in her living room, "It's a very complicated problem, more like hatred. . . . And it's only getting worse." As they spoke of hatred and land competition, Sarah and Ofra sat in two of the segregated communities that result from and feed into this conflict. Four years later, a government plan to settle claims and relocate residents raised debate and street demonstrations as a government initiative called the Prawer Plan was debated and subsequently tabled. The uneasy détente remains.

To understand how this segregation has become so pervasive in the Negev's socioenvironmental landscapes and how land conflict has come to seem so inevitable, this book addresses three central questions. What kinds of attachment to land are people fighting over? How are particular lines of opposition entrenched as "natural," such that conflict is taken for granted? Do avenues of conflict resolution being explored move beyond these naturalized oppositions?

These land struggles in the Negev have developed within the larger context of Palestinian-Israeli battles over sovereignty and security, as well as the shifting political sensibilities and personal identities that make Israel a deeply and multiply divided society (Ben-Porat and Turner 2011; Rabinowitz and Abu Baker 2005). Conflicts over "the Land" of Palestine-Israel are often expressed in historical and political terms, and a large body of scholarship provides intricate analysis in these terms. A brief historical summary, below, demonstrates how the leadership strategies, economic demands, and ethnic tensions buffeting the region over the past 120 years are directly relevant to contemporary land struggles. The book then builds on this history by examining environmental factors at the heart of this conflict. Through detailed analysis of the Negev case, I offer a political dwelling perspective as an alternative lens for viewing land conflict.

Creating a Conflict

Scholarship on the history of the Zionist movement and Israeli state-building before the 1980s was largely celebratory, avoiding criticism of Zionist leaders or military bodies, and neglecting violence and discrimination directed against Arabs. However, critical scholars of more recent decades, such as Avi Shlaim (2000) and Benny Morris (1999), have pointed out these limitations and developed lively debates about the causes and course of nationalist struggle between Israelis, Palestinians, and a wider Arab populace.[6] These accounts often begin in nineteenth-century Europe, where, amid a number of movements advocating different approaches to alleviating the anti-Semitism and exclusion of Jews from civil and political society, Zionists gathered around a shared belief in the need for a Jewish state. Though the World Zionist Organization (WZO), founded in 1897, initially considered several possible locations, including Cyprus, Argentina, Uganda, and other parts of the Ottoman Empire, by 1905 the leadership had ruled out these other possibilities, for both practical and ideological reasons (Laqueur 1989). Thereafter, the WZO focused its efforts on building the small-scale Jewish settlements already underway in Palestine into a strong *yishuv* ("settlement," or Jewish society) that could lead to a Jewish state.[7]

Whether analyzing the unique ideological origins of Zionism or engaging a more materialist approach that views Zionism as a case of settler colonialism best understood through comparison with other cases, scholars explaining the origins of Arab-Israeli conflict often focus on the First Aliya and Second Aliya. Historians typically distinguish several waves of *aliya*, or Jewish immigration (literally meaning "ascent"), to Eretz Israel between 1882 and 1948.[8] These waves trace international events, such as the shift from Ottoman to British Mandate rule over Palestine (1923–1948), and changing ideologies and economic organizations of immigrant groups (Tessler 1994). Though early settlers initiated plantations of grapevines and orchards with aid from wealthy Jewish philanthropists, the rising influence of a faction known as Labor Zionists marked the Second Aliya. Labor Zionists, a political subset of the Zionist movement who called for self-sufficiency through labor in the land, established the agricultural settlements, *kibbutzim* and *moshavim*, which became emblematic of Zionism. *Kibbutzim* were founded beginning in the early 1900s, and *moshavim* from the 1920s. Both types of settlement were co-operative but to different degrees, as *kibbutz* members pooled resources and labor in fields and homes, and *moshav* members pledged financial support to each other, but also established and managed fields and homes individually.[9] As exclusively Jewish communities, both types of settlement contributed to the segregation of Jews and Arabs, which was a cornerstone of the Zionist movement (Piterberg 2008).

Zionism was not a singular effort but rather a diverse movement that included wealthy land purchasers and unskilled laborers, groups aiming for politically negotiated sovereignty and those seeking immediate safe havens for Eastern European Jews being persecuted in pogroms.[10] However, these groups held a common goal of territorial gain (Shafir 1996). The Holocaust in Europe fueled the urgency of this territorialism, as it seemed to prove the need for a Jewish state as a safe haven (Zertal 2005). As Jewish immigration increased, as Jewish individuals and organizations bought more lands, and as the territorial and sovereignty goals of the movement became clearer, Palestinian resistance to the movement grew. Arab leaders reacted with more violence, and Zionist leaders rallied around a security focus, deprioritizing cordial relations (Caplan 1978). Particularly influential in building this security concern were events like the attacks against Jews in Jaffa in 1921 and the more widespread violence of the 1936–39 Arab revolts.

During the late 1800s and early 1900s, Zionist groups initially settled most intensively along the coasts of Palestine and in the Jezreel Valley (Kimmerling 1983). In the arid, less fertile Negev, little Jewish settlement occurred before the 1940s. This began to change when in 1939 Zionist leader David Ben-Gurion called in earnest for Negev settlement. Several observation outposts and agricultural research stations led the way for a handful of settlements by 1946. Then in 1947, as part of a bid to include this large and strategic area in a future Jewish state that was being debated in the United Nations (UN), several Zionist organizations cooperatively undertook a tower and stockade campaign to rapidly establish small, fortress-like outposts in carefully selected, dispersed Negev sites (Kellerman 1993, 1996).

In 1947, Zionist expansion and Palestinian (now also wider Arab) resistance came to a head. After the United Nations voted to partition Palestine and Arab leaders rejected this partition, Great Britain withdrew its Mandate government, and the war that later became known by most Jews as Milkhemet ha-Atzmaut, the "War of Independence," and by most Arabs as al-Nakba, the "Catastrophe," broke out.[11] Fighters on both sides killed Jewish and Arab combatants and civilians, and in the end Zionists gained the most, while Palestinians suffered the greatest losses. The war drove hundreds of thousands of Palestinians permanently away from their homes and gutted Palestinian communities of their educated and wealthy residents (as these groups were most able to flee during fighting).[12] The war led in 1948 to the declaration of Israeli statehood and the formation of a government, and it gained considerably more territory for Israel than would have been assigned under the UN Partition Plan.[13] Those Palestinians remaining within the new state's territory (about 150,000) were granted Israeli citizenship (Tessler 1994).

Following the war, Ben-Gurion, who had become Israel's first prime minister, championed the Negev as the country's prime frontier for development. The region made up approximately 60 percent of Israel's territory at the time of statehood and contained 2 percent of its population (Lithwick, Gradus, and Lithwick 1996), making it a vast area of potential for absorbing Jewish immigrants. The Negev was also a critical buffer zone between the Arab states of Egypt and Jordan. Without protecting their military conquest of the region by settling Jews there, Ben-Gurion maintained, Tel Aviv and the more densely settled narrow coastal strip would be merely a vulnerable city-state (Kellerman 1993).

Initially, Zionists' "conquest" of the Negev, like other European colonial projects, involved extensive projects of infrastructure building and landscape transformation (Lines 1991; Scott 1998). Labor Zionism dominated politics in Israel's early years, and because these leaders strove to modernize the desert with large-scale agriculture, water provision was critical. Ben-Gurion's government began work in 1953 on the National Water Carrier to pump water out of Lake Kinneret in the north and carry hundreds of millions of cubic meters to the arid southern region (Tal 2002). The project entailed great costs. It required significant investment from a young and cash-strapped state; its implementation escalated border disputes with neighboring countries, which threatened war; and the long-term ecological impacts of rerouted streams, depleted aquifers, and a shrinking Dead Sea are still being realized (Orenstein, Tal, and Miller 2013; Tal 2002).[14] Yet bringing water to the desert was worth these costs for the Labor Zionist government because it enabled agriculture and Jewish settlement throughout the country. Twenty-six new *moshavim* and eight development towns were established in the region during the 1950s.

In addition to building infrastructure, Israel's new government used legislative and policy tools to "Judaize" various frontier regions, settling more Jews there and curbing Palestinian populations (Rabinowitz 1997). The Negev was a particular frontier of focus during the state's first decade. Bedouin tribes had been practicing extensive farming and seminomadic pastoralism, primarily raising fat-tailed sheep and goats, rather than intensively farming or building large, permanent communities (Hillel 1982; Abu-Rabia 1994). In the 1950s, the Israeli government designated a restricted area known as the *siyag* ("fence"), which covered about 10 percent of the lands formerly inhabited by the Bedouin tribes (Marx 1967:14), and compelled Bedouins in the Negev, who were also Israeli citizens, to move into this area. Until 1966, the *siyag* existed under military administration, and Bedouin residents needed permission to move about within the restricted area, as well as for any trips outside (Meir 1998; Abu-Saad 2005). In addition, the Israeli High Court ruled in the 1950s that most areas of the Negev were *mawat* ("dead") lands because they had not been "improved" according to specific agricultural criteria (Kedar 2001). The government claimed these as state lands and then, with the 1965 Planning and Building Law, outlawed Bedouin residence on them by establishing a scheme for zoning lands (as agricultural, residential, and so on) and declaring all building outside of this scheme as illegal (Abu Hussein and McKay 2003).

As Jewish-Arab tensions mounted, an additional social cleavage grew in Israel. Ashkenazi Jews (those with European ancestry) had led early Zionist settlement efforts, and their cultural expectations had set the norms of progress and civility among Jews. Jews from the Middle East and North Africa, once called Oriental Jews and now Mizrahim, were pushed to assimilate to Ashkenazi norms when they began immigrating to Israel in large numbers in the 1950s. Government officials, social workers, and teachers in the Zionist movement treated Mizrahi immigrants as dirty, disordered, and in need of training to become "modern" members of Israeli society. Fearing an "engulfment by the East" that would threaten the separation of Jewish and Arab societies, Zionist leaders invited Mizrahi Jews into Israeli society on the condition that they excise any signs of Arabness from their language, dress, religious rituals, and so on (Shohat 1999:8). They also directed large numbers of these newcomers to Israel's frontier regions, exacerbating tensions over land and ethnic identity. This included the Negev, where government planners aimed for a tenfold increase in the Jewish population through immigration (Tzfadia 2000).

After the 1950s, Israel's frontier of focus shifted again, and the Negev slowly fell into neglect. It became a remote periphery, due in part to geopolitical changes. During the mid-1960s, Prime Minister Levi Eshkol championed the Galilee, in the north, as Israel's most crucial frontier and redirected governmental resources accordingly (Kellerman 1993). When Israel occupied Gaza, the West Bank, and the Sinai Peninsula during the 1967 War, these territories became the most critical frontiers. Though investment in new Jewish communities in the Negev slackened during this period, efforts to protect "state lands" from settlement by Arabs continued. The government constructed townships for Bedouin Arabs from 1969 onward and combined threats and incentives to remove Bedouin Arabs from their more dispersed patches of land and concentrate them in urban settlements (Dinero 2010; Yiftachel and Meir 1998).

The Negev's peripheral status deepened in the 1980s–1990s when the national trends of economic liberalization and the concomitant reordering of national priorities reduced government funding for remote settlements. Low socioeconomic indicators and high unemployment figures further indicate the region's peripheral status (Kellerman 1993; Teschner, Garb, and Tal 2010). Successive national governments proposed ambitious development plans to raise living standards, increase Jewish residence in the region, protect larger areas from Arab settlement, and more recently, ameliorate pollution problems.[15] But there has been little implementation of recent development plans (Teschner 2007). The few governmental initiatives aimed at the south in recent decades, such as quarries, waste facilities, and military bases, have tended to respond to and perpetuate the Negev's image as a wasteland and wild space.[16] As a result, Israelis refer to the contemporary Negev as a periphery, and residents often complain of disregard from politicians and fellow Israelis living in "the center" (the Tel Aviv and Jerusalem areas).

Living in Landscapes of Conflict

This book builds on this commonly told history in two key ways that attend to the political charge of everyday interactions with Negev environments and the ways that basic understandings of people and "their" landscapes drive political developments. First, while Arab-Jewish Israeli conflict consists of settler colonialism and increasingly ethnic nationalist conflict, as many scholars note, it is also an environmental conflict. In a basic sense, this is a conflict over land—the ability to use it and the authority to govern it. As in other colonial contexts, this land conflict has been fueled by divergent "environmental imaginaries" (Davis and Burke 2011), which are visions of the ideal relationships between people and a given landscape.

"Desert" has long been a symbol of desolation, emptiness, and exile for the Zionist movement (Zerubavel 2008). For decades, Zionism's advocates have justified their efforts as the greening of desert wastelands and contrasted the progress of Western agriculture with backward Arab lifestyles. As the region most different from Zionism's ideal agrarian landscape, and as Israel's most sparsely populated expanse of land, the Negev was initially a challenging and tempting frontier. It embodied both threat and promise. Early immigrants and Zionist leaders alike described the Negev as "an empty and gloomy desert" (Zerubavel 2008:35), "lifeless, dying earth" (Sened and Sened 2009:16), and "an enemy" to be defeated (Zerubavel 2008:38). It was a forsaken swath of sand and rocks that needed to be turned into productive farmland to support the Jewish nation. In contrast, from the perspective of Bedouin Arabs living there at the time, the Negev consisted of tribally claimed territories with grazing lands and seasonal agriculture, which was still remote enough from urban seats of power to allow for free movement and self-governance. Contrasting environmental imaginaries are also evident in competing notions of land ownership: flexible, tribally organized land control conducive to seminomadic herding clashes with European notions of land ownership through labor investment and written documentation that facilitate intensive agriculture (Shamir 1996). Investments by the Zionist movement, and later the Israeli state, in settlement construction, agricultural training, and farming infrastructure have attempted to create a productive, agricultural landscape that meets their environmental ideals. Meanwhile, some Bedouin Arabs have complied with government programs shifting them away from agropastoralism and toward wage labor, while others have resisted restrictions and continued farming, herding, and living in dispersed settlements.

Particular environmental discourses have driven these contrasting environmental imaginaries and practices, thus building and entrenching the Negev's current conflicts. The term "environmental discourse" draws on a broad notion of environment and a practice-oriented definition of discourse. As political ecology scholars point out, "environment" need not connote simply rurality and wilderness or focus solely on conserving particular ecological relationships (Biersack and Greenberg 2006). My use of the term includes landscapes and ecosystems, whether urban neighborhoods or desert plateaus, and it is not prescriptive. A discourse is environmental, in my usage, if it makes claims about relationships between inhabitants and their landscapes, whether it lauds the progress of skyscrapers and concrete or prefers forest restoration.[17] And environmental discourses are not fixed ideas or phrases. They are both the products and the tools of power (Foucault 1990). I enlist Foucault's notion of discourse, which attends to a range of discussions, bodily practices, and institutional norms, in order to foreground the individual and institutional actions that are immanent to discourses (Foucault 1977). Environmental discourses express notions about human nature, what a "natural" landscape is, and the relationship humans ought to have with these landscapes.

Environmental discourses are so effective for staking claims because, even though they are constructed by groups of people in historical contexts, they draw on the symbolism of nature (Williams 1985) and seem to be part of an essential reality. It is precisely those discourses least in need of explanation for residents that hold the most power to shape society (Li 2005). In Israel, several dominant discourses—about social belonging by rooting in the land; the moral and economic value accorded to agriculture, and the concomitant understanding of desert as wasteland; and a purportedly natural Jewish-Arab opposition—both shape and naturalize Negev land conflict.[18] This focus on environmental discourses highlights important overlaps between clashes over geographical boundaries and group boundaries. Environmental discourses in the region draw boundaries around and naturalize opposing groups of Jews and Arabs, establish land relations as a competitive clash between these groups, favor certain land-use practices and aesthetics over others, and privilege a circumscribed notion of property rights over other types of land claims, such as historic occupancy. This is not to say that the whole conflict would be better understood as environmental, but rather that environmental discourses have been key tools used by people on all sides of the conflict to naturalize it along binary lines of opposition.

Second, this book contributes a more embodied dwelling perspective to politically oriented accounts of land and resource conflict. My encounter with Sliman that day in 2009 provided one of countless demonstrations offered by Negev residents of the deeply emotional and enduring attachments they hold to contested landscapes. Before we looked out from the rooftop to view the divided Negev from above, Sliman had led me down a walking path amid tall pines. He wanted to show me the water well his grandfather had made. He explained how his extended family was scattered in Israel, the West Bank, and Jordan by the war in 1948. One great-aunt who had lived in Jordan since 1948 had recently returned to visit with Sliman. She was amazed at how the place had changed. Pine forests had been planted and the *kibbutz* houses, factory, and museum had been built. Yet amid these changes, she walked around pointing out a house that was here, and here. And your grandfather's well was here, too, she had recalled, standing just where Sliman and I paused along the path. Sliman described how they searched for the well that day in vain. Weeks later, Sliman noticed a piece of wood along this same path, overgrown with brush. Lifting the wood as he spoke to me, he revealed the cap of a narrow well. After more than fifty years, she remembered just where the well had been, Sliman concluded quietly. He said no more but silently led me back up the path, leaving me to interpret the meaning of this long-held memory. This elderly woman had invested herself in remembering this social landscape for decades and staked her identity to its former configuration. For Sliman, this *kibbutz* landscape is now infused with his great-aunt's powerful recollection.

Such everyday acts of memorialization in place demonstrate how the drawing and policing of group boundaries and the staking of land claims happen not just through the maneuverings of political leaders and governmental bureaucrats, but also as residents build fences, houses, and factories, herd sheep, plant crops, and speak about these and other land-use practices. These dwelling practices have shaped—and continue to shape—power relations in the Negev, as well as the broader Palestinian-Israeli region. In the burgeoning field of political ecology, many scholars look to the nexus of material and symbolic factors to explain how power shapes relationships between people and the land and resources upon which they rely (e.g., Biersack and Greenberg 2006; Heatherington 2010; Ogden 2011; Robbins 2012). We know that residents of contested landscapes vie over land and resources through their dwelling practices. From class conflicts in Brazil's cities (Holston 2008) to rural contestations for territory in Zimbabwe (Moore 2005), residents plant trees, build houses, and till fields in disputed territories to stake claims (McKee 2014). These are the "micropractices" by which inhabitants vie for territory (Moore 2005). At the same time, large-scale power struggles and political maneuverings in the form of ownership laws, governmental land-use policies, and economic structures all selectively enable or inhibit residents' dwelling practices. Anthropologists, political ecologists, and other social science scholars have long recognized the importance of historical hierarchies and powerful discourses in shaping our understandings of particular landscapes and people's access to them (Hirsch and O'Hanlon 1995).

A growing but still nascent body of literature is now exploring embodiment theory and phenomenologically influenced approaches to dwelling to understand conflictive experiences of place (Campbell 2005; Heatherington 2010). One challenge for examining understandings of the Negev's divided landscapes and their social consequences is to adequately account for embodied senses of politics, that is to understand how political practices such as state-building and ethnonationalism become part of people's phenomenological experiences of place. This requires investigating how individuals come to believe and invoke these discourses themselves, how residents of a contested landscape see evidence of hierarchies encrusted in the roads, fields, and fences around them, and how such senses of place influence their dwelling practices.

To do so, this study draws elements from two typically separate scholarly approaches to place: phenomenological investigation of dwelling and political ecology scholarship. As one of many phenomenological approaches, the dwelling perspective elaborated by Tim Ingold (2000) focuses on the co-formation of inhabitants and landscapes by viewing landscapes as the products of ongoing "taskscapes." Tasks are particular acts of dwelling—whether explicitly work, like plowing or hammering, or simply walking—and an ensemble of tasks constitutes a taskscape.[19] A landscape, then, is never static; it is constantly reshaped through the tasks of dwelling. This understanding of landscape is distinctly different from its common treatment in anthropological literature and everyday speech as a framing backdrop for the true object of study (Mitchell 1994) or as a metaphor for understanding the place of people in a globalized world (Appadurai 1996:27).[20]

Equally importantly, inhabitants see traces of past dwelling practices, making landscapes meaningful. Whether a well that one's great-grandfather dug, a row of greenhouses that one's fellow *moshav* residents built over the past several decades, or the tin shack one's neighbor built on disputed land, it is the tasks behind these landscape features that make them so meaningful for Negev residents. One does not inherit cultural norms or biases, but learns them by doing (Bourdieu 1977). And this learning process happens not in abstract space, but in particular landscapes. Contemporary Negev residents learn lessons of, for example, distinguishing right from wrong or the difference between one social group and another, while dwelling within the region's segregated landscapes.

Though Ingold (2005) has noted of his own scholarship that politics have been notably absent from a dwelling perspective, the political dwelling perspective I propose for this Negev case study draws on the more cross-scalar analyses of political ecologists to highlight power and hierarchies in local places. These analyses highlight the global processes that complicate any simple notions of "the local" or "community," because translocal forces such as newly capitalized markets (Schmink and Wood 1992), new technologies (Gardner 2005), and migration (Lambek 2011) all intervene in local places. In the Negev, both local residents and extralocal agents, such as state institutions, shifting global markets, and international nongovernmental organizations (NGOs), are participants in taskscapes. Looking at communities within a context of global mobility, Michael Lambek (2011) suggests a situated understanding of how place and practice intertwine by redefining "the local" as that which is constituted by a shared ethical life. Thus, in socially divided landscapes, multiple senses of the "local" may exist within a single geographical place. Indeed, the fault lines of socioenvironmental disputes are often defined by disagreements about what should constitute the shared ethical life of particular places—ecological stewardship, protecting livelihoods, or bringing modernity to backward places, to name a few possibilities (Heatherington 2010; Li 2007; Ogden 2011). As residents try to define "local" places according to their own, often conflicting, ethical projects, they participate in the Negev's land conflict.

Researching across Borders

One sunny day in May 2008, several young boys trailed behind a group of people following a community elder along the dusty paths between their houses. I was taking part in and recording observations of an environmental justice tour that aimed to teach visitors about environmental health hazards in this unrecognized Bedouin village. Walking at the back of the tour group, I spoke with another participant, a woman my age who wore a headscarf and a long skirt. I wore slacks and a button-down shirt. Overhearing our conversation in Arabic, one boy on a bike approached and asked me to explain myself:

"Are you Jewish?" he asked, pausing, "or Arab?"

"No, and no," I replied, trying to sound friendly despite my short response.

After another pause, the boy repeated his question, seeming to think I had not understood. "Are you Jewish?"

"No," I repeated.

"So, you're Arab," he persisted.

"No," I said again. "I'm not Arab and I'm not Jewish."

The boy stood looking at me with confused eyes. "Then where are you from?" he asked. I told him I was from America, but he continued looking at me with questioning eyes.

Because I was speaking Arabic, I seemed to be local rather than an international tourist. But my appearance did not match what the boy knew of Arab women, so he suspected I was Jewish. When I denied both identities, the boy continued trying to fit me into the dominant categories of his social world. While he astutely noted my out-of-placeness, his questions suggested that he had grown up in an atmosphere dominated by "us" and "them," Jewish versus Arab. Indeed, working across multiple sites in the Negev, I found a pervasive set of nested binaries that reinforce each other to enframe social relations: Arab/Jew, nature/culture, tradition/progress. The rigidity of these binary oppositions and the specific ways they have been imagined and enacted have changed over time. However, the set of nested oppositions itself has remained remarkably consistent.[21]

Equally striking, the boy attempted to clarify my identity not by asking *who* I was, but *where* I was from. He lived in a social context of deep links between place and identity. Nationalisms draw their emotional and rhetorical force from claims of real, natural connections between "a people" and "a land" (Herder 1803; Smith 1987), but actually form by building on other divisions, such as colonial power and race (Anderson 1991; Moore, Kosek, and Pandian 2003), gender (Peteet 1991), language (Gal 1995), and ethnicity (Zubrzycki 2001). Understanding the real force of group belonging and exclusion in Israel requires examining how group boundaries harden *and* how identities become emplaced. Ethnic and nationalist identities are social events, like my encounter with the inquisitive boy, rather than fixed analytical categories (Brubaker 2004).

Decades of concerted effort through residential segregation, separate schooling, social censoring of "intermarriage," and differential access to social services and political representation have done much to make the purported separation of Jewish and Arab societies a material reality (Kanaaneh 2002; Rabinowitz 2001). Faced with this material reality, most contemporary Negev residents continue to remake Jewish-Arab group boundaries both through public projects involving organizations and institutions and through individual cognition, for example in the founding of a *kibbutz* and the choice of a marriage partner based on religious identity. Thus, group boundaries are both cause and result, as actors on all sides of this sociopolitical conflict participate in drawing them.

Because of my aim to study processes of group-making, I chose not to research within one group. Drawing inspiration from ethnographic studies of land and resource conflict in other settings (Kosek 2006; Merlan 1998; West 2006), I adopted a regional focus on the northern Negev to learn from those on multiple "sides" of this conflict. While absolute objectivity is not possible in ethnography, it is an important goal, and my research design strove for objectivity by seeking multiple perspectives on land relations. I planned fieldwork that took me across not just Jewish-Arab divisions, but also potentially crosscutting lines of affiliation, such as political orientation and religiosity. For approximately sixteen months, I moved between field sites within the Negev, learning from environmentalist NGOs and community members.[22]

I gained my first introductions in the region via participant observation with Bustan. For about seven months, I studied in the informal, though somewhat institutional setting of this grassroots environmental justice NGO. Living in Bustan's volunteer housing in Beersheba, I participated in the organization's daily routines and conducted in-depth interviews with Bustan members, campaign audiences, and members of other environmentalist and social activist groups in the Negev. I collected data on tactics of activism and campaign design, as well as the frustrations, large and small, that these activists faced.

I began research with this focus on environmentalist activism because it promised moments of rupture, when taken-for-granted associations between national identities, social groups, and contested lands would be challenged (Dawson 1996; Kosek 2006). Nationalist movements around the world and in different historical moments have shared a preoccupation with rooting people in their purportedly native lands (Geschiere and Jackson 2006; Malkki 1992; Zenker 2011). These movements draw on the nature imagery of homelands, often asserting connections between the characteristics of the land and the character of the people (Schwartz 2006; Smith 1987), and excluding those deemed not to have natural connections to a place (Kosek 2006). Claims about the natural inhabitants of a place and about ideal land uses are central to these processes. Environmentalist activism, in challenging existing norms of land use and advocating new relationships between people and places, also grapples with these nationalist associations.

Thus, I began learning about land conflict and its underlying environmental discourses by studying efforts to disrupt them. Participating in the planning and implementation of the NGO's campaigns taught me about the rhetoric and practicalities of environmentalist activism. Coordinating one of their outreach classes helped me understand from an experiential standpoint. A few activists shared longer life histories with me and invited me into their homes, where I met their friends and families. By following these individuals' social networks and personal histories, I learned how they incorporated environmentalist work into their everyday lives, and vice versa. While traveling with Bustan for both formal projects and home visits, I met residents from the region's towns, cities, *moshavim* and *kibbutzim*, and unrecognized villages, some of whom became my host families during a second research period.

During this second period, I explored land-use practices in the Negev in more mainstream social contexts by living for four months in one of the area's Bedouin Arab townships, 'Ayn al-'Azm, and for four months in the neighboring Jewish *moshav* of Dganim.[23] I chose these neighboring towns, only two kilometers apart across a dry riverbed, for their potential to reveal both social divisions and overlooked commonalities between Bedouin Arab and Jewish residents. In each community, I lived with families and took part in daily life. Informal leaders in each community introduced me to a range of individuals and families with whom I cooked, cleaned, tended gardens, built homes, tutored children, spent time with elders, and shared meals. In addition to casual conversations during these activities, I conducted lengthy interviews focused on individuals' and families' histories of residence, land-use practices, and perspectives on current environmental issues.

Living and working in these communities, I experienced Israel's residential segregation (Rabinowitz 1997), but during each period, I continued visiting friends, colleagues, and host families from prior periods. These individuals taught me about particularly meaningful social boundaries by expressing shock or wariness when I crossed them. As I moved back and forth between Dganim, 'Ayn al-'Azm, Beersheba, and surrounding villages, I also learned when and how to shift languages and manners of comportment and to rearrange clothing. Learning these adjustments required attention to the subtle gestures of others, like adjusting a headscarf, as well as more obvious features in the landscape, like fences. Such social and environmental cues participate in the drawing and policing of emplaced group boundaries. Taken for granted in the typically segregated dwelling practices of residents, they became more obvious in journeying and interacting across social boundaries.

It became clear to me that, though practiced in many other settings, this regional approach is rare in Israel (McKee 2013). When I arrived in Israel and began introducing my research as an ethnographic study in the Negev, I was struck by how consistently both residents and fellow scholars assumed I was studying either the Bedouin or (less often) Jewish collective settlements, rather than both. After I heard these assumptions repeated several times, I reexamined the anthropological literature and realized how segregated most ethnographic research in this region has been (Furani and Rabinowitz 2011; Rabinowitz 2002). Ethnographic research has tended to assign topics such as collective communities and nation-building as metonymic of Jewish communities, while it designates tribal structures, gender roles, and development challenges as metonymic of communities identified as Arab or Bedouin.[24] Rarely does nuanced interpretation of overlapping differences and similarities encompass people across the Jewish-Arab division. These norms of anthropological research risk intensifying the segregation of an already divided society. In recent years some ethnographers critiquing colonialism and Orientalism have begun to diversify these research topics (Furani and Rabinowitz 2011).[25] More work of this kind must be done if we are to understand how these social categories are constructed and how conflict between groups of Jews and Arabs in this region has come to seem so primordial.

Conflict is a status quo in the Negev, but it is not the whole story, as some people are striving to ameliorate social and political disparities. Though other scholars have addressed potential legal remedies (Forman and Kedar 2004; Abu Hussein and McKay 2003; Shamir 1996), few have looked beyond the legal realm. Looking to everyday dwelling politics, I found elements of socioenvironmental change in a variety of social milieus. Through innovative juxtapositions and new associations, some Negev inhabitants attempt to unsettle dominant discursive frames. For example, insurgent tree-planting campaigns assert that Bedouin Arabs can be farmers who "green the desert" like their Jewish counterparts celebrated in Zionist pioneering mythology. Organized activist campaigns offer one obvious milieu to study these dynamics. I distinguish activism from other social practices as consisting of more concerted, and generally collective, efforts oriented toward particular goals of sociopolitical change. Organized and collective activism offers people the tools and relationships to challenge dominant discursive institutions more deliberately, and potentially more creatively (Burdick 1995; della Porta et al. 2006; Tarrow 1998).

However, the activism of social movements and strikes is not entirely compartmentalized in people's lives (McAdam, Tarrow, and Tilly 2001). In homes and fields, news media, and Knesset (Israeli Parliament) proceedings, people also used environmental rhetoric and practices in new ways. While researching in 'Ayn al-'Azm and Dganim, I sought out interlocutors who were grappling with similar questions as I was about land struggles, emplaced identities, and conflict resolution. I found residents undertaking projects that were less concerted, though sometimes equally creative, aimed at righting inequalities and mending the rifts of land conflict. Being pointed by local residents to those they deemed to be experts on these issues, I not only gained expertise, but also learned about wider perceptions of knowledge and authority. In 'Ayn al-'Azm, this approach led me to a woman reputed by fellow residents to be wise in "old ways" and local flora and fauna, and to a man building his home from mud, straw, and recycled trash, as well as to the woman known across the township for her entrepreneurial project in tourism and herbal medicines. In the smaller community of Dganim, I was pointed to the charismatic local council leader spearheading his community's shift from agricultural to tourism-based liveli-hoods, the two remaining large-scale farmers, and a woman charged by the local council with environmental beautification of the *moshav*.

Projects in both these settings also introduced me to an underappreciated approach to social change. While more attention is often paid to those engaged in confrontational politics and blunt attempts to reverse power relations, some of the more creative projects I witnessed were about softening boundaries—physical, rhetorical, and symbolic. This boundary softening is a social change effort that proceeds (though it may not be articulated in these terms) from the perspective that change can happen through continuity, that resistance occurs from within existing relations of power (Butler 1993). A critical question for Negev land conflict, then, is can this politics of softening work in Israel, and can it effect significant change?

Ethics in Studying Conflict

Conflict and violence, both acute and structural, have become central to Israel's social relations (Kemp et al. 2004; Kimmerling 1983; Sheffer and Barak 2010; Smooha 2004). Open warfare has killed many people and shaped the lives of those who remain. During my fieldwork in 2009, armed conflict in Gaza and the northern Negev killed more than 1,100 Palestinians in Gaza and 13 Israelis. Once again, in 2014, acts of brutality (in this case, the kidnapping and murder of three Jewish teens, followed by the murder of a Palestinian teen) exploded into a seven-week ordeal of Israeli air strikes and ground invasion into Gaza and Hamas missile launchings, which killed more than two thousand Palestin-ians and scores of Israelis. Though such extraordinary events of violence domi-nate depictions of the region in international news media, violence has become a routinized part of the Negev's social landscape and residents quickly continue in their daily routines, as in comparable contexts around the world (Nordstrom 1997; Scheper-Hughes 1993).

Still, bursts of brutal violence continue to influence people's lives long after the missile firings and shootings have subsided, though in more subtle ways than news coverage would suggest (Swedenburg 1995b). The context of conflict manifests in the "everyday violence" (Scheper-Hughes 1993) of interpersonal prejudice and state-sanctioned structural inequalities. Resentment and suspicions shade interactions between Jewish and Bedouin Negev residents. As Victor Turner (1957) tells us, conflict and disharmony can be just as constitutive of a society's structural relationships as continuity and consonance, as the upheavals of social dramas most often reinforce preexisting divisions. This wider context of Palestinian-Israeli conflict profoundly affects individuals' senses of place, policies and practices of land use, and the stakes of personal identities and affiliations.

Researching across social cleavages, including a focus on efforts to shift or soften boundaries, was methodologically important because it helped me understand these divisions as dynamic negotiations within the social landscape rather than fixed, immobile features. My choices of study topic and regional approach were also ethical matters. Conflict has become entrenched in the lives of Israelis and Palestinians—specifically in the Negev and in wider Arab-Israeli strife—to the extent that an entire generation of young adults has grown up not having known any other state of affairs. I feel a responsibility to engage in research that facilitates resolution efforts that go beyond divvying up land and resources wherein active clashes halt but basic inequalities and resentment remain. By demonstrating how the seemingly natural categories of Arab and Jew are historically contingent and socially constructed, I hope to contribute to efforts, both within scholarship and in the social change movements of some Negev residents with whom I worked, to challenge the naturalization of existing social inequalities (Rabinowitz 2002; Tzfadia and Yacobi 2011; Yiftachel 2006).

My commitment to study across conflict lines has shaped logistical and ethical considerations of fieldwork. Being non-Jewish, non-Muslim, non-Arab, and without any family connections in the Middle East, I was often approached as an outsider. The pressure for "unaffiliated" researchers to choose a side can be strong in Palestine-Israel. For ethnographers in the Occupied Territories, where Jewish-Palestinian relations involve much violence, this pressure may come through stones and shouts (Swedenburg 1995a). Within Israel, it is likely to be subtler (Dominguez 1989). As Negev residents offered to help me convert my religion or marry a local man, they were also gently pushing me to affiliate. My multisited fieldwork created productive tension with this pressure to choose.

I certainly developed social, emotional, and practical ties to particular families and communities, but I was often imagined to be an external arbiter and candidate for education. Many people exhorted me to understand and agree with their interpretation of "the situation," and some referred directly to an imagined audience of readers they hoped I would similarly convince. But my agreement was rarely demanded. I was surprised many times early in my fieldwork, after worrying that I had squandered my welcome by expressing disagreeable opinions during what felt like a particularly contentious debate, when I was then offered another cup of coffee, given a comfortable place to lie down and rest, or invited back for dinner.

At an interpersonal level, boundary crossing challenged me to establish rapport with residents while also maintaining the physical and social mobility to move between people who may have less than cordial relationships with each other. While working with Bustan and meeting with rival organizations, I was careful to assure all involved that I would not pass potentially sensitive information about finances or tactical planning between these groups. On the other hand, as a long-term participant observer with Bustan, I acted as a "committed critic" (Burdick 1995), sharing preliminary analysis of my research regarding Bustan's social and environmental messages and their fit with the priorities of their intended audiences. Living among the reluctant neighbors of Dganim and 'Ayn al-'Azm, I found that my potential role as liaison was more sensitive. Decades of divisive social boundaries and a contemporary lack of intercultural communication between residents of these towns have fostered caricature portraits of irrational, often hateful opponents. Traveling across these lines, I was sometimes treated as a conduit of information or social interpreter. This role became more fraught during periods of violent conflict, such as the 2009 outbreak of armed conflict in and around Gaza, when group boundaries hardened and enmities festered more openly. During kitchen-table conversations in each town, my hosts asked me to explain what "they" were thinking, and how "they" justify "their" actions. In such circumstances, I strove to disassemble caricatures and report the fears and hopes I heard in each community, while protecting personal confidences.

Arab-Israeli conflict tends to be dealt with polemically, in the most warlike and belligerent connotations of that adverb's Greek roots. In such a setting, I have sought—in research and writing—to address Arab-Israeli conflict at large, and Bedouin-Jewish Israeli conflict in particular, not in order to identify righteous and victimized parties, but rather to answer "how" and "why" questions by seeking out situated knowledge (Haraway 1988). I believe that confrontations can move understanding of the conflict forward through difficult contradictions, opposing viewpoints, and evidence of injustice. Unmasking the power dynamics that shape social relations can open more space for minorities to advocate for themselves (McKee 2010). However, I aim to do this without vitriolic attack.

These goals inform the structure of this book. The first half focuses on how dominant environmental discourses have carved Israel as a whole, and the Negev in particular, into segregated spaces. Chapter 1 examines the use of several dominant environmental discourses in the competing historical narratives of Zionist and counter-Zionist land claims. It outlines a discursive genealogy that continues to influence the tactics and strategies of contemporary land struggles, particularly for Bedouin Arab residents telling histories of the Naqab. Chapter 2 examines the stakes of these environmental discourses and the land claims they support by comparing two cases of "illegal" land use. In one case, Jewish farmstead owners built houses on agricultural land, and in the other, Bedouin Arab residents built on lands declared as state owned. In both cases the government threatened eviction, and residents sought governmental recognition of their land claims, but they faced very different public and governmental responses.

The second half of the book zooms in to focus on the everyday practices and experiences of residents in the Negev, exploring how residents shape and are shaped by the state-planned landscapes within which they dwell. A bridge introduces the two case study towns that provide the bulk of this dwelling analysis, as well as the in-between spaces that constitute such an important part of the region's divided landscapes. Chapter 3 focuses on life in the Bedouin Arab township of 'Ayn al-'Azm, where most residents felt strong attachments to family and neighborhood but felt alienated from the township as a collective landscape, and where many adapted some rural taskscapes to cope with life in this planned township. Chapter 4 presents the Jewish *moshav* of Dganim, settled by a group of new immigrants from Cochin, India, in the 1950s. From their early years building a cooperative farming community to recent shifts to new economic sectors, residents have worked to maintain their communal identity and negotiate a changing role within the Zionist movement. Chapter 5 probes the potential of deliberate engagement with the everyday politics of dwelling to shift dominant environmental discourses. It examines three environmental justice campaigns through which Bustan aims to change norms of land ownership and ethnopolitical identification in Israel: political and environmental educational tours, an alternative energy campaign, and sustainable design classes. The chapter considers the potential and limitations of Bustan's efforts to challenge the status quo of land conflict.

Throughout the process of researching and writing this book, I have tried to recognize the humanity of all those involved—with their attendant frailty, anger, generosity, and ingenuity—and to point out where and how the humanity of certain groups of people is threatened through this conflict. My goal here is not to provide simply a dispassionate accounting of facts. Nor is it to make as passionate an argument as possible in favor of a particular solution or against a particular party. Rather, I hope that this book will explain where the passion, polemics, and virulence of this conflict come from; that it will highlight basic structural inequalities in Israel which perpetuate strife by discriminating against some citizens while privileging others. I aim to translate across sides, and perhaps even move a step toward softening these currently hardened group boundaries.

1 Narrating Present Pasts

INVOCATIONS OF THE PAST are everywhere in Israel's contemporary land conflict, from the land claims of individuals to governmental justifications for regional land-use plans. In 2007, two-meter-tall corrugated metal Hebrew letters sitting on a hilltop just west of Jerusalem asserted one link between past and present. "AGRICULTURE WILL WIN," they declared across the valley. These letters lined the steep entrance road of one of the few remaining collective *kibbutzim* in Israel. *Kibbutzim* of the early 1900s were small agricultural settlements run as economically and socially cooperative communities. They played a significant role in Israeli nation-building, not primarily through economic contributions but as social and ideological keystones of the Zionist movement.[1] Since then, most *kibbutzim* have privatized, and many have shifted away from agriculture (Grossman 2004). The *kibbutz* I was visiting, for example, had many productive acres of vineyards, orchards, and vegetables but also a glass factory and a children's water park that supplied much of the community's income.

Mark, a proud resident of the *kibbutz*, explained the message his community hoped to send via these metal letters to the other Israelis who drove through the valley or bought the new housing plots that encroached on the *kibbutz*'s farmland. Mark explained how the founders of this *kibbutz* and others across the country had transformed a barren landscape into lush and productive agricultural plots. We are struggling to keep the agriculture and the green space, Mark said. It is not as profitable as using land to construct buildings, but we think agriculture will win, he concluded. To some extent, Mark's *kibbutz* was struggling against status shifts common in any society undergoing a transition from an agrarian economy to one more reliant on industrial production, tourism, and other services (Cronon 1991; Harvey 1996; Heatherington 2010). But in certain ways, this struggle is unique to Israel and the Zionist movement. The rallying cry for agriculture invokes an Orientalist historical narrative of campaigns to civilize a Middle Eastern wilderness with European farming technology and a work ethic that prizes agricultural labor as redemptive of both workers' character and a neglected land. While it speaks most pointedly to fellow Jews who would replace farming land with condominiums, the sign also speaks to non-Jews, asserting Jewish claims to land through their productive use of it.

Yousef, a middle-aged Bedouin man living in an unrecognized Negev village, invoked agricultural practices during an interview with me, too, to strengthen his land claim. However, he did so by telling a very different kind of history. He spoke of an unbroken chain of forebears who had worked the land where his house now sat. Long ago, the land was covered with shrubbery, he told me. His ancestors cut down shrubs, dug furrows, and farmed. This was before Ottoman times, he explained. It was before his grandparents; it was seven grandparents ago. Yousef's assertion of a steadfast line of grandfathers counters Zionism by contradicting its erasure of non-Jews from the land. But in the same breath Yousef asserted a work ethic familiar to Zionist accounts. His forebears fulfilled the requirements for agricultural labor and suffering espoused by Zionist leaders.

Though Naqab Bedouins' land claims are often denied because of their supposed nomadism, Yousef asserted that his tribe was only "quarter-nomadic." Rather than simply living in one place and then moving to the next, he told me, they settled the village of Tel Assha'ir as a base for growing wheat and barley. Residents stored these crops underground through the winter in wells they dug. The families also herded sheep and goats, and if vegetation was scarce, one year a portion of each family, such as one of a man's wives and her children, might travel north to graze the herds above the rain line (in an area recognized within the family's *dira*, its tribal territory). Meanwhile the second wife and other residents would stay in the village. Yousef emphasized that the graves were always here, along with the water well and the storage places.[2] He carefully accentuated the sedentary and farming aspects of his heritage, like growing rain-fed wheat and barley, and depicted shepherding as a complement to farming.

While Mark's and Yousef's uses of history contradicted each other indirectly, other historical claims-making can be more blunt. At a Shabbat dinner in 2009, my host, Chaim, asked what I had learned in the Bedouin township where I lived before moving to his *moshav*. I began describing different ways families had adapted to that urban township, including some who continued past lifestyles of agriculture and raising animals. "No," Chaim cut in suddenly, "the Bedouin never farmed. They only do it now to hold onto land." Chaim then contended adamantly not only that Bedouins were manipulating the ideological weight of agriculture within Zionism, but also that Israel's collective agricultural communities were "a beautiful dream" of the past that could not survive humanity's individualistic nature. His community members had done what was necessary, he contended, by quitting agriculture and finding jobs off the *moshav*.

Chaim and Mark both draw on variations of Zionist foundational narratives, which hold high status in Israel. Official Israeli historical accounts of Eretz Israel, told in school classes, governmental documents, a voluminous published literature, and the celebration of national holidays, recount the expulsion of Jews from the Holy Land during Roman rule, followed by a period of neglected landscapes, and the eventual return of the Jewish people to rehabilitate these landscapes. Zionist Negev residents told me of brave predecessors taming a wild and dangerous desert to create a new society. A robust historiography examines how Zionist narratives have been mobilized for these nation-building purposes (Attias and Benbassa 2003; Kellerman 1993; Piterberg 2008; Zerubavel 1995).

Critics of Zionist land policies, both Palestinians and Jewish Israelis, tell counter-narratives that contest official accounts as well as their meanings and moral lessons. In the Naqab, these narratives focus on a long line of Bedouin Arab protagonists, with Jewish settlers arriving as interlopers. Contradicting the barren desert wilderness of Zionist accounts, counter-narratives depict sparsely peopled, yet social landscapes. They describe long histories of family land use as legitimate claims to lands.[3] Unlike Zionist narratives, these accounts rely primarily on informal reminiscences; they are less tied to published sources and include fewer facts and figures.

What is striking about these competing histories of the Negev/Naqab is that despite their contradictions they often rest on shared environmental discourses: agriculture's value for rooting persons, depictions of Bedouins as traditional desert dwellers and Jews as progressive and civilized, and the characterization of certain lands as "Jewish" or "Arab." Moreover, these environmental discourses interlock and strengthen each other, as they contain overlapping binary oppositions of Arab versus Jew, nature versus culture, and tradition versus progress. These discourses are not innately given, but rather trace back to the development of Zionism as well as the wider Orientalist and ethnic nationalist discourses that shaped the movement. As Zionism's dominance grew, these discourses were associated both with successful settlement projects and with ongoing nation-building narratives, giving them tactical power in making moral arguments and practical claims (cf. Silverstein and Urban 1996).

Contemporary land debates draw force from discourses with long genealogies. What this chapter offers is not a comprehensive history of Zionism,
nor a full historical account of nationalism and state-building in the region
of Israel-Palestine.[4] Rather, this chapter traces the consolidation of three key
environmental discourses in mainstream Zionist accounts and examines
how Bedouin residents negotiate with these powerful discourses when telling
counter-histories of the Naqab. Placing Naqab narratives alongside textually
and institutionally strengthened Zionist narratives highlights the unequal foot-
ing of these accounts. If done naïvely, such a juxtaposition would risk delegiti-
mizing Naqab narratives. However, when done with attention to the political
and material histories surrounding these narrations, this juxtaposition highlights the sociopolitical constraints with which Bedouin Arabs must contend
when narrating their connections to land.

Making Jewish Territory

The first of these Zionist discourses asserts the imperative of establishing and
protecting a physical territory for the Jewish people. In contemporary Israel,
it is common to hear Zionist residents bolster their claim to a particular area
of the Negev by asserting the Jewishness of the place. When I asked Yaron, a
moshav resident, how he and his fellow *moshav* members had come to settle
in their particular area of the Negev after immigration, he said their parents
were drawn to the place. "And that's because in the Bible [Tanakh], they talked
about Beersheba, and Abraham our father, long ago. . . . [So,] they came here."
Yaron came from a religiously observant community, and this proclaimed desire to resettle his biblical forefather's land asserts both the immigrants' Zionist
dedication and their religious piety (Shahar 2008). The importance of "Jewish"
lands is not necessarily religious, however. When Jewish residents of a different Negev town established in 2004 described their move to that "remote" area
as important because "otherwise, Bedouins would settle here," they invoked a
discourse of Jewish territory as state territory.

Territorialism may have religious or secular meaning, but both versions
share the conviction that territorial integrity is critical for the survival of the
Jewish people. Equally importantly, both look to a long genealogy of Jews in
Israel to make their claim. Zionism and its drive for territorial integrity developed in the nineteenth century in the context of European colonialism and
nationalism. Early leaders viewed the sovereign nation-state as the ideal—indeed, the natural—form of community (Laqueur 1989). Responding to widespread attitudes in Europe, Theodore Herzl, the widely proclaimed "father of

Zionism," agreed that Jews were materialistic and morally weak, but argued that these character flaws resulted from Jews' distorted relationships with their states. Anti-Semitism barred Jews from gaining the full benefits of citizenship, he argued, and thus denied them the motivation to uphold responsibilities, such as military service, to the wider community. The solution, he claimed, would be for the state to expect Jews' full participation, making them honorable contributors to the common good (Kornberg 1993). The emphasis on civic duties shaping citizens corresponded with French ideals of nationalism at the time (if not its practices, as demonstrated by the discrimination of the Dreyfus Affair in the 1890s). The goal of aligning ethnic and political borders in a nation-state, and the particular tactics used during Zionism's early years of settlement, drew from the ethnic nationalism that Zionist leaders experienced in Germany and elsewhere in Europe (Brubaker 1996; Piterberg 2008).

Though sharing much with European territorial nationalism, the notion of "return" has been more particular to Zionist understandings of territory. Statements like Yaron's justification for settling describe individual Jews' connections to landscapes within Eretz Israel as reconnecting with an interrupted national ancestry. Particularly during early statehood, school curricula, youth movements, and popular rituals brought this ancient connection into Jewish Israelis' everyday lives. Children's literature drew on archaeological finds and stories of the first-century Bar Kokhba revolt to teach lessons of strength and integrity, for example, and youth hikes and military initiations at ruins of the ancient fortification of Masada instilled a sense of common purpose between ancient Jewish rebels and contemporary defenders of the Jewish state (Zerubavel 1995). Indeed, the belief in a natural connection between the Jewish people and Eretz Israel has become central to Zionism (Selwyn 1995). In contemporary conversations, the simple use of the word "return" to describe Jews' immigration to this area indexes this larger narrative of ancient connection, and a claim of rightful repossession. The geographical focus of this "return," however, was far from certain during the movement's early years (Attias and Benbassa 2003; Elon 1971). The amorphous bounds of the project are reflected in the common term *ha-aretz*, which literally means "the land" and refers to the area over which Zionists assert historic claim. The term may include only the territory of the current Israeli state or a much wider area.

Following anti-Semitism's fevered and genocidal pitch in Europe, Zionists also invoked the Holocaust to justify their territorial intensions. The place of the Holocaust within Zionist politics and historical accounts has been complex. During the 1930s and increasingly in subsequent years, Jewish leaders argued that the extreme anti-Semitism that eventually fueled the Holocaust proved the need for a Jewish state as a safe haven (Zertal 2005). Yet there was a "less than compassionate response [from] the Jewish community in Palestine to the destruction of the European Jews" during the Holocaust, as leaders like David Ben-Gurion rebuked European Jews for not having heeded the call of Zionism earlier (Segev 2000:11). Symbolically, the urban and migratory image of European Jews became an important antithesis against which Zionist leaders sought to forge a Jewish society in Palestine that would be deeply entrenched in place.

This discourse of Jewish territorialism—the need for Jewish sovereignty over Jewish land—has had widespread implications for the development of the region since the early 1900s. Chief among them was the materialization of a "dual society" separating Arabs from Jews. Zionist leaders strove to establish a "dual society paradigm" that would naturalize a separation between "two completely separate and self-contained entities in Palestine," the *yishuv* (the community of Jews living in Palestine) and Palestinian Arabs (Piterberg 2008:64; Lockman 1996). This paradigm was based on a premise shared by other forms of colonialism, that natives could be kept external to the settler society (Cooper and Stoler 1997). Looking to the "working people's colony" used in nineteenth-century Germany to induce Germans to establish agricultural settlements in Polish-majority regions, settlement administrators for the World Zionist Organization created collective settlements that segregated Jews and Arabs in different territories (Bloom 2011; Piterberg 2008).

With Israel's declaration of statehood in 1948, the Zionist movement's discourse of territorialism became more concretely geographical. Previously, the movement's imagined territory had been the amorphous bounds of *ha-aretz*. Suddenly, with the establishment of armistice lines, the state had a clear and contiguous, but insecure, territory. The Labor Zionist movement, which led Israel's first government and dominated politics for the next thirty years, used new military and legislative tools to continue securing this territory by establishing "presence," specifically Jewish presence (Kimmerling 1983). Guided by their conviction in the power of the state to shape citizens, Labor Zionist leaders built centralized institutions to help establish this presence.

Because the Jewish National Fund (JNF) had managed to purchase only a portion of the land that came under Israeli control, legislative redefinition of additional lands was one key method of control.[5] First, successive legislative measures reclassified Palestinian-owned lands for which owners were not present on or after November 29, 1947 (when the United Nations voted to partition Palestine) as "abandoned land," and then "absentee land." The government needed these legislative measures to legalize land use for nation-building purposes such as housing new immigrants and providing them with established agricultural fields. Under David Ben-Gurion, the government made the JNF a semigovernmental organization and transferred one million *dunams* (approximately 250,000 acres) to it. However, the state did not own this land by any existing laws, so new laws retroactively legalized these transfers (Forman and Kedar 2004). Then, in 1960, control over these redefined lands was further consolidated when new legislation gathered the lands held by various state and semistate bodies under the unified control of the Israel Land Administration.

In addition to these practical measures to control territory, the government named places to tame and claim frontier lands.[6] In 1949, Prime Minister Ben-Gurion established a special commission to lay nominal claim to the Negev. The Committee for the Designation of Place-Names in the Negev Region (NNC) spent two years poring over British Mandate-era maps of the Negev and assigning Hebrew names to hills, valleys, and any newly established settlements. Often these replaced former Arabic names, deliberately declaring these lands to be Jewish. As the committee chairman asserted, "Just as the Bedouin of the Negev did not sink roots in this place, so also are the names not rooted here" (Benvenisti 2000:18). In contrast, the NNC often assigned Hebrew biblical names, using the linguistic genealogy linking ancient and modern Hebrew to assert deep Jewish roots in these places (Masalha 2007).

Thus, in the years of prestate settlement and early Israeli statehood, a discourse of Jewish territorialism became increasingly geographically defined and enmeshed with state power. In the 1970s, though, shifting internal labor markets, slackening immigration, and inconsistent external financial support weakened the ability of Labor Zionism's state institutions to play such a direct role in staking territorial claims. Labor Zionists lost political dominance, and economic liberalization began to take hold. In recent years, reform groups champion economic liberalization, such as the 2009 legal reforms to allow the sale of state lands, as an opening of equal opportunity (Hananel 2012). This shift has not signaled the end of Zionism's territorial drive, however. Free market real estate transactions in recent decades have continued to reproduce the ethnically territorialized landscapes of earlier state projects, particularly in "mixed" cities that have defined "Arab" and "Jewish" neighborhoods (Tzfadia and Yacobi 2011). Instead, land reforms aim to make economic development more efficient and make Israel an appealing place for wealthy, urban Jews, allowing Jewish territorialism to proceed through privatization (Tzfadia 2008).

Thus, the projects justifying Jewish territorialism have changed over the years, from particularly stark and statist tactics in early years to land reforms that signal an expanded economic definition of territorial control in more recent years; but a discourse of Jewish territory remains a driving force within Zionism.

Redemption through Agriculture

A second key discourse that developed in Zionism and shapes land contestations in contemporary Israel is a discourse of agriculture as redemption, both of individual laborers and of neglected land. While Zionists have claimed the territory of *ha-aretz* in a variety of ways, establishing farming taskscapes has long been central to both the practical and ideological goals of the movement. Since Herzl's leadership and more so under Labor Zionism, Zionists have asserted the necessity of physical labor in service to the collective and the importance of land as the basis for collective redemption (Sternhell 1998; Zakim 2006). Ber Borochov and other Labor Zionist leaders spoke of the need to invert the labor "pyramid" of the Diaspora, in which Jews had rarely filled the agricultural and industrial labor positions widely viewed by socialists as the foundation of a society. This inversion, Labor Zionists believed, would dispel the negative qualities of urban Diaspora life by "rooting" a restless, exilic Jewish identity (Almog 2000; de-Shalit 1995).

These leaders strove to foster a generation of physically strong "New Hebrews" who, distanced from their immediate forebears in urban Europe, were the imagined grandchildren of ancient Hebrews in Eretz Israel (Piterberg 2008; Shapira 2012). Literature, photography, and promotional posters of the time extolled the firm muscles of farm workers confident in their bodies (Biale 1992).[7] In strengthening their physical bodies, farming immigrants also aimed to strengthen the national body, a relationship of metonymy shared with other nineteenth- and twentieth-century nationalisms (Mosse 1985).

This transformation would also be moral, Zionist leaders believed, by creating strong collective bonds among Jews of the *yishuv* and the land of Eretz Israel (Almog 2000). Poems, plays, and paintings propagated imagery melding improvement of the soil with improvement of the Jewish soul (Sternhell 1998; Zakim 2006). Particularly among the earliest pioneer farmers, known as *chalutzim*, values of collective responsibility were influential. In the social structure of the *kibbutz*, the collective community was the most important social unit. Raising children in communal residence halls weakened nuclear family connections, and rotating workers through branches and leadership levels reduced internal social divisions (Talmon 1972). As the *kibbutz* was the vanguard institution of the Zionist movement, this sort of attachment to the collective also represented a wider ideal within the *yishuv*. For example, the reported dying words of a *kibbutz* defender in 1920, "Never mind, it is good to die for the country [*ha-aretz*]," were invoked for decades in textbooks, songs, and children's stories (Zerubavel 1995:43).

Key to this agricultural discourse, early Zionist leaders believed that Jews' tasks, their labor in the land, could make landscapes Jewish. During debates over the rightfulness of Jews' land claims in Palestine, A. D. Gordon wrote in 1909, "One thing is certain, and that is that the land will belong more to the side that is more capable of suffering for it and working it. . . . That is only logical, that is only just, and that is how it should be in the nature of things" (Sternhell 1998:68). The supposedly barren and uncultivated state of Palestine's landscapes in the late nineteenth century was proof for Gordon and other Zionists that the Arabs living there had not gained rights in the land through their labor.[8]

To achieve these goals of agricultural redemption, Zionist leaders during the British Mandate followed socialist ideas of governance to build a set of centralized institutions. Since 1901, and increasingly after World War I, the JNF collected money from Jews around the world to purchase and manage lands in the name of "the Jewish nation." The JNF could only lease lands (because sales would remove lands from centralized control), and only Jewish labor could be employed on its lands (Levensohn 1941). The Jewish Agency (JA), formed in 1923, was recognized by the British Mandate government as the representative body for Jews living in Palestine and later became a semigovernmental arm of the State of Israel. As a rough division of tasks, the JNF, the JA, and a third influential organization, the *yishuv*'s trade unions (Histadrut), bore responsibility for shaping Jewish land, people, and labor, respectively.

The leaders of these organizations prioritized cooperative agricultural settlements less for their fit with Palestine's ecological qualities or their ability to contribute economically, and more for their potential to support a particular agricultural vision of the Jewish nation. Early cooperative farming villages were often placed in arid or swampy areas ill suited for growing crops. They were also impractical because of their proportionately low economic contribution and high infrastructure costs, the lack of agricultural experience among most immigrants, and the hostility that they aggravated with resident Arabs.[9] However, Zionists' belief in agriculture's power for character building and moral territorial claims encouraged what economic historian Dan Giladi calls "the romantics of soil cultivation" (cited in Kellerman 1993). The taskscape of farming became a goal of Zionism in and of itself, not just a means to an end, and Zionist leaders emphasized their own participation in and enjoyment of agriculture, both in public fora like propaganda literature and speeches, and in private diaries. As David Ben-Gurion wrote:

> The plough is in my left hand, the goad is in my right hand. I am walking behind the plough and I see black clods breaking into crumbs, and the oxen are stepping very slowly and peacefully, and there is time to wonder and dream. Is it at all possible not to dream while you are ploughing the land of Israel and see around you Jews ploughing. . . . Is it not a dream? (in de-Shalit 1995:74)[10]

Cooperative labor to bond Jews to each other and to the land continued to influence the next generation of the *yishuv*. Jews born in Palestine from the 1930s through the end of World War II became known as "*sabras*," derived from the word *tsabar*, or prickly pear cactus (Almog 2000). Popular etymology emphasizes the rooting metaphor of the term, identifying members of this generation with the hardy desert plant (Doleve-Gandelman 1987). Members of the *sabra* generation were expected to embody many of the same characteristics as *chalutzim*, but with an even greater emphasis on rooting in the land and melding with its nature. Young Jews attended schools with lessons in the regional flora and fauna, read "homeland" textbooks, and joined youth groups for hikes and fieldtrips to *kibbutzim*—all aimed at raising a generation who would "know the land" and be adept in settling new "wildernesses" (Zerubavel 1995). Those raised most directly within these Zionist institutions, though constituting only about 10 percent of the Jewish population of Palestine, eventually filled many of Israel's military and political leadership positions and became the role models guiding their entire generation (Almog 2000).

For the waves of Mizrahi immigrants who reached Israel after 1948 in the first decades of statehood, the discourse of agricultural labor remained influential but shaped their immigration experience differently. Because the lands in central Israel had already been settled, and because Zionist leaders were concerned with consolidating control of land in border regions, they sent many new immigrants to arid frontier lands of the Negev and along the Jordanian border in *moshvei olim* (immigrants' *moshavim*) (Kimmerling 1983). For these new arrivals, agricultural success became an important means of assimilating into Israeli society (Kushner 1973; Weingrod 1966).

The environmental discourse of redemption through agriculture was not unique to Zionism. The discourse relied on an environmental imaginary of Palestine, common in many other European colonial contexts, of land degradation under native use and the need for restoration through colonial intervention (Cronon 1983; Davis and Burke 2011; Grove 1995). Zionist leaders held a particular variation of this common imaginary, contending that when the Jews were forced into exile, a previously lush landscape went into decline, eventually becoming the "ruined" landscape of "dreariness" and "desert" that Zionist immigrants saw in the early 1900s (de-Shalit 1995:74). As the Jews returned, this argument continued, they would repair the land through cultivation.

Because the discourse resonated with European and reformist Ottoman notions of ownership, agricultural settlements also facilitated property claims during the British Mandate (Kellerman 1993). From a legal standpoint, the Ottoman system of land tenure, which continued under British administration, enhanced the strategic importance of agricultural settlements. Under certain circumstances, the act of cultivation could shift land from classification as *mewat*, or "dead land," over which no ownership rights could be claimed, to secure tenure, known as *miri*. By the end of Ottoman rule, much of Palestine was classified as *mewat*, and large areas also remained unclassified (Abu Hussein and McKay 2003). In this context of unclassified land rights, cultivating land strengthened ownership claims.

Where agricultural settlements could not be established, tree planting became a substitute for asserting land claims. Large-scale afforestation projects began during the *yishuv* period and intensified after 1948. Tree planting has long been symbolically significant in Judaism, particularly associated with the holiday of Tu B'Shvat, and scripture passages call for the protection of trees, even during war (Deuteronomy 20:19–20). Following the Holocaust, the JNF and other organizations depicted tree planting in *ha-aretz* as a symbolic revival, each tree being akin to one of the six million Jews killed (Zerubavel 1996). Israel's first prime minister also promoted sapling donations from Diaspora Jews to forge lasting ties between Jews around the world and the land of Israel, and afforestation employed large numbers of new immigrants in the kind of labor thought to be so important to their integration (Cohen 1993; Lehn and Davis 1988).

This afforestation has reshaped landscapes, including large areas of the Negev that are now tree covered. Often linked by name to an adjoining Jewish settlement, like Lahav Forest and Be'eri Forest, the forests clearly claim land for the Jewish state. The instrumental value of afforestation is downplayed in official sources, however, particularly in recent years. The JNF describes its tree-planting activities not as the defense of Jewish national lands, but as ecological improvements, creating "'green lungs' around congested towns and cities, and provid[ing] recreation and respite for all Israelis" (Jewish National Fund 2010). In this case, the familiar narrative of redemption is posed in ecological terms, rebranding ethnic nationalism as ecological nationalism.[11]

In fact, the discursive centrality of agriculture in Zionism has undergone a more general shift in the decades since Israeli statehood. Following Labor Zionism's loss of political control in 1977, ties weakened between agricultural unions and political leaders, eroding public assistance for farming communities, such as water allocations, loans, and subsidies (Schwartz, Lees, and Kressel 1995). Greater integration in global trade also pushed policymakers to evaluate farming in terms of economic markers such as gross national product and numbers of Israelis employed in the sector, which have been declining.[12] Creeping concerns about environmental degradation and high water use in arid regions also began tempering agriculture's redemptive status for land.

Agricultural labor has also lost its vaunted status. As Israel consolidated its control over territory, farming lost its strategic importance for building the nation-state. From the 1970s, as Israel industrialized and higher-wage jobs became more plentiful, *moshavim* and *kibbutzim* began hiring low-wage Palestinian workers. Agricultural labor became understood as an acceptable interim job for youth, but as a group of young *moshav* residents opined in 1972: "A person who respects himself . . . cannot remain in agriculture beyond the age of thirty. When one is established one ought to be far, far away from it" (Kressel 1995:161). These youths labeled an agricultural career as the path of a fool, challenging *sabra* ideals of labor on behalf of the collective and the character-building role of agricultural work. By the 1980s, *moshavim* and *kibbutzim* stopped receiving priority in state budgets, and they played only a small role in immigrant resettlement. Agriculture's decline shocked the many *moshavim* and *kibbutzim* built to rely on farming (Sherman and Schwartz 1995). Because settlements' locations and farming plans were based on ideological and territorial priorities more than their ecological fit, many depended on subsidies to survive. But by the mid-1980s, governments were refusing requests for assistance. The ideal of national advancement through collectivism that was so strongly associated with earlier agriculture has been challenged by an ideal of improvement through competition and the individual profit motive (Bloch 2003; Sherman and Schwartz 1995).

However, the genealogy of the discourse of agricultural redemption continues to make it salient in contemporary debates over land use. Debates in the Knesset continue to reference farmers as the quintessential national workers, as when proposals to reduce farmers' high water allocations were opposed as "national larceny" because they reneged on Israel's commitment to its farmers (Tal 2002:228; see also Shuval 2013). There is now great ambivalence about agriculture's place in Israeli society. Despite budgetary and legislative shifts away from supporting cooperative agriculture, recent opinion surveys suggest that farmers continue to be seen as necessary for Israel's security and success, even when they regularly face economic losses (Lipchin 2007). Farming continues to carry rhetorical power, particularly through its perceived historical role in redeeming neglected lands and rooting a scattered people, but this power is tempered by Israel's increasingly economic and individualistic contemporary priorities.

Defining Arab-Jewish Difference

While a focus on Jewish territory and building Jewish character through labor have clearly been central to Zionist narratives, these narratives are also predicated on particular notions of the Arabs who lived and continue to live in the lands they claim. A third central discourse of Zionism asserts a deep, natural distinction between Jew and Arab. Though it has become taken for granted, this discourse of difference has actually grown and shifted since the early 1900s. When early Jewish immigrants reached Palestine, they encountered rich natural and social landscapes that included a complex Palestinian society of farmers, merchants, small villages, and cosmopolitan cities. Both Zionist leaders and individual settlers of this period developed notions of the New Hebrew's ideal character and behaviors through ambivalent relationships with Arabs. In different circumstances, they viewed Arabs as potential enemies, peaceful competitors, knowledgeable neighbors, and Semitic cousins (Zerubavel 2008b).

To some extent, this ambivalent relationship involved emulation. While agricultural rooting has been a strong element of Zionism, Palestinians were agriculturalists long before the rise of Zionist movements, particularly in northern Palestine. Many *fallahin*, Palestinian peasant farmers, lived around new Zionist settlements, and as early immigrants attempted to adjust to their new agricultural lifestyles, many borrowed techniques from these *fallahin*. Even more than other Palestinians, Zionists enlisted Bedouins of the Negev as a symbolic bridge linking new and ancient Hebrews. Influential groups of Jewish settlers emulated elements of Bedouin dress, horse-riding, and shepherding in an effort to establish themselves as natives (Almog 2000). Some even promulgated a "Hebrew Bedouin" identity, suggesting that the Bedouins they observed closely resembled their ancient Hebrew patriarchs, and that by emulating them they could demonstrate their ties to the land (Zerubavel 2008b).

However, early settlers also socially and temporally distanced themselves from Arabs. Zionists' claims of bringing a civilizing influence to the neglected wastelands of Palestine included drives both to "green the desert" and to civilize the Arabs, particularly Bedouins. The notion of the Bedouin-Hebrew desert dweller erased time between ancient and contemporary Bedouin tribes.[13] And while *chalutzim* borrowed individual agricultural techniques from Arabs, they cultivated contrasting images of themselves as farmers. They organized along socialist values of collectivism rather than along family or tribal lines, and the more open sexuality, exposed skin, and joint work of Hebrew men and women farming together (which challenged traditional gender roles) were seen as progressive practices and contrasted with popular images of Arabs (Biale 1992). At the same time, in literature, textbooks, and settlers' diaries Bedouins were depicted as a natural part of the landscape (Shamir 1996), and Jewish settlers wrote of their struggles to conquer the land, with its mosquito-infested swamps in the north and searing desert heat in the south (de-Shalit 1995). Both of these civilizing drives rested on an imagined contrast between the desert and the sown, between the *yishuv*, as civilized settlement, and wilderness as its opposite, "counter-space" (Zerubavel 2008a).

As Jewish immigration to Palestine proceeded, Jewish settlers came to see Arab inhabitants as increasingly threatening (Zakim 2006). In the 1920s and 1930s, as the Zionist movement's colonial ambitions became clearer, encounters with Palestinian residents strained romanticized visions of cousin affiliation. Arab leaders reacted to Jewish settlement with more violence, and Zionist groups increasingly used forceful and violent tactics of territorial defense (Caplan 1978; Shlaim 2000).[14] When these tensions escalated to war in 1948, the war, in addition to its direct death and destruction, became a key element in Zionism's construction of Arab-Jewish difference. Leaders framed the war in ethnoreligious terms rather than as a confrontation between competing nationalist groups; it was depicted as proof of Arab violence in contrast to Jewish reason (Chafets 1986).

Following the war, two historical developments made a Zionist discourse of Arab-Jewish division even more fraught. The Israeli state became responsible for Palestinian Arab citizens. Simultaneous Zionist aspirations to build a democratic state, which would treat all Jewish and non-Jewish citizens equally, and to create a Jewish state, which would be threatened by too much Arab integration, clashed (Ben-Porat and Turner 2011). At the same time, large numbers of Jewish immigrants began arriving from Arab countries.[15] These Mizrahi newcomers threatened the neat separation of Jew from Arab as naturally distinct. The physical separation of Arabs from Jews within Israel, through the *siyag* (the enclosure zone in the northern Negev) and a similar military administration in Israel's north, as well as efforts among the primarily Ashkenazi personnel of the JNF and JA to excise Mizrahi immigrants' Arab-influenced customs and languages can both be understood as Zionists' efforts to shore up a separation between Jew and Arab (Shohat 1988).

Some new settlers emulated Palestinian practices during this period, too. For example, one elderly *kibbutz* resident recalled his service during the 1950s managing friendly relations with neighboring Arab communities as his *kibbutz*'s "*mukhtar*," an Arabic term for a chosen leader. However, he also painted an anachronistic portrait equating his Hebrew ancestors with his contemporary neighbors. "The Sons of Israel," he told me, "were a Bedouin tribe." Importantly, this resident was Ashkenazi, and this sort of imitation, even buffered by this temporal distancing, would have been riskier for Mizrahi settlers. Indeed, I never heard such accounts of imitation from Mizrahim during fieldwork.

Sociological and anthropological scholarship of the 1950s and 1960s demonstrates the importance of Arab-Jewish opposition in defining the ideal character of the New Hebrew. The era saw intensive production of ethnographic knowledge, of both Mizrahim and Arabs in Israel.[16] Accounts of Mizrahim focused on their assimilation into Israeli society (e.g., Harman 1951; Weingrod 1966). Israeli scholars consistently characterized Arabs as politically weak, traditional, and having "backward" family structures, in direct contrast to Jewish Israeli self-portraits of the time, which emphasized Jewish unity, modern outlooks, and progressive gender roles and family structures that placed individual character and contribution to the Jewish nation over family cohesion (Furani and Rabinowitz 2011; Rabinowitz 2002).

Within this landscape of hardening social boundaries, Bedouin Arabs occupied a unique position, retaining a romanticized image within Zionist discourse longer than their *fallahin* counterparts (Cohen 2010). Many Zionists viewed Bedouins as loyal because many tribes assisted Zionist fighters in 1948 or remained neutral during the war. At the same time, their association with the Negev desert gained Bedouins the mixed compliment of "noble savage." While Zionist calls for the "conquest of the wilderness" (*kibush ha-shmama*) were repeated in speech, on posters, and even on postage stamps through the 1950s, those pushing to settle the Negev also depicted Bedouins as primitive nomads in need of modernizing by a "benevolent state" (Almog 2000; Shamir 1996).

Arab-Jewish difference lies at the heart of "ours, not theirs" debates about land in the contemporary Negev. In more recent decades, widespread efforts to foster Jewish multiculturalism have worked to dispel negative stereotypes of Mizrahim. However, most have done so by affirming the core Jewishness of these immigrants and their descendants and distancing them from "Arab" practices (for example, language). This has left many Orientalist stereotypes, particularly a discourse of Arab-Jewish difference, intact (Mizrachi and Herzog 2012). This discourse along with those contending the necessity for Jewish territory and the value of agricultural labor in land hold great influence. Sometimes mobilized explicitly, as in Mark's statements about the agricultural work of his *kibbutz's* founders in shaping that Jewish territory, but often left implicit, these discourses and their genealogies serve as the main criteria for evaluating land claims in Israel.

Changing Mobility

Historical accounts of Jewish "return" and the reclamation of neglected lands through agriculture meet counter-narratives in the histories told by Bedouin residents of the Negev. Bedouin poetry and historical and ethnographic accounts demonstrate that mobility, not sedentism, has long been prized in Bedouin culture as a source of strength and sign of freedom, both in the Naqab and beyond (el-Aref 1974; Bailey 1991; Marx 1967; Meir 1998). Deep genealogical roots and a strong territorial connection have indicated a tribe's honor, and protecting this status through honorable behavior has been of primary importance (Abu-Lughod 1986; Shryock 1997). Historically, nomadic tribes used their mobility to leverage power over sedentary communities by controlling trade routes and exacting payments, to avoid military conscription, and to prevent the direct involvement of central governments in daily life (Bailey 2009; Kressel, Ben David, and Abu Rabia 1991; Meir 1998). From this perspective, mobile animal husbandry was a more laudable livelihood than agriculture.[17] When speaking to me of the distant past, Bedouin residents associated mobility with freedom, and valued land—or more precisely, access to wide expanses of land—for supporting that mobility and freedom.

The relative advantage of nomadism over sedentism began changing in the Naqab under Ottoman rule, though, and more so during the British Mandate. Participation in the regional economy developing around Beersheba began making more consistent residence in the region preferable to wide-ranging yearly migrations (el-Aref 1974). Like centralized governments around the world, governing regimes encouraged sedentarization to control "roving" populations, making them easier to monitor and tax, and in order to reserve land for more profitable agricultural or industrial development (Ginat and Khazanov 1998; Nelson 1973; Ramos 1998).[18] Associations of mobility with freedom and strength underwent a more severe upheaval after the creation of Israel, when the rules of land access changed suddenly and dramatically. As the Zionist government worked to root Jews in the land physically, legislatively, and symbolically, simultaneous measures uprooted Bedouin Arabs from family lands and agropastoral lifestyles. The Black Goat Law of 1950 limited the number of goats allowed per *dunam* of land and prohibited grazing on forested lands.[19] Implementation of the *siyag* forced many families to move off their lands and crowded these displaced families onto lands claimed by other Bedouin groups. Israeli definitions of land ownership required documentation and excluded the oral agreements that most Bedouin used to track land claims (Shamir 1996). Sixty years after this dramatic shift, Naqab Bedouin residents spoke of mobility with ambivalence. Celebrating one's family's proud nomadic past in narratives would further separate the speaker from powerful Zionist norms of land use.

Instead, many residents recounted long family histories within the Naqab. Some, like Yousef, tapped into the moral weight accorded to farming in Zionist discourse by stressing the sedentary and agricultural practices of their forebears and downplaying nomadism.[20] Even more commonly, Naqab narratives established a discourse of nativeness interrupted, depicting themselves as native to the Naqab desert and others as outsiders. Structurally, speakers often did so by describing life before 1948 in ways that elided historical change. Like Yousef's account, descriptions of the yearly cycle of agropastoral practices emphasized how attuned Bedouin Arabs were with the local ecosystem: The people worked hard and stayed healthy. They moved their herds in accordance with fluctuating vegetation growth. Their crops depended on the rains, and the year's rains depended in part on the people's just and generous behavior, as God rewards and punishes through the rains.

Often a handful of practices and material objects indexed this whole cyclical way of life in the past (see also Bahloul 1993).[21] Tents featured prominently. In particularly sparse accounts, "We lived in tents" was deemed sufficient to evoke a whole lifestyle, despite the variety of forms tent-dwelling could take, from seasonal mobility to spending decades in the same place. Others explained tent life in more detail, describing family clusters of tents; well-established gender roles through which families produced basic necessities like housing, food, and tools; and economic cooperation that linked family units along tribal ties, as well.

Growing one's own food figured as a labor-intensive, but wholesome practice of the past. One afternoon, I sat with several elderly women on cushions in the entryway of a house in Rahat, a township that has grown to a city of more than 40,000 residents. Sipping soda from plastic cups and glimpsing the tower of speakers rising in the courtyard for a wedding party one afternoon, the women and I discussed life in the Naqab. Led by Um Khalid and Um Rashid, the women contrasted their former agriculture and eating habits with the present. They once grew barley, cucumbers, tomatoes, okra, and other vegetables, ground their flour, and made bread. "Now," Um Khalid said regretfully, "we eat out of the refrigerator." This phrase, it became clear as our conversation continued, was metonymic for a whole range of dietary habits, including relying on prepackaged foods, eating pesticide-laden produce, and consuming too much sugar. The women told me how they used to draw clean well water to drink and water vegetable plots. In contrast, due to pesticides on produce and the gray water (filtered and recycled water) used for irrigation, the women told me, "Today we eat illness."

Drawing water from wells, and the distance walked to reach these wells, was another common element of reminiscences. Some speakers emphasized the difficulty of this daily routine during the Ottoman era, estimating and repeating the number of kilometers they walked daily, carrying water on their heads. Others conceded the difficulty of chores like this in the past, but also insisted it was a healthier way of life. Walking kept people fit. And that well water was pure, many told me, not like the polluted tap water of today.

Each of these items or practices not only stood for a past lifestyle, but also drew a nostalgic contrast between a relatively harmonious past and a dysfunctional present. Nostalgic accounts of past tent life and provisioning food together depicted families as warmer and more dependable than today. Wafiq, who was seventeen years old when his family moved from their tent into a house in a government-built township in the late 1980s, longingly recalled:

> We used to . . . gather all the family together and to be in the same place, to have meals together, to eat together, and to sleep in the same place, one next to the other, like a domino [chuckle]. It was a special thing that really connected us together. . . . We were warm and loving. And supporting each other. This is the lifestyle that we had.

Food preparation and eating were social events. The labor required to turn stalks of wheat into bread drew women of the family together for preparation, and people ate in large groups when the freshly prepared meal was ready. Now, the group in Rahat told me, each person eats by himself. Although contemporary practices, such as the many large family meals I joined while living with Bedouin families, challenge this assertion, the perceived contrast between past cooperation and eating alone today is meaningful because it regretfully asserts a trend toward less cohesive family life, along with a shift away from seasonally attuned life.

This depiction of former cyclical continuity works to strengthen Bedouins' claims to Naqab lands, but it also coincides with popular Zionist and other Orientalist conceptions of Bedouins "as if they were separate from the rest of the population and somehow outside of, or beyond, history" (Cole 2003:238). The Negev desert was the quintessential wilderness for Zionism, both a threatening void in need of cultivation and a romantic natural space of "refuge from the social order" (Zerubavel 2008a:214). The Negev could only be this wilderness, though, as long as the desert's Bedouin inhabitants were more "natural" than "social," and as long as they fit within Zionism's opposition between modern Jews versus Arabs in need of modernization. The narratives Bedouin residents told me similarly posited Bedouins as internal to the local ecology. Bedouin pastoralists, their herds and crops, and the seasons all moved in synchrony, and changing any element of this system would throw other elements out of balance.[22]

The romanticism in this narrative of native equilibrium could be challenged by a variety of sources. Bedouin historiography highlights the importance of migrations, battles, and trade relations between Bedouins and others (Shryock 1997). Newer ecological models challenge the notion of stable equilibrium as the basis for relationships between people and landscapes, contending that all such relationships involve dramatic fluctuations and uncertainty (Scoones 1999). And ethnographic and historical accounts from this region describe interactions of trade, technologies, and people prior to 1948, denying a strictly bounded and unchanging culture (el-Aref 1974; Marx 1967; Abu-Rabia 2001; Rosen 2008).[23]

However, rather than simply dismissing this notion of natural connection and native equilibrium as counterfactual, these environmental discourses must be recognized for their significance in counter-narratives and land claims. In contrast to their accounts of natural Bedouin connections and equilibrium, many Bedouin residents depicted Zionism as a cause of ruptured equilibrium. Their narratives mark the end of a socially and ecologically harmonious cycle with the rupture of war in 1948 and a shift to more historical accounts thereafter. These residents recount war and the creation of the Jewish state as initiating a series of upheavals that threw the Bedouin out of balance with their natural environment. Bedouin elders who had lived through the period simply referred to "the war" or "when the Jews came into the country," rather than using the common Arabic term "al-Nakba" (the Catastrophe).[24] Many families who were dwelling in tents and living "from the land" fled to escape the fighting. They thought they would soon return to resume their lives, but instead the war began a series of permanent dislocations. Political boundaries, such as those between Israel and Egypt or the Naqab and the West Bank, disrupted what narratives described as natural migrations. Those families who sheltered in areas that fell outside the newly established borders of Israel could not return home. Others, who had sought refuge by foot or donkey-driven cart in closer areas, such as the southern Hebron hills, did return to their old homes after the fighting. But governance, family structures, economic relations, and food habits all began to change. Thereafter, narrators spoke of Bedouins losing their connection to land.

The *siyag* was central to Bedouin Arabs' accounts of these lost connections. Because the term is common in everyday speech, residents rarely explained the *siyag* as a policy. Instead, they focused on the social upheaval caused by this physical dislocation. During the *siyag*, the government granted some families from favored tribes rights to farm and herd on lands around the townships, but oftentimes these lands were already claimed by other Bedouin Arabs. Such families faced the choice of violating other Bedouins' land claims or ceasing agropastoralism themselves. Severing access to Bedouins' wide ranges of grazing land also severed ties between the smaller units of an extended family that once used these lands cooperatively (Kressel 2003; Meir 1998). These dislocations exacerbated the slicing of kin networks that had occurred in 1948, when political boundaries suddenly became rigid, leaving siblings, aunts, and uncles spread across Israel, Gaza, the Sinai, and Jordan. The internal dislocations caused by the *siyag*, the much greater residential density it imposed, and the various measures used by the Israeli government after the *siyag* was lifted to move Bedouins to planned townships splintered families and raised tensions between Bedouin residents over land claims.

In more indirect ways, too, speakers lamented how dislocations after 1948 divided families. Many Bedouin Arabs still prefer for a married couple to settle with the husband's family, but I heard repeatedly how the scarcity of land in recognized townships prevents sons from building such patrilocal homes. In unrecognized villages, because recently built structures are most likely to receive demolition orders, sons have difficulty building homes in their parents' villages. When sons did not settle in homes near their parents, grandparents were less involved in raising their grandchildren and cousins felt less bonded. Isolated nuclear families had gained influence in Bedouin society at the expense of extended families, I was told. Bedouins' greater dependence on wage labor, often seasonal and short term, exacerbated this splintering tendency by requiring frequent relocations (Meir 1998). Such relocations involved mobile individuals, or at most nuclear families, rather than entire tribes or lineages.

This was a new kind of mobility, as wage laborers rather than agropastoralists. While sitting in the courtyards of government-built townships or unrecognized villages in the *siyag*, some residents described how the Israeli military forced them to relocate from their family lands. Others described how their fathers, unmoored from their former homes and cut off from the means to subsist as agropastoralists, went in search of wage labor, sometimes on their own and sometimes moving their families with them. Bayan, now a mother of five, described how her father had moved their family from *moshav* to *moshav*, as seasonal harvesting work changed, and then to a large city when an injury forced him to shift from agriculture to work as a warehouse guard. In these accounts, mobility felt like dependence rather than freedom.

Honorable Land Ties

The measures that made mobility practically problematic have also placed moral constraints on Naqab narratives because they outlawed many Bedouin tasks and taskscapes. They defined legitimate land use in the Naqab according to Zionist priorities (agriculture and sedentary residence as the deepest and most valued tie to land) and supported a dominant narrative of law and order that casts Bedouins as roving law-breakers (Shamir 1996). As a resident of the Jewish *moshav* of Dganim explained, if you go up to any high point around the *moshav*, you will see that other than the land on which the *moshav* sits, everything else is full of Bedouins. "They have come and settled on every area of land," he said angrily, "and it's all illegal!" Such simplistic invocations of contemporary laws ignore the political interests of Israeli territorial control that shaped those laws.

Some Naqab residents attempted to oppose the dominant legalist discourse of land claims by enlisting a discourse of land and honor. While associations of Bedouin and lawlessness are strong in Israel, popular understandings of Bedouin society as a culture of honor and fierce independence also circulate widely. Without the power to actually change laws, many residents drew on this alternative image to implicitly or explicitly challenge the legitimacy of Israeli ownership laws. Counter-narratives like Yousef's depict the previous Bedouin system of ownership as clear and honorable. He stated:

> Everybody knew where one man's land ended and another began. There was no need to lay down markers. Nobody would claim this land if it belonged to someone else. It's a matter of honor. You can trust the word of a Bedouin; it's bound to respect for God. . . . We had natural borders, like the top of a hill, for example. If you pour water on the top, all the land where water flows one way is one person's, and where it flows the other way, it's the second man's.

Yousef commended this system of property recognition as honorable and correlated with natural boundaries. In contrast, he described governmental property registrations as systems imposed by outside occupiers. Bedouins didn't "make *Tabos*" (deeds of ownership) under the Ottomans, he said, because the Ottomans were an occupying empire that just came to take taxes. And later, he continued, the British started the *Tabo* up north but never finished in the south before they left.[25] To drive home his dismissal of this official ownership system, Yousef stated, And besides, even if we'd had *Tabo*, they'd still have taken the land. "They," here, refers to the Israeli government after 1948. Yousef recognized that property law is a social negotiation (Verdery 2003) and suggested that calls for documented property rights are a ruse masking the real basis of land ownership in the Naqab: might makes right.

Many counter-narratives contrasted Bedouin Arabs' honorable behavior with the betrayed loyalties they experienced under Israeli rule. Elderly Bedouins told me they had avoided fighting in the 1948 war and were led to believe that in exchange, they would be allowed to continue living peacefully on their lands.[26] Nuri's sense of betrayal was common. He was a child living in the northern Naqab after the war and recalled his father, a *sheik*, receiving military orders for Bedouin tribes to evacuate their lands. His father went in protest to a Knesset member and said, as Nuri recounted: "Why does Israel want to take away from us our lands and houses, when we had arrived at an agreement that we would protect the security and the borders, and the state should protect our land and our houses, so we can plow and farm?" His father was told the army "only wanted the area for six months in order for the army to do exercises on it, and then you can return."

Nuri was nine years old, he told me, when Israeli soldiers forced his family out of their village of mud-brick houses, agricultural fields, and grazing lands. "They moved us to the area of Hura," he told me, which was inside the *siyag* area. "There was no water. And in the beginning, we had no land of our own." Because of his father's status, the government granted Nuri's family rights to farm and herd on some of these new lands. However, as Nuri recalled:

> In the first year, we farmed the lands. And then the owners of the land began to come to us. Each one came after a period of time and said this is our land that you're farming. And my father . . . said, "You say this is your land? Okay, you take it. We aren't going to take someone's land. We don't want to settle on anyone else's land."

Faced with the choice of violating other Bedouins' land claims or ceasing agro-pastoralism themselves, Nuri's father chose the latter. Despite the hardship, Nuri proudly portrayed his father's response as more honorable than the government's behavior.

Despite earlier promises that transfers would be temporary, tribes were never allowed to return to their lands. As Nuri grew older, he said, he came to believe that removing non-Jewish people from lands in order to make room for Jewish people was "a racist idea of the first degree." Nuri grew up attending Israeli schools and participating in a youth program at a *kibbutz*, and this land seizure and transfer went against the rhetoric of democracy and citizenship that he learned there. As an adult, Nuri began publishing articles denouncing the government's treatment of Arabs. As a result of his convictions, and in honor of his father, who died before being able to move back to his former lands, Nuri took up residence in these lands again in 2006, living in a tent and his car. State agencies consider this to be illegal squatting, and Nuri has been embroiled in legal battles ever since. Nuri showed me documents supporting his ownership claims, such as tax records and old maps showing his family name of el-Okbi labeling large areas. However, he spoke less of this documentary evidence and more of principles like honor, respect, and loyalty that Bedouins have upheld but the state has forsaken.

This connection between land rights, honor, and loyalty to the state was even more pronounced in connection with military service. Bedouin Arab service members and their families forcefully expressed a sense of betrayed loyalties. In accordance with their status as "loyal Arabs," Bedouin Arab volunteers were accepted into the Israeli Defense Force (IDF) beginning in the 1960s (Cohen 2010).[27] Because of its status as the overriding mark of state loyalty in Israeli society, advocates for Bedouins' land rights often cite military service as evidence that they have earned recognition of land claims. Residents spoke of their disappointment that the state had not behaved honorably toward these military volunteers. A frequently circulated story captures this sense of betrayed loyalty with irony. One day, a young Bedouin man who had volunteered for the IDF returned to his home to find two notices from the government waiting for him. One was a summons to report for reserve duty with the IDF. The other was a citation warning him that his house, built in an unrecognized village without a legal permit, would be demolished. Similar reports appear in newspaper articles and the publications of Bedouin rights groups as moral ammunition against the dishonorable actions of the state (Kanaaneh 2009).

Constrained Claims

The Negev's Jewish and Bedouin Arab residents make competing claims to lands, and to justify these contemporary claims, residents like Chaim, Mark, and Yousef interpret and narrate particular pasts. Because Zionism became the guiding ideology of the state, its central environmental discourses of agricultural redemption, territorialism, and Arab-Jewish difference have profound consequences for all those involved in Israel's contemporary land conflict. All the Negev's residents must negotiate the complex genealogies of these discourses. Narratives of the past stake explicit land claims, and they also make implicit ethical claims using the taken-for-granted relationships between people and landscapes embedded in environmental discourses. When a Bedouin resident of an unrecognized village invites human rights advocates to witness his planting of trees by his home, he is asserting his rightful claim to the land through the roots of the trees and the agricultural labor he has invested in them. When a *moshav* resident extols the success of her *moshav* in growing and selling apricots, she is not only speaking of financial success, but also asserting her agricultural community's value in protecting territory for the Jewish state as well as asserting her belonging as a valuable member of society. Thus, historical narratives continue to shape political disputes, often in unacknowledged ways.

When Yousef, Nuri, Um Khalid, and other Bedouin residents told me their historical accounts, they were narrating not the Negev but the Naqab, a place with an Arab heritage that predates Zionism's waves of Jewish settlement. This was not always exclusively Arab space, as some spoke positively of early Arab-Jewish relations, noting how they helped individual Jewish settlers find water or navigate other difficulties of the desert. The Naqab, in Yousef's account, is not a frontier periphery of a larger state project, but a center of livelihoods and intertribal activity. But as he narrated, Yousef, like other Naqab residents, also negotiated Zionism's dominant environmental discourses and the genealogy they claim.

At times, Yousef was defiant. Gesturing across the road to the *moshav* where I was living, he countered the common depiction of unrecognized villages as recent squatters' settlements, proclaiming, They lie if they say this village was not here until recently! He then proudly narrated his forefathers' labor in these landscapes. At other times, Yousef lamented the fall of a once proud people. After recounting his village's past lifestyle as a seasonal routine of growing crops and raising animals, he emphasized how this routine has disintegrated. They don't have land for farming or to hold big weddings anymore, Yousef told me. They have lost their community gatherings and tradition of poetry, as each person now sits in his own house watching television. They have suffered many years of drought because God is punishing their poor behavior, he asserted, and they don't get water for farming from the state as do their Jewish neighbors. Thus, they can't make a living anymore from farming. "The Bedouin have taken a blow" (*al bedu akhathu darab*), he said, "and the damage has spread."

When they choose their words, speakers like Yousef must acknowledge the authoritative weight of a more widely known and accepted Zionist version of history that is fixed in books and archives and supported by Israeli institutions, while also finding ways to assert their own authority and gain acceptance for their contradictory accounts. A discourse of disrupted native life was key to many Naqab narratives, and it contradicts certain elements of Zionist discourse, including the separation of a dual society paradigm. In these Bedouin Arabs' accounts, Zionist immigration caused profound changes to the existing Bedouin society, often by coercive means of dislocation but also by more subtle modes of influence, such as improved transportation and the availability of new foods. Rather than confirming the development of parallel and independent Jewish and Arab societies, these narratives demonstrate the profound impact that these groups in the making had on each other, or at least the impact Jews and the Israeli government had on Bedouins. Even more directly, the narratives challenge the Jewishness of territories claimed by the Jewish state. However, this narrative of disrupted native life also coincides with key aspects of Zionist discourse. Both associate Arabs with nature and blend them, and Bedouins in particular, with the desert landscape, while associating culture, modernity, and progress with Jews.

This contrast can be mobilized for very different sorts of land claims. Faced with Zionism's drive to root Jews in the land of Israel, this narrative of Bedouins embedded in particular ecosystems implies potentially powerful claims of "indigenousness" or prior rootedness.[28] Yet this discourse of nativeness also risks restricting land claims in the present and future. Like "noble savage" depictions adopted in indigenous rights campaigns throughout the world, asserting that "true" Bedouin identity is traditional, nonmodern, and tied to landed subsistence risks assigning Bedouin Arabs to an "indigenous slot" that identifies them as a part of nature and denies them the flexibility to change and still remain "authentic" (Brosius 1999; Li 2000; Trouillot 1991).

What happens to land claims based on native connection when a group's lifestyles change? In their reminiscences, as residents' connections to landscapes were disrupted, so too was the *bedaawa* (bedouinness) of their identities. When explaining the term "Bedouin," residents I spoke with all asserted the same origin: "Bedouin" comes from the Arabic word *baadiya*, which means desert. Thus, they said, Bedouin identity is inherently attached to life in the desert, and to be Bedouin means to live in the desert and move from place to place. It is a lifestyle, not an ethnicity, many informants told me, or clarified that one is ethnically Arab and culturally Bedouin.[29] But in contemporary Israel, such a desert lifestyle is impossible, and often undesirable, to follow. Yousef, for example, did not narrate his family's history with the desire to relive it. When we spoke in his cinderblock guest room, he was working at least three jobs to support his family while remaining on their lands. He yearns for elements of a vanished Bedouin lifestyle—the remoteness of a seasonal 'izbe (a sort of camp or retreat) and life in a tent—but he also stated firmly that he wants modern lifestyles for himself and his children. He wants educational opportunities and municipal services comparable to those of Jewish Israelis.

To complicate matters, the environmental discourses that underlie many alternative historical accounts also contradict the very structure of governance and land laws in Israel. Enlisting alternative environmental discourses such as the value of seasonal, nomadic land use would also entail a confrontation with Israeli norms of law and order. The constraining power of law and order norms operates primarily through the language of formal property possession, which Carol Rose (1994) describes as a form of communication. Like the American legal system Rose discusses, Israeli property law relies on criteria such as "suitable use" and a "clear act" of possession, which must be communicated between a possessor and an audience with the power to recognize that possession. As Rose notes, though, "this must be in a language that is understood" (1994:16), and different audiences will understand different acts as legitimate claims to possession, thus setting the rules of ownership from a particular perspective.

Among Bedouin audiences, communal tribal rights, periodic use, undocumented (oral) agreements, and long-term family occupation establish ownership. But Israeli courts, and Israelis who cite court decisions as definitive, do not share these criteria and do not "hear" Bedouin land claims spoken in these terms. Instead, Israeli law and popular discussion of those laws use "conceptualist" logic (Shamir 1996), which imposes fixed notions of residence, individual ownership, and documented dates and boundaries of property. Occupation that did not leave clear traces of "suitable use" according to the standards of an intensive agricultural and commercial audience, such as houses and fenced fields, has not been recognized. Because Bedouin Arabs' traditional norms of land ownership do not fit within these strict boundaries, they, like indigenous land claims elsewhere (Biggs 1989; Nadasdy 2003), are rendered incomprehensible in the Israeli legal system.

Faced with the deafness of the legal system to land ownership that is tracked orally and leaves few physical traces, some speakers shape their accounts to fit Israeli legal norms of communication. Absent are the heroic poems and genealogical histories of sheiks, leading families, and intertribal disputes told by

Bedouins in other places and with different audiences (Shryock 1997). Such tales are troubling to land-rights advocacy efforts in Israel that assert a united Bedouin community. Missing too are discussions of ancestors controlling trade routes or livelihoods based on smuggling (Bailey 1991). Amid widespread stereotypes of Bedouins as wild and lawless, such associations would further strain acceptance into mainstream society. Mobility has become a liability in Israel for land claims, not only in practical terms but also in ethical terms. Instead, Naqab Bedouins often directly enlist a Zionist discourse of land claims through agriculture and, like Yousef, narrate a long history of farming in the region. Indeed, much testimony on behalf of Bedouin Arabs' land claims in court focuses on proving long-term land modifications (Kedar 2001; Shamir 1996).

Some Bedouin residents also attempt to standardize their accounts to conceptualist standards of dating and documentation. Nuri's case provides one example of this standardization. Embroiled for years in legal cases over his family's land claims, he has testified before numerous courts, written newspaper articles about his case, and spoken publicly in many fora. As we sat in the small office of the Bedouin rights advocacy NGO he cofounded twenty-nine years ago, Nuri told me his story. From his first sentence, "I was born in 1942," he made use of calendrical dates. Without pausing to reflect, he listed the day, month, and year when the military evacuated his family, when he and his father returned to farming the family's lands, and when he returned to live on those lands. From birth through his adult life of social activism, Nuri traced a smooth trajectory of causes and effects, with few tangents distracting him from the linear story. The maps, photographs, and tax receipts he showed me furthered his effort to fix his family's residence in place and time. It was clear he had recounted his narrative many times, and that he had done so in formal settings that privilege this narrative style. Nuri's case is also an example of the fruitlessness, thus far, of Bedouins' attempts to meet these standardized expectations. No Bedouin land claims have been affirmed as legal ownership by the Israeli courts (Yahel 2006).

Conclusion

Without significant influence in legislative processes to redefine property law, counter-narratives are one tool Bedouin residents can use to object to current norms of legality and ownership. Naqab Bedouins tell counter-histories that not only contest the historical narrative of Zionist accounts, but also assert alternative justifications for land claims. They assert long-term residence, "natural" connections, and honorable behavior as legitimate bases of contemporary land claims. But while I refer to these accounts as counter-narratives, they are not entirely contradictory to dominant state histories. Rather, these "unofficial" histories refuse elements within "official" history, but also reveal how aspects of official history gain their hegemonic status (Bryant 2008).

As Naqab Bedouins spoke of landscapes and inhabitants, they told selective stories of the past that met the expectations of imagined audiences and made claims about land attachments and social belonging. I was the most immediate audience, but many of the themes in these private narratives also coincide with more public narratives given by Bedouin leaders at political events and asserted in advocacy groups' publications. These speakers were aware of my plans to write and teach about my research findings, and of the international and NGO audiences this implied. Speakers chose their words carefully, attempting to appeal to a broad audience. As such, these reminiscences were not some sort of pure resistance to Zionism's hegemony. Residents opposed Zionist histories through their style of narration and the practices and people they recalled. However, as in many relationships between minority and majority groups, these subaltern narratives were filtered through dominant discourses and often reproduced them (Shryock 1997). When both Zionists and Zionism's critics assert Arab-Jewish difference, the primacy of agricultural labor, and exclusive territorialism, these discourses gain strength.

Both the inclusions and exclusions of accounts about land use responded to sociopolitical pressures. To speak of tactical narration, though, does not declare these narratives to be false. Rather, examining which stories are told and why others remain untold demonstrates the power of dominant environmental discourses to structure and constrain personal narratives of place and belonging.

This is not only a question of limited expression, because material claims over land are interpreted and their legality evaluated with reference to historical narratives of land use. Thus, Bedouin residents' possibilities for land use, as well as the interpretations that fellow residents like Chaim hold of those uses, are both structured by dominant environmental discourses. Residents sometimes push back against these limitations rhetorically, by engaging dominant discourses in counter-histories or enlisting alternative ethical standards, but they do so within limits. Struggles for legal recognition of land rights in the Negev test these limits both through spoken claims and through material dwelling practices. How do dominant discourses and their historical genealogies shape illegality and the possibilities for legalization?

2 Seeking Recognition

BEFORE DAWN ONE JULY MORNING IN 2010, hundreds of police officers and heavy machinery rolled into the Bedouin village of al-'Araqib.[1] Police officers, helmeted and holding large shields, evicted families and moved all the residents away from the houses. As some residents shuffled away, others attempted to hold their ground. Police formed a line between residents and their homes, and destruction teams with bulldozers moved in and crushed the village's eleven cinderblock buildings and thirty-four homes made of corrugated metal, while approximately three hundred residents and several dozen allied Bedouin rights activists looked on. Crews uprooted olive trees, carefully keeping roots intact so that they could be replanted elsewhere. Some residents wailed while others sat quietly staring. By afternoon, as the midsummer heat was peaking, the demolition was complete. Several witnesses video-recorded the events, which they later posted on YouTube and sent out with announcements to the email lists of various social justice NGOs.[2] I watched these events on my computer screen in Michigan the next day, having finished fieldwork the previous year, and recalled my earlier visits to the village.

In newspaper articles following the al-'Araqib demolition, governmental representatives claimed that the Israel Land Administration's (ILA) demolition crews were simply enforcing building laws.[3] A spokesman for the ILA described the crews as "implementing a verdict for the evacuation of the area which has passed all legal instances," including an initial eviction notice in 2003 and a series of appeals that reached the High Court of Justice (JTA Wire Service 2010).[4] Al-'Araqib lay on "state land," and the Israeli government, which claimed the authority to determine these lands' use, had not recognized it as a legal place of residence. Without governmental permits, all al-'Araqib homes were subject to demolition.

Residents and land-rights advocates, on the other hand, claimed that these demolitions were unjust because the laws used to deny ownership rights were based on overly restrictive criteria that ignore Bedouins' land ties and occupancy predating the Israeli state (Kedar 2003; Abu-Saad 2005; Shamir 1996; Yiftachel 2000).[5] Residents were unable to obtain building permits, despite these villages being their historic homes. As one member of Gush Shalom, a left-wing peace activist group, declared following the demolition: "Residents of al-Araqib are neither squatters nor invaders: Their village existed many years before the creation of Israel in 1948. Residents were evicted by the state in 1951, but returned to the land on which they live and which they cultivate" (Hartman 2010). Or as one elderly resident of al-'Araqib stated succinctly, "This is my home. . . . Why should I leave?" (Sanders 2010).

Following this demolition, residents replaced their homes, erecting tents and metal structures. One week later, these structures were destroyed when the ILA returned to carry out another demolition. This process repeated over the next several years, and by 2015, advocacy groups reported the eightieth demolition of al-'Araqib.[6] Residents rebuilt homes, often as makeshift structures, and governmental authorities demolished them. Over the years, village residents have appealed their eviction in courts, but judges have repeatedly rejected their ownership claims.

Al-'Araqib is one of approximately forty villages in the Naqab that are similarly denied the legal right to exist.[7] In blunt, material form, these residents encounter the power of state planning driven by discourses of territoriality, Jewish-Arab difference, and the primacy of intensive agricultural land use. State officials order residents of these unrecognized locales—roughly half the Bedouin residents of the Naqab—to relinquish their lands and move to one of seven government-planned townships. Government agencies assert that without ownership documents or evidence of long-term, settled agriculture, Bedouin residence is "squatting." Residents and their advocates make counter-arguments of morality and justice to assert the legitimacy of their homes and livelihoods and resist demolition. The razing of al-'Araqib was the most extensive act of demolition in recent years, but houses in most unrecognized villages have been demolished and many additional residents throughout these villages have been served with demolition orders that may be carried out at any time (Gottlieb 2008). While the national government has granted provisional legal status without recognizing any ownership rights to several villages on the premise of facilitating social service provisioning, residents have seen little material change in living circumstances.[8]

In the spring of 2008, eviction orders were given to a different constituency of Negev residents. The Israeli newspaper *Haaretz* reported that the ILA and the State Prosecutor's Office sent notices to twenty-three Negev farms instructing farmers "to clear their land and restore it to its original state, because they were violating planning and zoning laws" (Golan 2008). These notices were not administered to Bedouin residents of unrecognized villages, but to Jewish residents living on *chavot bodadim*, or single-family farmsteads.

The farmsteads existed in a planning gray area, between government approval and illegality. In 1992 the Knesset established the Negev Development Authority (NDA) to encourage "the settlement of the Negev and the increase of its capacity to absorb immigrants" (Knesset 1992). Development officials planned a corridor of agrotourism running through the Negev and invited farmers to establish small vineyards and goat farms that would sell wine and gourmet cheese directly to tourists—a "Wine Route." Although small-scale agriculture alone had not proven profitable in this desert region, officials hoped that tourism would supplement farmers' earnings, helping settlement flourish (Moskowitz 2007).

Political interpretations of these farms vary. For some Jewish farmers who had difficulty finding land elsewhere for independent farms, this development initiative was a personal, apolitical opportunity.[9] However, because the NDA sought to increase Jewish settlement in Negev regions from which the government pressured Bedouin Arab residents to leave, many interpreted it as a thinly veiled effort to "protect" land from Bedouins (Tzfadia 2008b). This development plan furthered long-running government efforts to "Judaize" both Israel's border regions and "internal frontier" areas having large Arab populations and proportionally small Jewish populations (Kimmerling 1983; Yiftachel and Meir 1998).

Though the lands granted to farmers were zoned only for agricultural, not residential uses, farmers also built homes and bed-and-breakfast units and brought their families to live with them. They were encouraged by spoken promises of support or benign neglect from governmental officials. In the late 1990s, watchdog groups became aware of these farmsteads and called for their dismantling. Economic development advocates asserted that the distribution of state lands to these farmers was unlawful, and environmental groups claimed the farms wreaked ecological damage on sensitive desert lands where settlement should not be allowed. After a series of court cases, the ILA ordered the evictions in 2008.

Farmstead residents raised a public campaign against eviction. These farmsteads were not numerous—between twenty-five and thirty existed at the time, each housing just one family[10]—but their threatened dismantling prompted widespread disapproval from Israeli citizens throughout the country and international Zionist organizations, such as the Jewish National Fund (JNF). After two years of threats, court cases, and Knesset debates, the Knesset passed legislation that, rather than evacuate the farmers, changed state development priorities in the Negev and retroactively legalized the farmsteads. Thus, by 2010, the interests invested in single-family farmsteads proved powerful enough to achieve what more than forty unrecognized villages housing tens of thousands of Bedouin Arab residents had not been able to achieve. In each case, residents lived in places and engaged in lifestyles that challenged the state's authority to govern behavior and structure landscapes. This case demonstrates that everyday dwelling practices become politicized, whether residents wish to make political statements or not, because much is at stake in whether or not one's dwelling practices are deemed properly Israeli. Comparing the struggles undertaken by residents and the very different resolutions in each case highlights the different opportunities and obstacles facing Jewish and Bedouin residents as they seek government cooperation to shape Israel's laws to fit residents' dwelling practices.

Unrecognized Villages

Today most unrecognized Bedouin villages are clustered near Beersheba in the northern Negev, within the boundaries of what was once the *siyag*. Interwoven factors of historical residence, state-building, and individual choices created the indeterminate legality of these villages. The Negev has long been most densely populated in the north. This high plateau area receives more rainfall than areas further south, yet it was hilly and arid enough to be relatively inaccessible to pre-Israeli central governments, making it a particularly attractive region for seminomadic pastoralists (Marx 1967; Abu-Rabia 1994).[11] As Ottoman and British governments expanded their influence in the region, making Beersheba an increasingly important administrative center, the population in the surrounding region grew. Both seminomadic and fully settled agropastoral families moved to the area, attracted by markets and schools (Marx 1967).

Following Israeli statehood in 1948, national attention to and investment in the Negev ebbed and flowed with the young state's shifting frontiers of military conflict and other national priorities. The upheaval of the 1948 war and the military-enforced relocations and imposition of the *siyag* during the 1950s moved many Bedouin Arabs off family-inhabited lands and further concentrated them around Beersheba. After 1966, with the end of military rule, some residents returned to former family lands while many continued living in the *siyag* where they had been transferred.

During the 1960s, a government policy of Iyur HaBedowim (Urbanization of the Bedouin) began, which aimed to relocate Bedouins from rural communities into towns and cities built specifically for Bedouins. In 1963, then minister of agriculture, Moshe Dayan, expressed the order government leaders sought to instill:

> We must turn the Bedouin into urban laborers. . . . It is true that this is a sharp transition. It means that the Bedouin will no longer live on his land with his flocks, but will become an urbanite who comes home in the afternoon and puts his slippers on. His children will get used to a father who wears pants, without dagger, and who does not pick out their nits in public. They will go to school, their hair combed and parted. This will be a revolution, but it can be achieved in two generations. Not by coercion, but with direction by the state. This reality that is known as the Bedouin will disappear.[12]

The 1965 Planning and Building Law declared all residences outside government-planned townships to be illegal.

The revolutionary change sought by Dayan and others did not aim for assimilation, as government initiatives worked to distance Arabs from Jews through separate school systems and governance under different ministries and regional councils.[13] It is crucial to note that in Dayan's eyes, primitive behaviors of dress and hygiene were inextricable from Bedouin culture and identity, so this change could only happen when Bedouins ceased to be Bedouin. Further, while government initiatives encouraged farming lifestyles for Jewish immigrants, they restrained Bedouin Arabs from farming by restricting land access and building only urbanized, nonagricultural towns for Bedouins.

This separate treatment follows from a discourse of fundamental Jewish-Arab difference and contributes to its instantiation in taskscapes and landscapes. A series of special offices designed to consolidate Bedouin affairs have mediated Bedouin Arab residents' relationships to the state for decades (Swirski and Hasson 2006); at the same time, government agencies stepped up efforts to force or entice Bedouin Arabs into government-planned townships (Dinero 2010; Yiftachel and Meir 1998).[14] About half of Bedouin Arab residents of the Naqab resisted the pressure to urbanize, staying within unrecognized villages instead. These unrecognized villages have no official local councils, and with no listed addresses residents cannot vote in regional council elections.

Though Israeli officials often blame this stalemate on the lack of a real negotiating partner, Bedouin Arab leaders have offered alternative proposals.[15]

In 1995, galvanized by a Beersheba district master plan that plotted industrial areas and city expansions over existing unrecognized villages, Bedouin Arab leaders established the Regional Council of Unrecognized Villages in the Naqab (RCUV). This body of local leaders aimed to offer a strong, collective voice in negotiations. The RCUV has raised the visibility of Bedouin Arabs' demands, primarily by testifying in governmental hearings and providing legal assistance to residents engaged in court cases involving land rights. However, the Israeli government does not recognize the RCUV as a representative body.

Governmentally initiated commissions, legislative measures, and court cases over the years have consistently denied all Bedouins' ownership claims to Negev lands and offered limited compensation to those Bedouins willing to relinquish ownership claims and move to townships (Amara, Abu-Saad, and Yiftachel 2013).[16] Recently, the government's tendency toward enforcement or negotiation has shifted somewhat with changes in Israel's ruling party (right-wing parties tending toward less compromise and harsher enforcement). In 2000, Ehud Barak's administration led a plan to legally recognize six Bedouin villages. In 2003, however, the state government escalated enforcement of zoning regulations, including home demolitions and the spraying of crops with herbicide (Brous 2007; Negev Coexistence Forum 2006; Qupty 2004). In 2005, the state established the Abu Basma regional council to administer to the recently recognized villages.[17] Yet by the end of my fieldwork in 2009, little had changed in the living conditions of these villages because the regional council existed primarily on paper. In 2008, policy recommendations from the Goldberg Commission, appointed under Prime Minister Ehud Olmert, seemed to promise flexibility in the government stance, including acknowledgment of Bedouins' "historic connection" to the Negev and the need to include them in municipal planning (Goldberg et al. 2008). But the Prawer-Begin Plan of 2013, under Prime Minister Benjamin Netanyahu, instead proposed more relocations and harsh punitive measures against those who resisted. Growing population pressure in Israel's center has prompted the national government to reprioritize Jewish settlement in the Negev and curtail Bedouin access to large areas of land. Thus, since 1965, residents and governmental planners have been in a stalemate.

The Push and Pull of Village Life

With this growing focus on the Negev as a frontier, the future of unrecognized Bedouin villages has become a larger topic of debate among Israelis around the country. External commentary tends to highlight primarily what the villages lack. For example, an editorial published in the Israeli newspaper the *Jerusalem Post* reports:

> Twail Abu-Jarwal can hardly be called a village. Home to some 450 Beduin [*sic*], members of the al-Tlalka tribe, the clusters of tents and tin shacks are sprawled over several barren *wadis* [dry streambeds] in the northern Negev. Reached by turning onto a dirt road off route 40 north of Beersheba, the community—or what remains of it—is barely accessible.
>
> This is Beduin country. . . . The results of the absence of planning and agreed-upon arrangements for the Beduin population can be seen in the chaotically expanding jerry-built collections of shacks and piles of refuse that are visible along the highways of the Negev; what was once a striking desert landscape has become an eyesore. The results can also be seen in the abject poverty and social neglect in which most Beduins live and in the growing alienation and rage that have gripped the Beduin community. (Golan 2007)

Similarly, my early visits to villages, led by land-rights activists, highlighted poverty and social neglect. In addition to a lack of services, because these settlements are not accounted for in regional plans, industrial zones and chemical waste and nuclear facilities have been built alongside many (Almi 2003; Tal 2002:332). In Wadi al-Naʿam, a village that surrounds a regional electricity plant and sits across the road from the Naqab's hazardous waste facility and industrial zone of Ramat Hovav, the toxicity felt tangible. I smelled the rank smoke from the industrial plants and heard the buzz of the high-voltage electricity cables strung overhead, from which residents could gain no electricity. Thick drifts of garbage seemed to hug every depression and wind-side hill face (see Ill. 1).

Illustration 1. One side of Wadi al-Naʿam, next to the electricity plant. 2008. Photograph by Author.

Thus, on two sides of a dueling commentary, Bedouin rights activists and governmental officials both emphasize the deplorable material conditions of the villages. Such portraits beg the question: Faced with possible eviction and living in uncomfortable, even hazardous conditions, why don't residents of unrecognized villages move? Outsider perceptions of these villages as places of lack make evacuation seem a logical solution. Residents, however, have compelling reasons to avoid this. Poverty and social neglect are real and pressing issues, but they do not fully encompass residents' experiences of these landscapes.

In conversations with me, residents discussed many motivations for staying, but most centered on attachments to the village as a landscape and anchor of identity. They felt comfortable in the open vistas and arid scrub of their villages, while the landscapes of large towns felt strange. I understood this attachment on one level. Anthropological theories of dwelling recognize how one learns the world through particular landscapes, gaining a sense of familiarity and security, no matter how uncomfortable its material circumstances may be (Ingold 2000). Indeed, I had given this explanation to others (mostly Jewish Israelis interested in my research) asking me why "they" live there. However, coming from a middle-class American culture in which mobility to find a comfortable home was the norm, I initially found it difficult to understand at a more visceral level why residents felt attached to these places. In Palestine-Israel, a house becomes an uneasy metaphor for a group's political struggle, and claims of property and collective rights can obscure "a different kind of valuation" that foregrounds the deep experiential importance of a place (Bishara 2003:143). To understand residents' motivations requires attention to these ways of valuing home.

After my introduction to unrecognized villages as places of neglect, one overnight visit with a family in Wadi al-Na'am, approximately halfway through my fieldwork, showed me another side of village life. The family lived over a hill and out of view of the industrial zone (see Ill. 2). A constant wind prevented chemical odors from lingering. It felt cleaner here. The surrounding hills were open, dotted with just a few other Bedouin homes. We worked outside all day building a community center, then sat in the blackening purple of evening. Bright lights began dotting the hills as generators turned on, and Beersheba glowed on the horizon. I started to see the landscape from the family's point of view. Aside from the aesthetic, romantic appeal of sweeping winds and the orange-brown of desert stone, there was a comfortable distance from neighbors. When the generators shut off, the night was quiet, punctuated only by crickets.

Illustration 2. The far side of Wadi al-Na'am. 2008. Photograph by Author.

This visit introduced me to the pull of village life. After my experience in Wadi al-Na'am, when I visited a family in the unrecognized village of el-Hawashla, I was more prepared to perceive the family's everyday dwelling practices for their benefits as well as their difficulties. Amna, a friend from 'Ayn al-'Azm, took me to visit her parents. When I first arrived, we sat in the parents' home chatting, and Amna's brother described the difficulties of living without building permits, never knowing when his house might be demolished. Later, happy to be out of the township for the day, Amna led me through the hills behind her parents' house. She knew the names and uses of seemingly every plant we passed. She proudly dug up the fuzzy, light-green root called *khukh barri* (wild peach) for me to taste and pointed out the *qasuum* that is good for easing stomach pains. Her son cleaned his hands by rubbing them on the leaves of a *slaameniya* bush. Her younger children ran about without fear in the open spaces around the house, and the women felt free to raise their voices and let their headscarves fall loose without worries of peering eyes from unrelated neighbors. They felt at home here. Though "home is not necessarily a comfortable or pleasant place to be" (Ingold 2005:503), the security that comes from knowing a landscape helps to make that place home.

Consistent with Naqab narratives of the past that associated open land with freedom, residents valued villages for providing a degree of independence. Farid, for example, lived in an unrecognized village where he kept a garden and grew wheat and barley in the lands around his house during rainy years. He used to work as an agricultural laborer, but had had difficulty finding work in recent years. He wanted to farm for himself, like the *moshav* residents who lived across the highway, but no such option existed for Bedouin Arabs. Farid had family members unhappy with their circumstances in recognized townships. He knew that if he moved to a township, he would give up his garden and grain growing. Given the choice between moving his large family to a small urban plot in a township or continuing to experience the long-term uncertainty but day-to-day freedom of life in an unrecognized village, he chose the latter. He explained that despite the physical discomforts of living with his village's limited infrastructure, he refused to move into a planned township where he would have added expenses (for municipal taxes), yet less freedom to determine the shape of his daily life and livelihood. Beyond Farid's personal preference for freedom, agropastoral production has been a safety net supplementing wage labor in insecure labor markets since the 1970s (Marx 1984). Today wage labor remains highly unstable for Bedouin Arabs due to competition and discrimination (Abu-Bader and Gottlieb 2008).[18] Maintaining some ties to the lands necessary for agropastoralism offers a measure of security (Abu-Rabia 1994).

Often residents who have already experienced one or more evictions feel different pushes and pulls related to village life. The tumultuous period of forced relocations during the 1950s and 1960s complicated the personal and formal legal ties between residents and the lands where they later lived, and the number of dislocations experienced varied from tribe to tribe. Many tribes live on lands to which the Israeli military relocated them. Some groups, such as the families of the Tarabin tribe, had already been evicted and relocated several times before the first governmentally planned township was completed in 1969. Current governmental orders to relocate are simply one more in a series, and residents are tired of being pushed about; but without long-term ties to the land where they live, many expressed a willingness to move to governmentally approved sites if given comparably rural plots. On the other hand, families whose traditional lands fell within the *siyag* may still live on lands held by their forebears for multiple generations, and some have documentation, such as tax receipts and photographs, that demonstrate this history of residence. Many with long-term family ties to a particular landscape described unassailable attachments of familiarity, connection to their extended family (both living and deceased), and rightful ownership. They adamantly refused to relocate.

The variety of responses residents have to land disputes is often ignored in public discussions of solutions to "the Bedouin problem" that assume "the Bedouin" to be a single group for which only one solution need be found. In fact the lack of legal options open to Bedouin Arabs deeply frustrated residents. Many asked me rhetorically why Jews in Israel should have so many options, including tiny *kibbutzim*, quiet towns, and bustling cities, while Bedouin Arabs have only the choice between a governmentally planned urban township or a rural, but illegal village.

Amid this heterogeneity of valuations, residents consistently repeated several priorities during conversations about their reasons for staying: freedom and rural livelihoods, fairness and betrayed trust, and a personal sense of comfort in open landscapes. Because residents frequently incorporated narratives of past land uses to explain their present circumstances, it is not surprising that current priorities draw on the same environmental discourses as counternarratives of the past. Past and present meld in residents' experiences of their landscapes, and the dishonor many see in the Israeli government's past land relations continues to frame residents' experiences in the present. Because past promises were broken, residents do not trust that contemporary promises— about improvements through the newly established regional council, new relocation plans that include agricultural options, and plans to improve the existing townships—will be kept. Together, this remembered history and these varied valuations of home influence residents' contemporary decision-making.

Sabr and Insurgence

Residents who remain in unrecognized villages all challenge government efforts to urbanize Bedouin Arabs and define their lifestyles, but residents do so in a variety of ways. Most "make do" nonconfrontationally (de Certeau 1984). For example, residents often built modest houses using inexpensive and poorly insulating materials like sheet metal. When I visited Amna's family in el-Hawashla, her brother explained how hesitant he and other residents are to invest anything in the external structure of their houses or landscaping. Such activity could invite attention from state authorities, and a great deal of money would be lost to the bulldozer. Instead, economic limitations and tactical considerations led residents to build simple structures and perhaps invest a bit more in furnishings to add comfort inside. Other residents "made do" by planting crops or grazing flocks on disputed lands simply because they needed shelter and income and saw no choice but to plant and graze without permits.

These residents discussed their management of daily life in unrecognized villages in terms of *sabr*, patience. They did not typically speak to me of their village livelihoods as part of a concerted effort to defy the Israeli government. Instead, they focused on personal and familial priorities and said they "just wanted quiet." 'Abd, an elderly man living in Wadi al-Na'am, was far from being a politically vocal opponent of the Israeli state. He had worked as a translator and liaison between the government and the Bedouin community during the 1950s and had great praise for the government during that period. He bought a house in the nearest township many years ago, but quickly regretted the move and returned to Wadi al-Na'am. He did not want electricity or any other state intervention now, he told me; he just wished to be left alone to live in the landscapes where his parents lived and died.

More public advocates of Bedouin land rights, including some village residents, fashioned the *sabr* of residents into the more politically provocative notion of *sumud*, steadfastness. Publications by the environmental justice group Bustan asserted, "Over 70,000 Bedouin in unrecognized villages are daily engaged in *sumud*, steadfast struggle to stay on their lands in defiance of a process of internal transfer" (Manski 2006), and promoted a proposed farming project for its ability to support the "'*sumud*,' or political resistance," of the villagers. Describing village residents' dwelling practices as *sumud* creates defiant connotations related to Palestinian nationalism, which has been narrated for decades in terms of the *sumud* of the idealized Palestinian *fallah* (Bardenstein 1998; Swedenburg 1990). Advocates' use of the term not only describes persistent Naqab residents, but also implies solidarity with a wider Palestinian community.

In addition to these everyday dwelling practices that may or may not be interpreted as political challenges, some residents engaged in more deliberately provocative tactics. These included insurgent building and planting, filing court cases, and public advocacy in partnership with NGOs. Insurgent building and planting refers to the deliberate construction of unlicensed houses and sowing of crops that solicits public attention in order to convey political, legal, and moral messages. James Holston (2008) discusses insurgent citizenship in Brazil, where working-class residents successfully used cooperative associations and home construction to destabilize the discriminatory forms of governance and ownership laws that have shut out segments of the Brazilian population for centuries.[19] Paradoxically, in their insurgence, residents used the same legal, material, and rhetorical elements—such as gaining power through private property—that supported Brazilian hierarchies. Negev activists engaged in insurgent citizenship through planting and building to oppose an Israeli land regime that excludes non-Jews. But they too used some of the same environmental discourses that underlie the exclusionary land-use management against which they fought.

The repeated rebuilding of homes at al-'Araqib, combined with residents' defiant statements to news reporters of their intentions to remain in place at all costs, offers an example of insurgent building. Like Zionist pioneers, Bedouin Arab activists attempted to buttress land claims through the physical labor of building homes and sowing fields. Some village residents tried to appeal to public perceptions of good stewardship and progressive politics. For example, one chose the globally trendy and eco-friendly straw-bale building technique to construct a mosque in his unrecognized village. The mosque's builder, an IDF volunteer, even offered his military service as evidence of his loyalty to the state when news crews interviewed him about the demolition order issued by the Ministry of the Interior. Despite framing such efforts in these widely valued terms, none of these buildings have proven immune to demolition.

Insurgent planters sought visibility through their chosen crops and public events for sowing and harvesting, and they used environmental discourses of redemption through agriculture to publicly call for state recognition of their land-use practices (McKee 2014). In the village of Twail Abu Jarwal, village leaders and an activist coalition called the Recognition Forum held periodic "solidarity plantings" to protest governmental practices of home and crop destruction.[20] In December 2007, I attended one such planting, which responded to the government's most recent home demolitions in an unrecognized village. Multilingual publicity for the event promised participation in "sow[ing] about 100 *dunams* with wheat and barley in the manual sowing [that is] traditional of the area" (Recognition Forum, 2007).

On a windy winter day, the carloads of guests who had traveled to Twail Abu Jarwal did not go directly to the fields. Rather, we were invited into a tent made of black tarpaulin and burlap coffee sacks that had been set up especially for the occasion. While sipping sweet tea, we listened to speeches from community leaders and Knesset members as young men from the village snapped pictures on their cell phones and several journalists filmed the gathering. An organizer then told us that it was time for the planting and led us from the tent out to the fields. However, after lingering along the edge of a field and being carefully shooed away from a tractor digging furrows, we were led back to the tent for more speeches. The village sheik and another elder spoke of the injustice of home demolitions and the inequality Bedouins face in Israel. A Knesset member insisted that the residents of this village have a rightful claim to these lands because the Bedouin "are an integral part of nature here." After a thank-you and farewell, we visitors drove out of the village along the rutted dirt track and dispersed.

Planting events like these reveal how advocates deal with contradictory sociopolitical pressures. Faced with dispossession, village residents and advocates sought to publicize a message of Bedouin belonging through long-term residence and cultural connection. However, to convey this message convincingly

Illustration 3. "Solidarity planting" of olive trees, east of al-'Araqib. 2008. Photograph by Author.

to large audiences this coalition of Jews and Arabs relied on an essentialized image of a Bedouin indigenous farmer. This image downplays any history of shepherding, which could weaken cultural claims to place with its connotations of rootlessness (Malkki 1992; Rosaldo 1988). Seeking both authenticity and convincing land claims, the event's hosts combined the discourse of labor in land favored by Zionist movements and discourses of Bedouin belonging through long-term residence and cultural connection (McKee 2010). They displayed symbols of Bedouinness, like tea and tents, and speakers discussed traditional farming and natural land ties.

However, in addition to sidelining part of their own heritage, this strategic essentialism risks perpetuating the very binaries that enframe Israel's contemporary land policies. It opposes "traditional" to "modern" and Bedouin nature to Jewish society, and attempts to identify land ties with a traditional, non-modern Bedouin lifestyle that bears little resemblance to most contemporary Naqab dwelling practices. Attempting to attract a wide Israeli audience, residents presented a truncated version of themselves and what they hoped for in the future. However, this frame of romanticized authenticity wavered when guests viewed the mechanized field preparation, and indeed, many residents chafed against such restrictive definitions. As one Bedouin Arab member of this coalition explained to me, "I can combine computers and agriculture." He can send his children to college and use new technology like mobile phones and wireless internet to make a more comfortable rural life for his family, he said. Such subtleties are easily lost in the publicity of insurgent planting campaigns.

Some residents advocated for land rights within the Israeli courts. Nuri el-'Ukbi, whose family was removed from al-'Araqib in 1952, combined legal advocacy with insurgent building and publicity. Beginning in 1973, he, his father, and brothers returned to al-'Araqib to farm on a temporary basis, requesting and receiving permission from the state each year to plant crops. However, they also wished to live on the land, so they filed a land claim. After his father died in 2005, Nuri feared the state would simply wait until all those with memory of the land expropriations had died and then reject all land claims, so he requested that the Department of Justice expedite his family's case. Meanwhile, Nuri decided to reassert their ownership claims physically and began living on these lands in 2006, sleeping in a tent and his car. The Green Patrol (enforcement branch of the Israel Nature and Parks Authority) ordered him to leave, leading to repeated evacuations and reoccupations over the next several years, another set of court cases, and fines against Nuri of more than 200,000 shekels (about $5,500).

In court, Nuri, like all Bedouin Arab claimants, faced the dilemma of either obeying the standardized definitions of suitable use and evidentiary rules created by the Israeli legal system, to which their historical land use has not conformed (Kedar 2003; Shamir 1996), or basing their arguments on discourses of historic family ties and honorable claims that do not resonate in Israeli courts. Repeatedly during court proceedings, Nuri attempted to speak about traditions of Bedouin land ownership and moral evaluations of right and wrong. Repeatedly, this testimony was deemed irrelevant, as judges and lawyers admonished him to "focus on the facts," "take the political issues out of this hall," and not discuss "if it is right or if it is not right."[21] Like appeals for cultural rights through other court systems, these courts censored political and ethical statements that explored events beyond the procedural boundaries set by Israeli law.[22] Nuri showed documents—tax records affirming his family's payments since 1937, British Mandate-era aerial photographs of their village showing stone houses, and published maps from the same era labeled with his family's name—to establish earlier use rights. But when he strove to argue the validity of these nondeeded use rights using cultural or ethical arguments, the court refused to hear.

Stymied in courts, some residents sought wider audiences where they could leverage moral and ethical arguments to advance claims. To do so, they cultivated far-reaching alliances with national and (occasionally) international NGOs and tourists (Keck and Sikkink 1998). These networks brought together disparate, sometimes jarring elements, such as the differing objectives of national and international NGOs; Palestinian nationalism and claims of Bedouin cultural particularity; the mingling in homes of family members and international volunteers; and multiple structures of authority including family, national government, and military. These collaborations demonstrate that even in seemingly local territorial struggles, participants actually work through "translocal" and "culturally hybrid networks" (Moore 2005:19–20; see also Escobar 2008).

Several social justice organizations, including the Negev Coexistence Forum, Gush Shalom, and the Association of Forty, helped al-'Araqib residents gather materials and publicly rebuild their village. They issued Hebrew press releases and email announcements in Hebrew, Arabic, and English that amplified a message of steadfastness and linked al-'Araqib's plight with that of all the unrecognized villages. Similarly, in Wadi al-Na'am, Bustan's volunteers and their network of sympathetic environmentalist activists spread word of a threatened eco-mosque, spurring public criticism of the government's demolition plans and delaying the mosque's destruction.

However, while these translocal networks offered the benefit of greater vis-ibility, they also demanded compromises in village residents' messages, because partnering NGOs are guided by their own goals and priorities (Cooley and Ron 2002). For example, following the Twail Abu Jarwal planting day, my Bedouin Arab colleague commented that he was pleased that journalists, politicians, and Bedouin rights advocates from Tel Aviv came. But he was also frustrated that the event dealt only superficially with the problems faced by Bedouin residents in the Negev and had been exploited by Knesset candidates and a few powerful community men as a platform for speeches.

Various advocacy NGOs also prioritized different aspects of recognition. Some, like the RCUV, focused on the attainment of formal recognition and ownership rights. Others, like the Arab-Jewish Center for Equality, Empower-ment and Cooperation (AJEEC), strove to improve substantive citizenship and were less concerned with juridical rights. AJEEC, working in both recognized and unrecognized settlements, led educational programs for Bedouin Arab children, training programs to build entrepreneurship among Bedouins, and collaborative Jewish-Arab volunteer projects. NGOs like AJEEC realized practi-cal goals by acquiescing to some of the state government's conditions for recog-nition that restricted traditional Bedouin taskscapes, for example, by quelling calls for open grazing land. Others, like the RCUV, refused to compromise on the acceptance of Bedouin Arab land-use practices in Israel and made little progress achieving structural changes. Villagers choosing to work with one type of NGO risked alienating the other.

Double Binds of Recognition

Musa, a resident of the unrecognized village of Al Sira, spoke in Hebrew to the audience gathered for a public education evening in 2008 entitled "The Future of the Arab Bedouins in the Negev." After describing his family's long history of residence in Al Sira and the unfairness of the state's demands that they leave, he ended not with a position of defiance, but with an appeal for help: "We need the government; we can't fix ourselves. We're children of the state, not like the Palestinians. We're not asking for a new state. We're asking for our rights. . . . We're citizens who want a solution." Musa cast himself and fellow residents as worthy subjects of the state, but neglected and in need.

Two days later, my discussion with Wafiq revealed a very different view of recognition. Wafiq, who lived through his own family's shift from an unrec-ognized village to a planned township, worked with an environmental justice organization. As we sat discussing his upcoming presentation at an international social justice conference, he stated that Bedouin Arabs must be more proactive in fighting for their rights and affirming their ties to the land. "You must recognize yourself," he declared. "You must not shoot yourself in the foot and then blame someone else!" Bedouins must demonstrate, he continued, that the struggle is not just over a house, but over "my land, my food, my economy, my health, my life. Right now, the people are doing ninety percent of the work, and the government just comes and knocks down a house, like that, easy." His voice rose as he asked, "Why are you running away from your traditions and your connections to the land, and running toward the city and modernization?"

These two statements, both made by men engaged in public advocacy on behalf of the unrecognized villages, highlight the double binds inherent in Bedouin Arabs' quests for recognition as legitimate members of Israeli society. Double binds are competing obligations or consequences that are equally valued but contradictory (Fortun 2001). Recognition on the government's terms—relinquishing agropastoral lifestyles and affiliations of tribe and family to make the "logical" decision to move to planned townships—promises access to the support available to other citizens. But this recognition is a self-contradictory compromise because it requires renouncing what many view as the pillars of their communal identity ("my land, my food . . ."). Rather than gaining rights as full participants in Israeli society, Musa's approach calls for recognition of vulnerable subjects in need of basic aid (Zeiderman 2013). It requires residents to trade their historically formed relationships with landscapes and the comfort of familiar taskscapes for uncertain and partial recognition. Even those who fully complied with state demands, such as IDF volunteers and those who moved to planned townships, found that this compliance was no guarantee of substantive citizenship or social belonging. On the other hand, to choose not to seek governmental recognition but rather to "recognize yourself," in Wafiq's terms, incurs punishments like demolitions and crop spraying, which threaten these same pillars. Residents practicing *sabr* lived in anticipation of demolition. Those who used proactive tactics like insurgent building and planting, public advocacy, and court cases found their efforts stymied by double binds.

Single-Family Farmsteads

Whereas unrecognized Bedouin villages housed approximately 80,000 people, Jewish single-family farmsteads in the Negev housed no more than 150 people in 2008. Yet these few tiny settlements raised considerable attention in news media and the Knesset when residents faced eviction. Advocates of the farmsteads pleaded for their recognition as essential participants in Zionist projects, as Israel's new *chalutzim*, pioneers. The JNF website lauded farmstead owners as "a new breed of true pioneers, who are leaving the overcrowded center of the country . . . in order to merge wide open expanses with Zionist action."[23] Newspaper editorials depicted farmstead owners as modern pioneers poised to lift the Negev out of economic stagnancy and "stop the rapid spread of the Bedouin" (Golan 2008).

Advocates of Bedouin land rights also viewed these farmers as agents of Zionist settlement. They pointed out that despite the farmsteads' questionable legal status, certain sectors within the state government assisted the farmers through loans and connection to national water and electricity infrastructure. Some associated the farmsteads with state security, suggesting that farmstead founders were agents of a security apparatus, "whose role is to contract and restrict Bedouin movement and development and to help the security forces keep an eye on the Negev's indigenous population" (Gordon and Tzfadia 2008).

In March 2009, to learn more about the environmental discourses and practices underlying the farmsteads, I scheduled interviews with a number of Wine Route farmers. As I drove south from Beersheba, and as towns and settlements became sparser and the dry, rocky hills dominated my view, I mused about the upcoming interviews. Given public commentary at the time, I expected to learn how individuals became so motivated by Zionist settlement imperatives that they left their home communities to establish these solitary farmsteads. However, when I began speaking with farmers, I found a more complex web of motivations and environmental discourses.

Elias lived with his wife and two children on a hillside along the Wine Route where they raised a herd of goats. Just above the goat pens, the family's two caravans sat in an L-shape around a small playground. Two railroad cars converted into a tiny store and café perched atop a promontory nearby. Visitors came to buy gourmet cheese and eat meals in the dining area overlooking a picturesque tableau of desert hills. As we sat in his caravan home, Elias told me of his dream to start a farm, and how he finally found the opportunity in this arid parcel of the Negev. Though he and his wife could have joined a *kibbutz*, Elias rejected this communal approach, saying he simply was not suited to it. "I grew up on a *kibbutz*; I won't return to a *kibbutz*," he stated firmly. "I prefer a place where nobody will bother me. I'm not in need of life in a community. It doesn't do well for me." He objected to the interference of community decisions trumping market demands in determining what to raise and how to sell it,

Illustration 4. Café catering to visitors on a single-family farmstead. 2009. Photograph by Author.

and complaints from neighbors who disliked the sounds and smells emanating from his goats. Instead, Elias preferred living with only his family, away from the annoyances of communal life.

Zionism is a widely valued ideology in Israel, and many other Jewish Israelis had volunteered their Zionist dedication to me. Since media coverage had primed me to hear this from farmers, I asked Elias if in addition to these personal motivations there was also "a piece that was ideological, or religious, or Zionist, or . . ." My voice trailed off as he shook his head.

> Zionist, no. Definitely not. It's very disappointing to people that I say that. Listen, I'm not Zionist, I'm not a patriot. I was practically born here . . . from the age of about ten, I grew up in the Negev. I love the Negev, through living in the place, the climate, the area. So, that's it! I don't know . . . if I can speak of Zionism. If somebody thinks that because I don't live in the center, I live in the south, I'm a Zionist, ok, I won't attack him. But it's hard for me to come and say I came because of Zionism. I don't feel that.

Though Elias valued Zionism, he saw himself not as an agent of state security, but as an individual working toward personal goals, including business success, independence, and connection to a landscape he loved. He moved where bu-reaucratic obstacles for establishing a farmstead seemed lightest.

Other farmers similarly noted multiple motivations. Some espoused Zion-ist dedication, while others denied it. All explained their decision to establish these farms primarily as a personal matter, undertaken because they wanted an independent lifestyle. Dov, the owner of a wine-producing farmstead, re-sponded to the same question about motivations by saying, "Not religious; Zionist, you could say, yes, but religious, no." Nir, a restaurateur who at the age of forty established his business of raising goats, making yogurt, and hosting tourists, described his decision primarily as a welcome career change, second-arily as a change in lifestyle that allowed for more solitary time, and thirdly for "Zionist-settling" (*tzioni-hityashvuti*) reasons.

Whether self-described Zionists or not, farmers drew on some of the envi-ronmental discourses that have long underlain Zionist movements. Dov was attracted to the Negev since his first visit during military duty because "there's a lot of potential in places that have nothing. And there's nothing here." Similarly, Shlomo and his wife moved to the Negev to realize their long-term dream of starting a small farm because the north of Israel is too crowded, while the open Negev holds great possibilities for development. When a person sees a place like this, Shlomo asserted, he sees enticing possibilities for developing something new, for starting something from scratch. Shlomo enjoyed the challenge.

This view of empty desert erases the sociality that Bedouin residents per-ceive and enact in the Negev, entrenching a dichotomy between settled, Jewish areas, and desert wilderness (Zerubavel 2008). Viewing Negev landscapes as empty also corresponds with a discourse of ownership through labor in land. In this sense, Dov, Shlomo, and the other farmers are part of a decades-long ef-fort following Ben-Gurion's directive to "make the desert bloom." At the same time, these farmers' motivations to establish agrotourism for personal gain, ex-plicitly avoiding the communal forms of settlement that underlay early efforts to build a strong Jewish society, depart from foundational Zionist priorities.

When asked about Bedouin Arabs' land rights and government land-use planning in the Negev, farmers expressed a similarly diverse set of opinions. They drew on some core Zionist environmental discourses yet also challenged the Negev's contemporary social segregation. These farmers all moved to re-mote places to do agropastoral work they described as "creative" and "produc-tive," in line with Zionist imperatives to shape themselves through agricultural labor. But some of the same farmers contradicted a discourse of Jewish-Arab difference by drawing parallels between their own and Bedouins' dwelling practices. Some even suggested that the same settlement model—agrotourism farmsteads—could benefit both Jews and Bedouin Arabs. "They're citizens of the state of Israel," Elias stated of the Bedouin. "Every citizen must be taken care of. You can't just throw people away like that." He noted that the urban townships built for them were poorly developed. Besides, he continued, there are many who "don't want something urban. They want something more outside, in nature, rural." If he can live this rural lifestyle, Elias wondered aloud, why can't they?

Shlomo supported rural options for Bedouin settlements in even stronger terms. It is important, Shlomo insisted, for Israel not to repeat the mistakes that the United States made in dealing with Native Americans. Bedouins cannot keep all the lands they used to live on, he said, but "we need to include them in a solution." Rather than evacuating an unrecognized village of two hundred people, he suggested, an agrotourism farm such as his could be established. This would preserve some Bedouin lifeways and provide employment opportunities, he suggested, which would have the added benefit of reducing theft and drug problems. "A Bedouin loves hosting," Shlomo explained, citing Bedouin traditions like inviting visitors to stay for at least three days and elaborate practices of coffee and tea service. Though citing somewhat simplistic tropes of Bedouin culture, Shlomo's comments also condemn the pressure that Bedouin Arabs face in Israel to abandon their cultural practices and collective identity. They suggest that forcing Bedouins to move out of landscapes they know and away from familiar taskscapes creates social disruptions that reverberate throughout Israeli society. Whether based on an individualistic interpretation of citizenship or the value of protecting Bedouin collectivities and cultural identity, opinions like these support the rooting rather than uprooting of Arabs from the land. They challenge common environmental discourses of land and Jewish-Arab relations.

Despite these discursive challenges, these farmers did not see their actions as pushing against state authority. They had searched widely and waited years to settle through legal means. Following passage of the NDA law that first authorized nonresidential agrotourism farms, a new, more right-wing government in 1996 began offering financial and bureaucratic support for individual farming ventures. Then the JNF assisted farmers by flattening areas in the hills (for example, for goat pens) and building dirt access roads connecting each farm to a highway, and JA grants covered some of the farmers' settlement costs. Because of this material support and spoken assurances from some government officials, farmers said they had not thought they would test state authority by moving to the farms with their families (contravening the officially nonresidential zoning of the land).

Proponents and opponents of the farmsteads offer different accounts of why the government's treatment of farmsteads shifted from supportive to confrontational. Opponents contend that legal cases initiated in 1999 by the Society for the Protection of Nature in Israel (SPNI) and the Israel Union for Environmental Defense (IUED) served as a wake-up call. The cases, which alleged that farmsteads damaged open areas of desert wilderness and broke land-use regulations, forced government officials to monitor the farmers' building more closely. Farmstead proponents argue that monetary interests are at the heart of the government's reversal. Land prices were rising, these parties argue, and though the SPNI/IUED cases were unfounded, they offered the government an excuse to repossess the farmstead land and offer it for public bidding. In either case, farmers were embroiled in a string of litigation culminating in the ILA's 2008 order to farmers to evacuate the farmsteads.

By the time I visited in 2009, Wine Route farmers had become reluctant rebels in defense of their farmsteads. They were in the midst of a two-pronged campaign to gain legal recognition as residential farmsteads. They had filed a joint appeal to their eviction in the courts and also formed a voluntary association headed by Dov to raise public support for their continuation. They issued statements to the press, and Dov offered free bumper stickers to his farmstead's visitors. One evokes a famous quote by David Ben-Gurion: "In the Negev the people of Israel shall be tested *despite* the Society for the Protection of Nature" (emphasis in the original).[24] A second reads, "Mani Mazuz. We are here and will not move." Mazuz was the deputy attorney general at the time and signer of the farmsteads' evacuation orders. A stylized *M* in Mazuz's name allows a play on words, so that the bumper sticker defiantly commands Mani to *zuz*, or "move," rather than the farmers. The sticker's blue stripes echo those of the Israeli flag. Both stickers insinuate that farmstead owners are the true patriots in this dispute. In addition to these public efforts, farmers countered SPNI and IUED claims that the farmsteads threatened Negev landscapes by showcasing environmentally friendly measures. Alon described the increase in avian diversity around his farmstead due to the greenery he planted, and Elias and Shlomo listed initiatives like gray-water recycling and composting.

Despite being engaged in this vigorous campaign, which farmers described as "a battle" or "a war," farmers did not see themselves as rebelling against state authority. They found themselves at odds with elements of the state government, despite having collaborated with other governmental bodies, and were exasperated with the inconsistent behavior coming from different branches of the government. Appeals to individual Knesset members garnered support, as five ministers proposed an amendment to the NDA law that would retroactively legalize the farmsteads as residences, including homes and some buildings for commercial use.

In establishing their farmsteads and then defending their rural livelihoods, these farmers asserted personal motivations and generally apolitical stances. However, like individual Bedouin Arab residents of unrecognized villages, though these farmers wished simply to be left alone to farm, they were participating in the grounded sociopolitics of the Negev in ways over which they did not have full control. They and their farmsteads were actors in the social, environmental, and political landscapes of the Negev, and their dwelling practices held political importance. In the placement of these farms, the material assistance they accepted from state agencies, and their campaign for legal recognition in the context of the long unsettled dispute over recognition of Bedouin Arab villages, these farmsteads had an unintended but consequential impact on Bedouin Arab fellow residents of the Negev.

Legislating Recognition

When the NDA amendment was introduced in the Knesset in 2009, it garnered support from many representatives. However, it also generated considerable debate, primarily based on the opposition of two Knesset members, Talab al-Sana, representative of the United Arab List, and Hana Sweid, a member of Hadash, the joint Jewish-Arab socialist party.[25] These debates made clear the strategic value of these farmsteads for state policy and the connection between policies regarding single-family farmsteads and unrecognized villages, both of which remain implicit in the language of the law itself.

Early during debate of the bill, in October 2009, al-Sana asserted that in addition to contradicting the government's own Master Plan for the Negev, the 2008 Goldberg Commission report, and other governmental plans, the amendment contravenes principles of distributive justice. He then challenged his fellow Knesset members:

> Why do we run to answer by law to 59 individual settlers and ignore 81,000 residents who live in 40 settlements, that don't have drinking water and have no roads, they have children and have no schools, no education and no welfare. Is this because these are Jews and these are Bedouins? Is this policy right? Is an individual Jew more important than tens of thousands of Bedouin residents?[26]

In response, Robert Ilatuv, a representative for the nationalist-territorialist Yisrael Beitanu Party, argued that there have already been many councils and resolutions to address "the Bedouin problem," and that government-planned settlements were an adequate solution. But nothing has been done yet to help these Jews facing imminent eviction, he complained. Ilatuv's comments perform two important discursive moves. First, they depict "the Bedouin" as an undifferentiated population while upholding the specific needs of these Jews. Second, they separate Bedouin from Jewish needs, refusing to address the two with the same legislation, and lending support to a dual-society paradigm. Al-Sana, himself a Bedouin and resident of the Negev, dismissed Ilatuv as ignorant of "the reality in the Negev," and countered Ilatuv's generalized depiction of the Bedouin:

> In the Negev there are more than 120 settlements of Jews, which are diverse. There are *kibbutzim*; those who want can live in a *kibbutz*. There are agricultural settlements, there are community settlements, there are development towns, there are cities. . . . The Bedouins, who make up about 30 percent of Negev residents, have not been given settlements to this day, only seven settlements that are all of a particular type—an urban sort. There are no agricultural ones, no trade ones, no tourist ones. Therefore, this course has been deficient. Let's go together to find a solution to the problem. Let's put an end to the phenomenon of "you" and "us."[27]

Al-Sana finished his statement by asking once again to place Bedouin and Jewish residents into the same legislative frame. Nonetheless, Ilatuv responded by repeating a "you/us" distinction: "I think we do give solutions. You do not accept them."

Throughout these proceedings, al-Sana and Sweid proposed rejecting this amendment and devising a broader bill that would provide residential and development options for all Negev residents. A guest expert from Bimkom, a nonprofit group promoting social justice in Israel's urban planning, proposed revisions to the amendment that would place "generations-old traditional farming" under its purview, in addition to the narrowly defined model of NDA-approved agrotourism farms in the existing text. However, other Knesset members repeatedly rebuffed attempts to place Bedouin settlements and Jewish farmsteads in the same legislative frame. They argued that the problems of "the Bedouin sector" were too complex to solve immediately and the farmstead residents needed speedy assistance. Over the next seven months, the amendment passed preliminary readings and moved closer to a final vote. Sweid and al-Sana shifted to recommending smaller revisions in wording and occasionally scoring rhetorical points regarding governmental mistreatment of Bedouin Arabs. They stopped advocating as energetically for a joint Jewish-Arab legislative approach.

Proponents most frequently argued for the amendment on the grounds that it would rectify a wrong inflicted through clumsy bureaucracy. Farmstead owners were portrayed as *chalutzim* who acted in good faith and were being victimized due to inconsistencies between local and national governmental practices. "This is an intolerable situation that, to people who settled quite a few years ago, we would say now: vacate," stated representative Yaakov Edri of the centrist Kadima Party (Knesset Economics Committee 2009). "They are doing something very important," Edri later continued, describing his visit to the farmsteads, "and also a Zionist enterprise. This must be said out loud." Sparking at the mention of "Zionist enterprise," al-Sana asked for clarification of the term and insisted that this is a state with laws and if a Bedouin transgresses the law he is expelled, implying that no special treatment should be given to Jews. Al-Sana and Edri then began shouting at one another.

In the end, though opposition to the farmsteads' land rights had come from multiple political directions, through arguments about environmental protection, eliminating Jewish favoritism, and upholding previous legislation, the Knesset approved the NDA amendment in the summer of 2010 and government offices pledged budgetary contributions to aid the farmsteads. Why was the government investing so much to help this small group of citizens who had not obeyed laws? When framed as part of a national mission to settle the Negev desert, the farmsteads proved to be unassailable. Establishing residence on these farmsteads, if transgressive at one point, became incorporated as state policy to meet a set of development, settlement, and symbolic imperatives. The NDA amendment promoted settlement through individual entrepreneurs rather than communal ventures, placing it in line with Israel's overall neoliberal economic shift. Knesset leaders avoided evicting these farmers because it would send a dampening message to other eager entrepreneurs. This tailor-made legislation also promoted Jewish settlement, as it was specifically designed to protect the farmsteads as residences rather than simply as business ventures. And finally, legislators appeared anxious to avoid the symbolically powerful act of governmental enforcers evicting Jewish citizens who were widely viewed as loyal pioneers, a move that would have garnered political criticism against the Knesset members from their constituents. Whether eagerly or in spite of themselves, farmstead owners gained recognition through their identification with Zionist projects, an avenue closed to Bedouin Arab residents of unrecognized villages.

De-cultural Accommodation

Laws that define illegal squatting and legal residence in any society are cultural products rather than expressions of universal principles. Particularly in societies like Israel, where a relatively recently arriving group gains dominance over prior occupants, property laws reflect the dominant group's understandings of "proper" land use and national belonging.[28] Legal amendments reveal the practices that shape these cultural products, and socially privileged citizens have more influence in defining legitimate and illegitimate land uses (Dennison 2014). Residents in both these cases lived dispersed, agropastoral lifestyles that were initially prohibited by the Israeli government. Thus, to ask how and why farmstead residents successfully gained legalization, while unrecognized village residents failed to, is to examine the sociopolitical processes and evolving discursive norms that shape relationships between land and people in the Negev.

Many scholars of Israeli land conflict have explained the differences between Jews' and Arabs' abilities to influence the legal system in terms of citizenship. This is not simply a matter of formal citizenship, which as scholars have shown in many contexts does not guarantee substantive citizenship (that is, a fair share of a society's civil and political rights and economic resources [Holston 2008]). Rather, "differentiated citizenship" (Holston 2008) or "graduated citizenship" (Ong 2006) means that social categories like class or race also mark the unequal distribution of government aid and other social goods. Whether describing Israel as an "ethnic democracy," based on ethnic nationalism but extending rights to citizens of other ethnicities as well (Peled 2011; Smooha 2002), or a nondemocratic "ethnocracy," in which ethnicity is the primary basis for the distribution of rights and opportunities (Yiftachel 2000), many studies have demonstrated the differential citizenship that exists within Israel (Ben-Porat and Turner 2011; Rabinowitz and Abu Baker 2005; Shafir and Peled 2002).[29]

This comparison of two eviction cases demonstrates how environmental discourses of legitimate taskscapes and personhood become mobilized in societal debates about substantive citizenship along a Jewish versus Arab division. The media campaigns, protests, court cases, and Knesset debates involved in these eviction struggles reveal the importance of leveraging cultural recognition in cases of land rights. Cultural recognition can shape legal rights in a variety of ways. Groups often achieve recognition through processes of "exclusionary incorporation," which means including individuals in a society "in a way that preserves and even depends on their position as outsiders" (Partridge 2008:668). Exclusionary incorporation may take many forms, operating within both assimilationist and multicultural frameworks. Assimilation promises inclusion in a collective "we" to those who successfully exclude elements of their cultural, ethnic, or national heritage that are identified as deviant by the collective. Mizrahi Jews have experienced this pressure in Israel, particularly from the 1940s to 1970s (Dominguez 1989; Shohat 1999). In exchange for assimilating to European norms of progress and civility and excising signs of Arabness from their language, dress, religious rituals, and so on, Mizrahi Jews became "internalized others," part of Israel's national story of integration (Dominguez 1989; Shohat 1999). They gained homes, subsidies, and other material goods in the process. Thus, through one sort of exclusionary incorporation, assimilation absorbed Mizrahi immigrants but refused many of their cultural practices as building blocks of Israeli society.

Liberal multiculturalism too presents dilemmas of selective recognition. These dilemmas may revolve around race. For example, in Aihwa Ong's (2003) account of Cambodian immigrants, naturalization in the United States "entails an inexplicable loss in exchange for a kind of dubious freedom" because it pushes immigrants to conform to a polarized racial geography of black and white. This polarization demands the excision of "primitive" aspects of immigrants' cultural practices (cf. Partridge 2008). Alternatively, double binds of authenticity can make recognition problematic, as for Aboriginal people in Australia (Povinelli 2002). To gain land rights, Aboriginal people must demonstrate "authentic" cultural ties to the land, yet Australian society has suppressed seminomadism, ritual protection of Dreamings, and other Aboriginal practices as primitive (Povinelli 2002). Thus, demonstrating "authentic" land claims requires practices that exclude Aboriginal people from Australian society. Despite the losses incurred in these double binds, the recognition of acceptable difference granted by liberal multiculturalism secures some access to substantive citizenship for minorities.

Like many societies with large immigrant populations, Israel has shifted in recent decades toward multicultural norms. Mizrahi, Ethiopian, and other minority Jews face both new possibilities for inclusion and expectations of performing authenticity in Israeli society (Chetrit 2000; Ein-Gil 2009; Ben-Rafael 2007). However, this selective multiculturalism has been paralleled by hardening boundaries between Jews and non-Jews, such as Palestinian Arabs and foreign workers (Drori 2009; Rabinowitz 1997; Shafir and Peled 2002; Willen 2007).

These two cases of eviction offer a particularly rich and dynamic view into Israeli land conflict and social relations because they demonstrate both the typically separate treatment of Jewish and Arab land claims and the provocative possibility of blurring this division. Some farmstead owners and civilian

Bedouin rights activists drew parallels between their struggles to legalize their homes, and for a brief window it seemed the new legislation legalizing agrotourism farms as homes might have opened space for legislative changes granting recognition for unrecognized Bedouin villages too. During private discussions and public debates, these individuals attempted to forge links of rhetoric, legislation, and social obligation between these two types of settlement and their residents. In so doing, they briefly broke out of the typical discursive framing that naturalizes Jewish-Arab difference, territoriality, and the primacy of Jews' agricultural attachments to land.

As it turned out, Sweid's and al-Sana's attempts to perforate the legislative separation of Jews and Arabs were quickly pushed aside. The calls from residents of unrecognized villages, their allies, and some farmsteaders for the recognition of Bedouin Arabs' cultural taskscapes and historical land claims also remained at Israel's social margins. They have not gained mass support or legal recognition for village residents.

Since 2010, other governmental plans and legislative measures have brought Negev land claims into Israel's public spotlight. Most notably, the Prawer-Begin Plan of 2013 (officially, the Law for the Arrangement of Bedouin Settlement in the Negev), which proposed a final resolution of Bedouin land claims through minimal recognition of title and widespread eviction and relocation of unrecognized village residents, sparked street protests, arrests, and vehement Knesset debates. However, again, this was only a brief window of public debate. Despite passing through preliminary rounds of discussion in the Knesset, the Prawer-Begin Plan was tabled after conservative politicians decried it as "a Bedouin take-over" and liberals called it "state-sponsored discrimination in the Negev" (Kestler-D'Amours 2013). A frame of Jewish-Arab opposition remained firmly in place. Government forces have continued using house demolitions and crop destruction to push Bedouin Arabs out of disputed lands, and Bedouin Arabs have persisted in building homes on these lands.

The pressures and possibilities that Bedouin Arabs in Israel face differ from the exclusionary incorporation of assimilation or multiculturalism. Instead, they face demands for what I call de-cultural accommodation. State agencies and many Jewish fellow citizens permit Bedouin Arabs within Israel as formal citizens, but only in ways that perpetuate their outsider status. Bedouins cannot gain inclusion through assimilation, because of Israel's definition as a Jewish state and national anxieties over Jews' cultural solidarity and their separation from Arabs. These anxieties limit multicultural celebration primarily to Jewish diversity. Instead, Bedouin Arabs must accommodate Zionist nation-building

projects by relinquishing cultural practices and ties to place in order to realize certain benefits of citizenship. This accommodation pressure is de-cultural
because it demands that Bedouin Arabs relinquish agropastoral lifestyles that
have been central to their cultural identity but also does not invite them to
assimilate by adopting Jewish culture. It pushes Bedouin Arabs to act *as if*
they were acultural, individual actors making the "rational" choice to move to
planned townships for better amenities. De-cultural accommodation is a particular mechanism of exclusionary incorporation that centers on simultaneous
anxieties about cultural differentiation and "rooted" ties to land. It attempts to
remove Bedouins as an obstacle to Jewish nation-building.

Comparing how the rights afforded to all Israeli citizens and those denied
to Palestinian citizens of Israel are differentially tied to land makes this pressure
particularly clear (Rosen-Zvi 2004; Tzfadia 2008a). The state grants all Israeli
citizens basic social welfare services that are not tied to the recipient's place of
residence, such as social security income, health care, and primary education.
Other services, such as electricity and running water, which are tied to places
of residence, are denied to residents of unrecognized villages. De-cultural accommodation creates direct and indirect pressures that push Bedouin Arabs to
abandon rural residences and deny them access to large areas of land for farming or shepherding.

Pressures of de-cultural accommodation also limit Bedouin Arabs' access
to legal reform. Farmsteaders eventually gained legal land-use rights specifically based on their recognition as Jewish participants in the cultural projects
of Judaizing the Negev and continuing the pioneering tradition that helped
to establish Israel as a Jewish state. This is a constraint of its own sort, as even
those farmers who did not identify as Zionist were hailed as such and expected
to govern themselves as such. However, in contemporary Israel, Bedouins settling and farming land are not recognized as relevant to Israeli nation-building
in the way that Jewish farmsteaders are valued for their cultural undertaking.
On the contrary, it is precisely the place-based character of the unrecognized
villages' campaigns for recognition that is most objectionable for the state because of the imperative to establish Jewish territory. Though the means have
shifted over the years, the Israeli state's goal of strengthening territorial control and the Jewish character of its territory has remained consistent. The state
government promises recognition to Bedouin Arab residents as law-abiding
citizens with ownership of their homes only if they relinquish their ties to particular landscapes and replace collective cultural and tribal affiliations with individual identities as neoliberal subjects.

Environmental discourses are particularly powerful in perpetuating this form of exclusionary incorporation because they naturalize social divisions. Common discourses of land claims through labor and of civilized Jews versus wild Bedouins naturalize the priority Knesset members gave to Jewish farmers over Bedouin Arab "nomads." The discursive linking of group identity to territory naturalizes the idea that Jews' security rests on exclusive territorial control. Legislative acts aid this naturalization by establishing cultural particularities with the veneer of universal rights and wrongs (Dennison 2014). When legalization—and failed legalization—are analyzed in practice, however, the social construction of these discourses becomes clear. The social and political maneuverings necessary to establish purportedly universal legal principles shows them to be anything but "natural."

Bridge: Distant Neighbors

IT WAS 8:00 A.M. AS I LEFT THE HOUSE, bundled in long pants, thick socks, and a warm fleece. A headscarf was tucked into my backpack for later. On this cold, dry February morning in the Negev, a breeze blew through, but it was gentler than the whipping gustiness that came most afternoons. I had been living in Moshav Dganim for two months, and that day I was going back to ʿAyn al-ʿAzm to visit the families with whom I had lived last year. As the bird flies, these towns are only two kilometers apart. But socially, the two communities—one of Jewish Israelis and the other of Bedouin Arabs—are much further distanced than that. This social distance is reflected in the landscape. No direct roads exist between them, and to travel from one to the other on paved roads requires a trip seven times longer than the bird's flight. Without a car of my own, I undertook a patchwork journey that day via public and shared means that highlighted the geographical, infrastructural, and social segregation of these landscapes.

I began walking up the road in Dganim past pretty houses with well-tended front gardens. The yards and street were quiet, as I had missed the rush hour when most of Dganim's residents left in private cars to drive to work in other towns and cities. Taking a shortcut behind the synagogue and through the now abandoned fields of this formerly agricultural community, I reached the main gate. This gate was part of a double-layer fence with barbed wire and electrification that ran the perimeter of the *moshav*. For most visitors, the gate may have been barely noticeable, as it was raised during the day. A nod and smile to the guard was usually all it took to pass. However, Bedouin Arab friends who drove to Dganim to drop me off were reluctant to approach the gate, reading it as a barrier in their social landscape.

Nehemiah, a friendly man my father's age, was the guard on duty that day. He greeted me and pulled up a chair so I could wait and flag down a car to hitchhike into Beersheba, the region's hub of industry, education, government, and transportation. Almost immediately, a sedan rounded the corner. Nehemiah knew all the small *moshav*'s residents, and he waved to this driver, Yaron. When Yaron pulled over, I climbed in and told him I was heading to the *shuk*, the open-air market. Riding for twenty minutes into Beersheba, we introduced ourselves, and Yaron asked the usual questions I received from new acquaintances: what am I doing here, am I Jewish, and why did I learn Hebrew if I'm not Jewish. As we talked about my research, I asked to interview him, and he invited me to stop by his house.

We drove along the highway, and eventually a string of gas stations and large stores lined our way as we reached the city's outskirts. Yaron turned onto the main road through Beersheba and stopped at the busy intersection by the market. As I stepped out, the central bus station, the public transportation portal between the Negev and the rest of Israel, was on my right. Public transportation has been a high priority since the prestate waves of immigration, and increasingly so after statehood in 1948, as a means of supporting Jewish communities throughout Israel and strengthening frontier settlements. Despite increasing privatization and fragmentation of the national bus system, vestiges remain of the ideological commitment to taming frontiers, and every tiny *kibbutz* or *moshav* has a bus passing through at least twice each day.

However, to reach 'Ayn al-'Azm, I did not enter this bus station. Instead, I crossed the road and entered the market's maze of covered stalls where merchants sold everything from fruits and vegetables to cell phones and radios. In the middle of these densely packed stalls was an intersection where delivery trucks and private cars serving as shared taxis competed for space. This was the Bedouin Arab public transportation hub of the Negev. None of the Bedouin Arab communities were included in Israel's public bus network. Instead, a gray economy of shared taxis, referred to simply as "cars," or *sayaarat*, served the six recognized Bedouin Arab towns, the Bedouin Arab city of Rahat, and many of the surrounding unrecognized villages.[1]

In this market of Jewish and Arab merchants and customers, Hebrew was the language of default. But in the taxi intersection Arabic dominated, as it was rare for Jewish Israelis to travel in the shared taxis. I walked in during the height of morning shopping. In a raucous swirl of older women laden with plastic bags of produce and couples juggling bags and children, young men called out the destinations of various taxis. I responded to a call for 'Ayn al-'Azm and was ushered to a white sedan where one other woman sat quietly in the backseat. I joined her to wait. Other passengers soon squeezed into the remaining seats, and the driver eased through the honking mass of cars, out of the market's alleyways.

As we sped down the highway, passing the malls and factories of Beersheba's industrial ring, I wrapped the scarf over my hair and tucked it under my chin as my friend Sarah had taught me. Though many residents I met in 'Ayn al-'Azm were not concerned with such things when I visited their homes, I found that wearing the garment allowed me to move more freely, drawing less attention, through the streets. Before long, the car pulled off the main road. We passed the entrance to the Jewish town of Meren, one of the wealthiest towns in Israel, and then turned into 'Ayn al-'Azm.

The driver turned to each of us to confirm our destinations. The town had no street signs, and few residents attended to the official system of numbered house addresses. Instead, the driver used the names of household heads to guide him. He wound through several neighborhoods, dropping off other passengers. From the street, only the tops of concrete or stone-faced houses were visible above the high walls abutting the sidewalk. Trees peeked over some property walls, but on the streets themselves little grew and trash fluttered in the wind. As we went over the final speed bump before my destination, I pointed out the Abu Assa home, and the driver pulled over. I handed him ten shekels and stepped out of the car. Walking into the family's courtyard, I was greeted with kisses and exclamations of *ahlan w-sahlan!* Welcome! and *keef al-hal?* How are you? On the return trip that afternoon, I would reverse the process, crossing from the market to the central bus station and the intercity bus, and then through the *moshav* to my apartment. But for the time being, I relaxed into a day of visiting with several households to catch up on family news, conducting an interview, and giving an English lesson.

Placed Apart

Residents of Dganim and 'Ayn al-'Azm are reluctant neighbors, and the barriers between them are constructed both "top-down" and "from below." As elsewhere in Israel, government projects in the Negev segregated people. They did so by building *moshvei olim* for Jews and townships for Bedouins; creating separate public transportation systems for Jewish and Bedouin Arab communities; and administering education, health care, and other social services for Jews and Arabs through separate agencies. However, residents also participated in this social distancing. People engaged in different norms of dress, like wearing long sleeves and a carefully draped scarf, or used one language versus another as embodied social markers. Particular places required specialized knowledge, like the informal knowledge of families required to navigate through ʿAyn al-ʿAzm. These boundaries divide and order people and places, and they teach travelers—both foreigners like myself and local residents—about the social order of the Negev (Stoller 1982).

Most residents of the two towns would meet each other only through the relatively anonymous commercial encounters that constitute most Arab-Jewish interactions in the Negev. I found that residents of each town held little detailed knowledge about the other, and if they spoke of each other it was usually as Jews and Bedouins rather than referring to neighborhood of residence, family, occupation, or other social grouping. Because my fieldwork took me between both communities, some residents viewed me as a conduit of social information and inquired about what life was like "over there." Most often, though, residents expressed little curiosity about their neighbors. Thus, in their everyday lives residents participate in the creation and re-creation of the Negev's segregated landscapes.

Though segregation dominates life in the Negev, it is not all-encompassing. Life in the region also involves Arab-Jewish encounters of employment and commerce, social friction, friendship, and activism.[2] Attention to the border zones and buffer areas of such encounters can shed light on how an Arab-Jewish line is drawn and policed and, equally importantly, where it is breached (cf. Modan 2007; Vila 2003). As Susan Bibler Coutin states, "Borderlands are marginalized yet strategic, inviolate yet conventionally violated, forgotten yet significant" (2003:171).

Between the outskirts of Dganim and ʿAyn al-ʿAzm exists one such buffer zone. A *wadi*, or seasonal streambed, lies between steep banks of rock and sparsely strewn shrubs, its bed of parched earth empty except for rare flashfloods in the winter. Beside the rocky banks, the former orchards and many fields of the *moshav* have gone fallow. During my fieldwork, most residents of both settlements felt this buffer zone to be a dangerous space. On a day-to-day basis, they actively avoided or simply ignored it. But on two occasions I accompanied residents of Dganim and ʿAyn al-ʿAzm into this stigmatized and typically avoided space.

Walk in the *wadi*

One warm Saturday in February, after relaxing with Einat's family in Moshav Dganim, I received a call from Sarah, a woman with whom I'd lived the previous year in ʿAyn al-ʿAzm. She invited me on the excursion she was leading for al-ʿUwaydi neighborhood children. For several months, Sarah had been mentioning her plans to lead children from 'Ayn al-'Azm to explore the *wadi* and see the old water well where their tribe had lived before the government moved them into town. I filled a bottle of water, laced on sneakers, and walked out of Dganim's front gate. "There aren't any buses today," a guard warned me, assuming I was heading for the main highway. I felt self-conscious as I thanked him and then turned off the road to walk around Dganim's fence toward the *wadi*, knowing that I was breaching *moshav* norms.

After hearing from so many residents of both the *moshav* and the township that "nobody goes to the *wadi*," I was surprised to find that I was not alone. An elderly man and a group of young boys were gathering weeds from the edge of a field for their livestock. Since Sarah's only directions had been to walk toward 'Ayn al-'Azm and meet them at "Cake Hill," I asked directions of the man. He flagged down a pickup truck that was bucking down a rough dirt track toward us, and the men inside, who turned out to be workers for a Dganim flower farmer and relatives of a woman I had befriended in 'Ayn al-'Azm, agreed to drive me to the hill. As we bumped down the path, the driver told me how unsafe it was for me, a woman on my own, to walk by myself in the *wadi*. *Shebab* (young men) who are no good hang out here, getting drunk and doing drugs, he warned. Kids come here to hang out and cause trouble, instead of going to school. He pointed to two boys with a donkey in the distance as proof of his warning. Later, though, I learned that they were boys in Sarah's group. They were children on a supervised trip, not delinquents, but the driver's expectation of illicit activity in this border zone led him to judge what he saw in a way that only confirmed his original view.

The driver let me out at Cake Hill, a recently constructed earthen mound at least 15 meters high with terracing that resembled a layered cake. The Jewish National Fund (JNF) built this hill as a tourist attraction, along with the grid of saplings planted at its base, the driver informed me. He then gestured around us to the bare, sandy landscape and opined that it could have been full of trees and well taken care of, but "these Arabs" don't take care. The driver, himself Arab, interpreted this landscape through the discursive frames propagated by Labor Zionism, which identify Israeli Jews as good stewards and Arabs as undeserving of the land. Underlying this contrast was a discourse framing good land use as intensive labor and the creation of greenery rather than adaption to an arid environment.

I spotted the children hiking out of the *wadi*'s ravine with Sarah and went to join them. We all climbed to the hill's top, where some relaxed in the shade of a circle of stone pillars and others frolicked in the sun and fed orange peels

to the donkey. As we rested, Sarah explained this place to me using a different discursive frame that valued nonproductive forms of dwelling as much as
planting or reaping. A fond smile lit her face, and her voice seemed to hold a
note of nostalgia as she described the orchards of Dganim that once lay where
the JNF's saplings now stood. Before Dganim's fence was erected, when Sarah
was a girl, her family members were employed to guard the orchards, and she
played among the trees.

Sarah's main goals for this excursion were to foster a similar sense of connection to the landscape among the children and let them enjoy simply being
outdoors. The children often sit all day indoors with school and video games,
and they don't know the landscapes around them, she lamented. As we cooled
in the shade and the children ate snacks, Sarah mentioned several nearby places
that were significant to the al-ʿUwaydi family's past taskscapes, including a
small stone house and an old water well, that we might visit. But she had set
no itinerary and said we would adapt our path to the afternoon's heat. Soon
we descended the hill, played a game of team tag, and then, with the children's
urging, set off toward the well.

We walked along the Dganim fence, atop the spine of an earthen wall (see
Ill. 5). I brought up the rear of a single-file line of children who were calling out,
running and walking, finding pretty rocks and pointing out snails. Several girls
asked me about the odd structures they saw across the fields in Dganim, and
I explained the agricultural uses of the dilapidated chicken coops and greenhouses. As we came upon the path's lone tree, Sarah stopped us under the shade
for a break. Three girls were excitedly showing me the tree's spiny seedpods
when I overheard Sarah describing a wide, flowing river to another cluster of
children. She's imagining what the *wadi* would be like here with a full river, one
of the girls explained. Then someone started singing a rain song and the rest
joined in, calling for the rains to fall. Sarah led the group in a call-and-response
prayer for God to bring the rains; she was demonstrating a sort of aspirational
stewardship over the *wadi* as their place. We continued on our way, and I wondered if anyone from Dganim was watching this brightly colored parade moving along the earthen wall.

Once we reached the well, Sarah steadied the children as they leaned over
the circular stone wall to peer into its depths. She narrated the cautionary tale
of a Bedouin man who had thrown a pebble down this well at night, angering
the dangerous spirit living in the well. Sarah then described another section
of crumbling stone wall as the remnants of a trough where shepherds once
watered their flocks. After the children clambered around the old trough, Sarah

Illustration 5. Sarah's group on an outing in the wadi, beside Dganim. 2009. Photograph by Author.

decided it was time to go home. She and the children climbed down into the *wadi* and up the much higher far bank to return to 'Ayn al-'Azm, waving and shouting to me as they went, while I walked back around Dganim's fence to reach the front gate.

Because the *wadi* was associated with danger and degenerate social groups, a trip like this was unusual, a rare opportunity for children living in 'Ayn al-'Azm to move through this border zone. Sarah led several excursions like this because she wanted children to enjoy "nature" in ways they could not experience within 'Ayn al-'Azm. With these trips, Sarah challenged the asocial or antisocial designation of the *wadi*. She invested value in this in-between space, both with stories of ancestors' activities and by labeling it as a destination for "nature." There was some didactic instruction, as Sarah warned the children not to litter and explained how they should behave as they moved through the landscape. But the socializing power of the excursion lay primarily in the physical experiences the children had and the associations made between their ancestors and this place, as in the stories of past Bedouins using the well. They made a social place by walking and playing through this buffer zone (Casey 1996), and this place became part of their developing senses of local identity (Gray 1999).

Tour of the Territory

The second time I ventured into the *wadi* was a month later, at the invitation of Gil, one of the *moshav*'s police officers. Gil knew of my research and offered me a tour of what he referred to as Dganim's *shetach*, or territory. This included the fields outside the fence and extended several kilometers to the *moshav*'s original, now abandoned settlement site. The *shetach* overlapped, as it turned out, much of the area I'd walked with Sarah's group. Gil picked me up one afternoon in a four-wheel-drive jeep, with a rifle slung over his shoulder. As we drove out the main gate and turned onto a rutted track along the *moshav*'s periphery fence, Gil described the security features protecting the *moshav*. He explained the progressive fortifications, from metal and barbed wire to electrification, that the community had erected over the years, interrupting himself to point out sections of the older fence that "they" stole to sell the metal for scrap. As Gil described the concrete tubes buried along the fence to prevent infiltrators from burrowing underneath, I realized that this security device was the narrow hill along which the children had skipped during Sarah's excursion.

The incongruity of this image highlighted the different interpretations of danger held by Dganim and 'Ayn al-'Azm residents. Gil's use of the term "territory" to describe the landscapes through which we traveled clearly claimed ownership, but by keeping his gun close to hand and repeatedly emphasizing security measures like the periphery fence, he also portrayed these landscapes as threatening. For most residents of 'Ayn al-'Azm, the *wadi* held moral danger; it was a place frequented by antisocial characters. The *wadi* was dangerous in a more violent, physical sense for Dganim residents. Had anyone actually tried to dig underneath the fence? I asked. Gil nodded but then referred to the recent news stories of Gaza residents digging tunnels under border walls to smuggle supplies.

Conversational associations like this, linking noncombatant Bedouin citizens of Israel to Palestinian militants, were common among Jewish Israelis, especially in 2009 when the Israeli army bombarded Gaza and Hamas sent rockets into nearby areas of the Negev. These associations, as well as worried statements about family ties between Gazans and nearby Bedouins, explained and perpetuated Dganim residents' fears of their Bedouin neighbors as threatening potential insurgents. As Gil and I continued bouncing along the rough path, he pointed to a missing section of guardrail along the highway. "They" stole that too, he informed me, explaining that it had been "the Arabs, the Bedouins," when I asked him to clarify. Jewish communities in the Negev are like guarded villas, he added, reinforcing the depiction of a small community beleaguered by surrounding violence, but also, perhaps inadvertently, highlighting the economic disparities that festered between neighboring communities (Kedar and Yiftachel 2006). Class, culture, and political agenda blended as Gil drew associations between Bedouin Arab citizens, Palestinian militants, and metal scavengers, and contrasted these with wealthy Israeli Jews.

As Gil drove us away from the *moshav* toward "old Dganim," he repeated the story I had heard many times before about the original inhabitants, who couldn't manage on this desert *moshav*, and how the *moshav* was refounded by Jews from India in the 1950s. He finished as we parked between the shells of two buildings. Gil left the truck running and took his rifle with him as we inspected the buildings' remains. I lingered for a moment, examining an old well, but Gil seemed more interested in the region's current Jewish presence as he pointed out and named Jewish towns on the horizon. Still intrigued by this well, I mentioned the other well I had seen with Sarah. Gil looked alarmed and, with shock in his voice, interrogated me as to when, with whom, and why I had been in the *wadi*. He appeared mollified by my description of an outing with children, and we climbed back into the truck to continue our tour.

Naming prominent features of the landscape was important to Gil. In addition to the Jewish towns, he identified a peaked hill across the highway as Abraham's Shoulder, so named because Abraham Avinu (our father, Abraham) had lived there, he said. Gil labeled Cake Hill as Mitzpe Dganim (Dganim Lookout). Both labels identified these features as part of a Jewish landscape.

Driving further, Gil took a cue from our surroundings to explain how Israeli Jews and Arabs are different. We passed the outer fields that Dganim used to farm, and I asked why some fields had fresh crops despite the departure of *moshav* residents from field agriculture. The *moshav* rents fields to large-scale, nonresident farmers, Gil replied, so that the JNF will not reclaim the lands while the *moshav* undergoes the slow, bureaucratic process of reclassifying these farmlands for commercial use in the *moshav*'s tourism plans. "We, the Jewish people, are a law-abiding nation," Gil averred. Unlike the Bedouins who just use the land as they please, he continued, sweeping his hand in a wide circle to indicate the unrecognized villages around us, Jews respect the law and obtain permits for different land uses.

Gil continued to narrate the landscape as we bumped through the agricultural fields in the jeep toward a "surprise" he wanted to show me. During a recent perimeter inspection, Gil had found that a large section of the earthen barrier surrounding Dganim's fence had been swept away by a powerful flash-flood. Gil's reaction to this breached barrier, like his attention to indications of

Jewish settlement in the area, suggested his dedication to shaping this landscape as a protective boundary around Dganim. Fascinated by this vivid demonstration of "the force of nature," he recorded a video on his cell phone of the swirling waters and then brought me to bear witness. Though struck by nature's power, Gil was not deterred. He explained how he planned to fix the breach with earthmoving equipment as he drove us back to the *moshav*'s front gate.

Each of these ventures into the *wadi* suggested different attachments to landscapes. Unlike my trip with Sarah, this was more explicitly an educational tour for the resident anthropologist, conducted so that I could return home and write accurately about the place. Gil used a more didactic style to teach me. We drove through, rather than walking and allowing the climate and shady spots to dictate where we went and when we stopped to rest. This tour was not simply of a landscape, but of Dganim's territory, the areas over which the *moshav* claimed control and the right to exclude others. Gil's demeanor, surveying rather than lingering in the landscape and carrying a rifle at all times, and his references to Jewish legality versus Bedouin illegality, all suggested his preoccupation with maintaining the barrier around Dganim. As a police officer, he was himself part of the state apparatus enforcing the particular legal structure that designated Jewish and Bedouin spaces, and he sought to maintain the physical barrier of the fence and earthen mound as impermeable.

A Place Between

These are not representative views of the two settlements. I would glimpse a different portrait if I joined the young men against whom the truck driver warned me, or if my Dganim guide was someone tending toward less bravado. But these accounts offer a glimpse at the gulf that can separate neighbors' perceptions of and interactions with the same landscape. Because of the region's segregation, most day-to-day experiences of the Negev's landscapes build on a limited experience of place. Most Dganim residents have not moved through the landscape or engaged in shared taskscapes with 'Ayn al-'Azm residents, and vice versa. Two settlements, though close together, are sundered by physical barriers, social norms of behavior, character judgments, and negative emotions of fear and mistrust. The same is generally true throughout the Negev.

As Dganim and 'Ayn al-'Azm residents dwell in the everyday politics of land conflict, they often reinforce—and sometimes destabilize—social divisions. Outings in the *wadi* were unusual, and precisely because they were anomalous the trips reveal that which usually remains unsaid and unacted. They suggest how neighbors understood and behaved toward the buffer zone that separates them, often reaffirming boundaries (Vila 2003). Some who ventured in, such as Gil and the truck driver who drove me to meet Sarah, read confirmation of their existing stereotypes from the landscape. Encountering physical barriers such as fences and the selective routes of a government bus system, as well as different norms of language, dress, and gender relations, can also reinforce divisions. Similarly, many studies of interaction across social barriers demonstrate that mere contact is no guarantee of improved relations (Hallward 2011; Hewstone, Rubin, and Willis 2002).

However, as a space of "cultural liminality" (Chapin 2003:5), where rules of interaction are less fixed, the *wadi* also allowed experimentation with new associations and new relationships between groups and places. Dwelling practices in and around border zones can challenge notions of absolute separation, revealing perforations in a binary Arab-Jewish division. Sarah's outing, in particular, demonstrated that although there are powerful social norms discouraging taskscapes in the *wadi*, these norms are not determinative. Traveling during the day as a large group of children and adults and framing the trip as a nature excursion for children, Sarah did not encounter any resistance from her neighbors. By hearing an instructive tale about proper behavior in this place from the story of the man and the dangerous spirit, learning how this place fit into their forebears' lives, and touching and climbing on the old buildings and constructed hill, the children brought this border zone partially into their socialized landscape of 'Ayn al-'Azm. The Negev has many of these culturally liminal spaces. Some activities, like those of the environmental justice group Bustan, strive to forge new relationships between Jews and Arabs through cooperative projects in these liminal spaces. Thus, transgressions of Arab-Jewish boundaries can reveal not only the dominant environmental discourses that fuel conflict, but also how some residents are enlisting the political charge of everyday dwelling practices to instigate incremental changes.

3 Coping with Lost Land

"AT THE BEGINNING, I WAS VERY HAPPY [moving out of the tent], because I was little and afraid of the rain, and everything. But after we moved, I realized that living there and playing in the mud was the best." This is how Sarah described her feelings when she moved off her family's lands and into their plot in the township of 'Ayn al-'Azm when she was young. 'Ayn al-'Azm was established in 1970 and by 2008 had reached a population of about 15,000. During the first several years, fewer than thirty families moved into the township, and the number of new families began to increase significantly only when, several years later, the state government adopted a strict policy of refusing services to unrecognized villages. To some extent, Moshe Dayan and the government planners of Iyur HaBedowim would be pleased with the state of this government-planned Bedouin township today (Dinero 2010). Children attend schools with nationally coordinated curricula, and many fathers dress as Dayan hoped they would and look for work as wage laborers in the nearby city of Beersheba. Already in 1994, anthropologist Aref Abu-Rabia found that "without a doubt, the economic centre of gravity has moved from livestock rearing towards wage labour in towns and villages" (1994:17).

However, because of the recency of its establishment, most adult residents, like Sarah, could recall some period of their lives before the township, and their parents had spent most of their lives in landscapes other than 'Ayn al-'Azm. Township planning contradicted many residents' priorities and barred practices they valued, such as raising livestock and growing food. Many residents remembered their moves from rural lifestyles in dispersed settlements to the planned townships as a shift from freedom to restriction, intrafamily closeness to interfamily friction, and self-sufficiency to dependence. Through these contrasts, residents perceived physical signs of loss and absence in their township.

Sometimes in deliberately provocative ways and sometimes less concertedly, residents faced landscapes of absence and adapted dwelling practices that sought to fill some of these gaps. What does this mean for the way residents understand home? In other words, do residents recognize themselves in the township landscapes, and do they look to these landscapes to tell stories about themselves and their society? (cf. Feld and Basso 1996).

The physical layouts of households in the township and the taskscapes they embodied offer some clues about the different, often creative ways residents responded to the limitations and opportunities of township life. Sarah's was the first household I joined upon moving to 'Ayn al-'Azm in 2008. Her family was part of the large al-'Uwaydi 'ashira (tribe or extended family) that dominated one side of town. The family's property, like most in 'Ayn al-'Azm, was surrounded by a high wall so that household goings-on were not visible from the street. Inside, a pair of two-story houses framed an open courtyard, and small pens for livestock ran along two edges of the property. In one house, Sarah's brother and his family lived on the top floor. The ground floor was a mixed-use space that included Sarah's workshop for skin-care products and room for occasional lessons with neighborhood children. Years ago, Sarah had gone to school in England to study business. When she returned, she began community projects to educate the children and women of her neighborhood about desert ecology and traditional Bedouin practices and had started a business both to further these aims and to earn a living. In this home workshop she started making soaps, creams, and oils derived from desert herbs, and on the outskirts of town she set up a shop and educational herb garden.

In the second house on the plot lived Sarah, her mother Um Fareed, and her three unmarried sisters. Several married sisters lived in the al-'Uwaydi neighborhood, having found husbands within the extended family, and visited often. Although the house had bedrooms for all the sisters living there, the sisters preferred to sleep together in one large room downstairs. Each night, thin mattresses and blankets were laid out, and each morning they were stacked against the wall so the room could be used to watch television, prepare food, and do innumerable other daily activities. The family maintained separate spaces for men and women, and when I moved in I was incorporated into this gendered division of space. Sarah asked me to cover my hair with a headscarf and remain with the women as well.

Sarah's father, Abu Fareed, split his time between this house and his other wife's house down the street. The formal guest room, where Abu Fareed hosted male guests and where the daughters lounged at other times, was the house's front room. The room accommodated multiple aesthetics, with a traditional Bedouin seating area of hand-woven pillows in brilliant hues of red, pink, and orange and a Western-style nook of brown and tan upholstered sofas. Each morning, Abu Fareed and his son left for work, often staying away until late in the evening, leaving the compound to the women doing household chores and tending the preschool-age children.

In the back of the compound was the *'arisha*, a gathering space for the household's women and their visitors. In a fire pit cut into the concrete floor, women made tea and coffee and toasted bread. Each morning, woven mats, mattresses, and pillows were laid on the floor around the fire pit. For much of the day, this space was full of family members preparing food, serving tea to guests, or just relaxing. This made it convenient to run a small neighborhood store from the back storage room. Neighborhood children ran in at all hours with pocket money for candy or to pick up cheese or milk for their mothers. Such neighborhood shops throughout the township allowed women and children to get supplies within the comfort of family networks.[1] Most evenings, women from the extended family, including Sarah's married sisters, aunts, and cousins, gathered in the *'arisha*, young children in tow, to talk and sip tea.

The family also had an *'izbe* on the outskirts of town. Though "*'izbe*" usually refers to a remote seasonal camp, the family used the term for the small plot of land that served a variety of purposes, including agriculture, Sarah's shop and garden, and formerly her brother's auto-repair shop. Sarah collaborated with NGOs like Bustan to bring in volunteers to help create the garden and then attract busloads of visitors, to whom she spoke about Bedouin culture. She was, it became clear to me, a "culture worker," someone dedicated to defining and representing a culture to a wide audience that includes both "insiders" and "outsiders" (Shryock 2004a). Her influence in promoting the revival of certain Bedouin traditions derived both from her position within a lineage that was large, cohesive, and well known within the township and from her skill in accessing NGO and media networks beyond the township. The *'izbe* was an important space for Sarah and her sisters. Often two or three of them walked there to work for the afternoon before returning home for dinner. It gave them a welcome respite from the densely packed neighborhood and a chance to gaze out to the landscape of open brush where their family used to live.

The family that hosted me for the second half of my fieldwork in 'Ayn al-'Azm lived on the other side of town. Members of a smaller *'ashira*, the Abu Assas lived in a neighborhood with households from several different extended families. I initially met Wafiq Abu Assa through the environmental justice campaigns in which he had been a leader for the last several years. He too was a culture worker, though his environmentalist vision of Bedouin traditions held less sway in 'Ayn al-'Azm than in the transnational activist networks in which he worked. When he invited me to live with his family, I joined his mother, Um Ahmad, and four unmarried siblings, who lived together in the concrete and stone house that the older brothers and their father had constructed together.

Unlike many in 'Ayn al-'Azm, Wafiq and his brothers recalled being initially eager to move out of their tents and into the township with its concrete houses. Ahmed, the eldest brother, had moved to northern Israel for several years to attend high school and had grown accustomed to the furniture and stone houses there, so he was happy when the family decided to leave their tents behind. He described with pride the attentive planning they had put into each room of their small house. The concrete house with stone cladding contained separate spaces for family relaxation and receiving guests. Two bathrooms, one with a more traditional squat toilet and one with a seated flush toilet, lay at opposite ends of the house. Not having enough money at the time to fully construct their planned house, they laid in stairs to a second floor, which, fifteen years later, remained unbuilt.

This sturdy house shared the family compound with two smaller, more hastily assembled structures where two married brothers and their families lived. With seven sons hoping to continue living near their widowed mother, space was tight in this small plot, and the family began building a two-story structure that would hold apartments for several brothers. But money was also still tight, so the cement skeleton of the apartments stood for years waiting for the funds to complete them. Unfinished houses lay throughout 'Ayn al-'Azm as in other Bedouin Arab townships, a visible indicator of economic vulnerability and unfulfilled aspirations (Melly 2010). Eager for housing, but not waiting for the money to build conventionally, another brother, Mufid, and his wife were constructing a unique, mud-brick-and-tire house.

Unlike the al-'Uwaydis, each household within the compound functioned independently to prepare meals and do chores. But they also mingled in the courtyard to have coffee and enjoy the afternoon sun or work together on the mud house. In the evenings, siblings and cousins squeezed into the living room of the main house to watch television while chatting, entertaining the youngest children, and preparing late-night snacks. Many Fridays, everyone gathered for a large meal. In this extended household, no spaces were specifically reserved for men and women, and I was not expected to wear a headscarf at home or keep my distance from the men.

Adult family members held a variety of jobs. Three of the older brothers worked in and around Beersheba for a large store and an NGO. One brother was a self-employed graphic designer, and another worked part-time in the local schools. Luna, Ahmed's wife, walked to work at a daycare center. Like Sarah's household, this family's compound primarily became the domain of women and young children during the day. Um Ahmed, her daughters, and her daughters-in-law stayed home, except when traveling to Beersheba to buy food. However, living in a neighborhood of unrelated lineages, unlike living in the spatially and socially dense *'ashira* relations of the al-'Uwaydis' neighborhood, there was little interaction with neighbors. Rather than hosting visitors for tea and chatting, this compound's evening gatherings consisted of a small circle of immediate family members.

Sarah's and Wafiq's families each engaged in notable experiments with 'Ayn al-'Azm's urban space—Sarah's with the *'izbe* and Wafiq's with the mud-and-tire house. Because my research aimed in part to explore new possibilities for escaping the Negev region's divisive strife, I sought out people who were proactive in thinking of and enacting new land relations in the Negev. However, these households were not unique. Some residents participated in the processes of their own urbanization by turning entirely to wage labor in the regulated labor market, dressing in mainstream Israeli fashions, and striving for a middle-class, consumption-driven lifestyle. Many others chafed against the township's grid of right-angle streets, restrictions on agricultural practices, and small residential plots. All these residents, like Palestinians throughout Israel, dealt daily with their simultaneous inclusion and exclusion from Israeli society (Kanaaneh 2002). Within this context of segregation and land conflict, even seemingly mundane dwelling practices are implicated in political contestations over identity, societal belonging, and land claims.

Encountering Loss

When describing their family histories to me, many 'Ayn al-'Azm residents looked toward the horizon and pointed in the direction of their former homes. The gesture to a physically close yet unattainable former home sadly admits to dispossession, while also asserting a lingering claim (Slyomovics 1998). Other residents, whose family lands were requisitioned to build 'Ayn al-'Azm, saw the past more directly within their daily traveled landscapes. One man pointed to his grandfather's land near the township's entrance, saying, "He bought it during British rule, and then the Jews came and . . . when the state came, they seized it." The land was then zoned as an industrial sector but still lies undeveloped.

He used to visit the place often with his father, who got very angry upon seeing it in its present state, with the crumbled remnants of the grandfather's house still evident. Another relative, who consistently foreswore political discussions, described this same landscape less darkly. But he too saw the past in the present. "I will explain everybody to you, where they were living then," he told me. Surprised and wanting to be certain I understood, I asked, "You still remember where everyone lived?" "Every tent, where was it! Even the sheep!" he exclaimed with a laugh.

In contrast to a remembered past tent life of freedom and wholesomeness, residents discussing contemporary life in the township were much more likely to cite problems and absences than to praise the place. Residents often complained of the poor planning that had gone into the township, noting that its neighborhood layout, original housing design, and the size of its schools were all incompatible with elements of Bedouin lifestyles. Like authoritarian modernization schemes elsewhere, planners followed an aesthetic assumption of what an ordered settlement should look like, sometimes neglecting empirical research about the plan's suitability for its intended population (Dinero 2010; Scott 1998). When 'Ayn al-'Azm was first planned, the housing units were small—just 70-square-meter houses set on 400-square-meter plots (0.4 *dunam*)—and designed according to what Western builders thought suitable for Bedouins (Falah 1983:314; Horner 1982). This was a commonly cited source of contention. Jaber, a Bedouin Arab social worker, described with an ironic smile how the planners had initially proposed houses without roofs over large sections because they thought "Bedouins like to see the sky." Later, because these government-built houses failed to attract families, a "build-it-yourself" policy was implemented throughout the townships, whereby families built houses on designated allotments according to their own desires and financial means.

As the past was present in 'Ayn al-'Azm's landscapes, so too was the future. Many parents, especially those like Um Ahmed with multiple sons, looked at their small plots (ranging in contemporary 'Ayn al-'Azm from 0.4 to 1.0 *dunam*), densely surrounded by neighbors, and sadly saw a future without room for their children to build houses nearby. This imagined future landscape of scattered children and grandchildren had prompted some who could afford it to buy extra adjacent plots when they moved into 'Ayn al-'Azm in the 1980s and 1990s. But by 2008, with few unpurchased plots remaining, most faced this future landscape with a mixture of resentment and resignation.

The small plots and the limited neighborhood area assigned to each extended family were unfair, some residents explained, because of the importance Bedouins placed on having many children and maintaining patrilineal solidarity (Kressel 1991). As Ahmed, a former school administrator, told me, it used to be "unacceptable" to Bedouins for sons to settle away from their parents (Ginat 1997; Meir 1998). But now, "they are forced to because there's no other place." He sighed heavily as he told me that it is now acceptable for sons to move away, but still very hard. A woman from a different neighborhood shared Ahmed's perspective, and she expressed her frustration with an explicit comparison to what she called "Jewish places" (Jewish municipalities), where "they have several thousand *dunams* set aside to expand in future generations. But in Bedouin places, there is only this much." She brought her hands very close together, peering into the narrow gap pensively. "So, the people can only build more floors; there is no space for people to have land." Many township residents worried about the effects of scattering families and raising children in a nuclear family (*usra*) without significant involvement from the uncles, aunts, and cousins of an *'ashira*. Though the growing independence of nuclear family units in 'Ayn al-'Azm is mirrored among urbanizing Arab communities throughout the world (Abu-Lughod 1990; Joseph 1999; Hopkins 2003), it has resulted from different taskscapes in Israel. Scattered family members in distant neighborhoods or towns reminded 'Ayn al-'Azm residents of government seizures of Bedouin lands and unfair regulations, the taskscapes of state planners.

The lack of jobs available within the township also troubled people. Employment opportunities in the formal labor market within 'Ayn al-'Azm are limited to a handful of small businesses operating along the main street and a few positions in the health clinic, community center, and local schools. An industrial zone that briefly supported several factories producing building materials had since closed down. This too residents attributed to negligent planning by authorities who were not guided by the best interests of Bedouin Arab citizens. As one former town council member told me, authorities knowingly planned the industrial zone on lands claimed by a Bedouin Arab family, and the property dispute forced the factories to close. Some residents find work outside 'Ayn al-'Azm, an opportunity open primarily to men. But unemployment rates are consistently high in the Bedouin Arab townships, compared with neighboring Jewish towns. Swirski and Hasson (2006:95) report a 2003 jobless rate of 34.7 percent among Bedouin men of "recognized" towns, and 11.6 percent among Jewish men in the Beersheba subdistrict.

Residents were not alone in their censure. Many researchers have also criticized the Bedouin Arab townships' insufficient land allocations, restrictive planning regulations for land use, small municipal budgets and limited governing power, meager economic opportunities, and inadequate provision of education, health, and recreation services (Rosen-Zvi 2004; Abu-Saad and Lithwick 2000; Yonah, Abu-Saad, and Kaplan 2004). These shortcomings were compounded for residents by the contrasts they drew with their pasts. Often rose tinted, these remembered pasts induced a collective nostalgia for lost lifestyles (Abu-Rabia 2010) and a sense of estrangement in the present that powerfully influenced residents' encounters with the urban landscapes of 'Ayn al-'Azm.

Making Family Space

Officially, the address of each house in 'Ayn al-'Azm consists of two numbers designating the neighborhood and individual plot. Planners designed the grid of streets to aid smooth traffic flow across the township and make houses easy to locate. This made the township legible and thus easier for government agencies to control without the mediation of local elites (Rose 1994; Scott 1998). But as I learned during shared taxi rides into the township, because residents interpreted township geography in terms of family groupings, it was not a set of numbers that the driver requested for directions, but a family name and perhaps the head of the household. Not recognizing place according to public paths and landmarks, as is common in well-established urban places (Lynch 1960), residents worked to carve private family space out of what had been planned as a town for Bedouin Arabs, regardless of 'ashira. Walking directions were given as, for example, "Go to the second street in the Abu Gweider family neighborhood and turn left; it's the fourth house on the street." The street layout of the township gave no indication of separate family enclaves, and no signs marked these boundaries. They were visible to those who were quite familiar with the social makeup of the township but less so to socially external government officials or visitors.

When I moved to 'Ayn al-'Azm, I was puzzled to see many streets blockaded by oil drums filled with concrete, lengths of sidewalk curb, or piles of rock and dirt. Wafiq later explained that families in many government-planned townships made these blockades to create family space. The roads that had been gridded to allow traffic flow and legibility also allowed strange men to pass routinely through the clustered homes of an 'ashira, bringing family women into public view. While standards of modesty are shifting in Muslim contexts around the world (Adely 2012; Falah and Nagel 2005; Mahmood 2005), standards in 'Ayn al-'Azm dictated against this exposure. Thus, in some places throughout town individuals reshaped urban plans, turning public space into private space with blockades. Similarly, the high walls surrounding most family compounds created visual barriers to separate family space from public space, protecting the family's *hurma* ("sanctity," also "women") (see Ill. 6).[2]

In these small ways, residents shaped 'Ayn al-'Azm's landscapes through their dwelling practices, shifting urban plans to meet residents' priorities. However, the "problem of land," meaning a lack of land available to one's family, was harder to overcome. Young couples were torn between ideals of lineage solidarity, that is, establishing households adjacent to other members of their *'ashira*, and the actuality of limited housing in dense neighborhoods. An image of modernity associated with nuclear family households in Israel (Kanaaneh 2002) also encouraged the dispersal of *'ashira* members. However, the meaning of *'ashira* affiliations is changing in uneven ways. Many residents confirmed the claims of scholars that lineages have lost influence in determining economic responsibility (Salzman 1980), but they continue to guide interpersonal relations in times of tension (Ginat 1997) and mobilize people during elections (Parizot 2001).[3] Residents complained of *waasta* (literally, "intercession," meaning "nepotism" or "family connections") eating into budgets and preventing the best people from being hired for local government jobs. Yet during 'Ayn al-'Azm's local elections, almost everyone I spoke to reported voting along *'ashira* lines. Fearful of losing out when those who gained political power continued operating through *waasta*, individuals were reluctant to break with this system of family affiliation.

Illustration 6. Street with high-walled family plots in 'Ayn al-'Azm. 2009. Photograph by Author.

Many residents explained 'Ayn al-'Azm's lack of security in relation to these troubled interfamily politics. Prior to Israeli statehood, the distance between Bedouin Arabs' family clusters helped avoid direct confrontation when disputes arose (el-Aref 1974). In the dense township, residents used street barricades and high walls to separate families and avoid confrontations. In the vast majority of cases, interactions between unrelated neighbors were smooth. But conflicts drew great attention, and almost every resident I spoke with characterized township life as involving greater strife with neighbors than life in the unrecognized villages. One day after being away for several weeks, I returned to 'Ayn al-'Azm and learned that two men had been killed earlier that week. I was having tea with a woman not related to the men involved, and she described the sequence of attack, retaliation, and further threats. A "blood revenge" (*taar*) was carried out between the al-'Uwaydis and al-Jibalis, she told me. The shooters were arrested, but young men from both families continued to make threats, saying the blood debt was not settled, and my host worried that more killings would occur. Though such killings were rare, a fear of violence between disputing families lingered for many residents, adding to their feelings of threat and alienation in town.

In other, less deadly confrontations there was considerable disagreement over when and to what extent the police should be involved. One night a van was set on fire in the Abu Assas' compound, and the family immediately suspected their neighbors. These families in adjacent plots had been involved in a long-running exchange of insults, threatening letters, and heightened fences, often sparked by building or other changes one of the families made to their plot. One of the older brothers in the family called the police after the van fire. While the police interviewed other family members, I sat waiting with a daughter-in-law who shook her head, upset that her husband and his brothers would call the police for "every little thing." "Are they grown men?" she asked rhetorically. She then asserted that men should take responsibility for defending their family. Though some residents reacted to these violent events with anxiety and sorrow, a constant anticipation of violence can make it feel commonplace (Scheper-Hughes 1993), and others, like this daughter-in-law, accepted such violent events as an unavoidable part of life.

This daughter-in-law and the other residents who grappled with issues of family cohesion, privacy, and protection in 'Ayn al-'Azm struggled to reconcile the imposition and possible protection of state institutions, like the police, with their desires for self-governance and respect within their community. As many older residents lamented, young people did not respect the authority of elders anymore. Urbanization had turned authority structures upside down, as the

decline of agriculture in everyday life and the more prominent role of state bu-
reaucracies and Hebrew-language interactions rendered the knowledge youth
gained from formal education more valuable than their elders' knowledge
(Marx and Shmueli 1984; Meir 1998). With the overturning of a past authority structure and decreased community autonomy, traditions such as taking
refuge, mediation by a tribal judge (*qaadi*), or reliance on a third-party guaran-
tor (*kafil*) of judgments, which used to settle disputes (el-Aref 1974), were no
longer practical. Yet the principle of family solidarity and defense remained
influential, leading to violent outbreaks such as these.

Residents were aware of the stereotypes of lawlessness and danger that
non-Bedouin Israelis hold against Bedouin Arabs (Kabha 2007), and they were
troubled by this reputation. When describing violent events, speakers were
often careful to remove them from association with Bedouins as a larger group,
explaining them along *'ashira* lines. The woman who told me about the blood
revenge noted that the al-'Uwaydis were known to be particularly volatile. They
have the wildest, most poorly raised children in town, she said, and their kids
sometimes throw rocks at cars driving through the neighborhood. But, she was
careful to clarify, this was not the case in her family. She and other speakers
managed the ambivalent connections they held to the township as a social place
by distancing themselves from other, more dangerous residents and emphasizing the family as a unit of belonging.

Urbanizing Rural Taskscapes

Like the spatial adjustments residents made—or attempted to make—for their
family structures in the township, their agropastoral taskscapes responded to
urban plans in contradictory ways. Bedouin Arabs throughout the Negev have
long earned their living by combining wage labor with farming rain-fed wheat
and barley and raising sheep and goats (Abu-Rabia 1994). However, imposition of the *siyag*, subsequent registration requirements and restrictions by the
Ministry of Agriculture, and the designing of Bedouin townships without space
for planting or pasture curtailed this agriculture and pastoralism. By 2008 in
'Ayn al-'Azm, a handful of families still made a living from raising herds, housing them in pens outside the township and taking feed to them. Most families,
though, did not have the financial means for this capital-intensive approach.
Instead, many adapted some elements of their former agropastoral lives to
township life. By farming and raising animals, they were "making do," in de
Certeau's (1984) sense of the phrase, living and working in a location in ways
that perhaps unselfconsciously create a meaningful place.

For many families, agropastoral practices provided economic benefits by supplementing the food bought with earned wages (Degen 2003). The al-'Uwaydis raised several sheep and goats in their family compound, along with a small flock of chickens and pigeons. These few livestock were not sufficient to feed the large family, but they did supplement their diet. After each meal, Um Fareed and her daughters salvaged and parceled out leftovers to the animals; Abu Fareed brought home grain feed. The chicken eggs and pigeon meat then reduced the amount of food to be purchased, and several sheep were slaughtered for the Islamic holiday of Eid al-Adha. In addition, the women grew herbs and a few vegetables in a small kitchen garden next to the 'arisha. Lemon and pomegranate trees lined one side of the house, and a large fig tree spread high between the two houses. On the family's 'izbe, Abu Fareed also tended a cluster of fruit trees and farmed a patch of wheat. This was "baladi wheat," the sisters stressed to me, meaning that they grew heritage varieties without chemical fertilizers or pesticides.

The al-'Uwaydis' neighborhood of interwoven family ties facilitated agropastoral practices, since resources could be shared between households. Some items were given or traded, and others bought. A relative up the road kept a camel and occasionally gave milk to Sarah's family, which they served with the sweet morning tea. Another relative raised two dairy cows. Usually, Sarah's family bought milk from the grocery store. However, when an investigative report revealed silicon in the milk of national dairy brands that spring, Um Fareed began buying fresh milk from her relative. The family's connection with food producers allowed them to switch easily.

To cope with housing shortages and zoning limitations, a few 'Ayn al-'Azm residents revived the mud-brick construction known as bayka that was once used for village buildings throughout the Naqab. Sarah's younger sister, Fawzia, was building a small mud-brick house on the 'izbe while I lived in town. She built because she loved the open view of the desert, she told me. The mud-brick house was unlicensed, but it was something she could do herself with a bit of help from her brothers without needing to hire a concrete layer. Fawzia also took pride in constructing "the way Bedouins used to build."

Responding to a more pressing need, Mufid built a home on the Abu Assas' crowded plot. He too used mud bricks, but combined them with a frame of used car tires. The stacked tires were filled with trash, like cardboard and cans, to weigh them down and sealed with a mixture of mud and straw to create a smooth wall. Mufid had been struggling for several years to find a house in this neighborhood for his wife and now two young children, and with mud-

Illustration 7. A mud-brick house under construction. 2008. Photograph by Author.

building he could provide shelter through his own labor and with free or inexpensive materials. Mud-building also fit his dream of a wholesome and productive home life. Mufid fondly remembered the family togetherness of living in a tent and nostalgically sought out "the simple life" of livestock rearing and farming that he imagined "real Bedouin" like his grandfather had enjoyed. By building this house and adding a vegetable garden in the future, he hoped to regain a lost sense of comfort and belonging.

This sense of comfort was a strong motivator for much of the agropastoralism practiced in 'Ayn al-'Azm. Some residents, particularly those who had moved into the township at a late age, created alternative landscapes within the township because they simply could not imagine living in a typical, boxlike house with only store-bought food. Um Yunis, now elderly, was middle-aged when she moved to a plot at the edge of 'Ayn al-'Azm, and though her son built her a concrete block house with two bedrooms and a large kitchen, she continued to live in a tent anchored outside the house. She was uniquely dedicated to her past taskscapes but was also a vocal proponent of modern conveniences. She appreciated the running water and gas burner, veterinary and medical services, and social security payments from the state that she could enjoy in the township. She was unwilling, though, to give up certain aspects of her taskscape such as raising a small collection of animals for milk and meat and living in a tent.

Some residents, like Fawzia and Um Yunis, "made do" to maintain or strengthen ties to familiar taskscapes that had been disrupted by the township's urban plan. But other residents made do to cope with feelings of double detachment, from both the place and the people of 'Ayn al-'Azm. The township gathered residents from disparate backgrounds, including some from very different landscapes. The first time I visited Muna's house, I saw from the street only a tall metal fence with thorny bushes spilling over the top. But when I entered her courtyard, I discovered flowering cacti and ornamental trees sprouting from pots and a few olive trees shading nooks of vegetation. It was expensive to coax this greenery out of the desert climate, Muna assured me when I asked about the cost of water, but she willingly spent large portions of her meager salary as a seasonal fruit picker on pots, seedlings, and water. Muna identified not as a Bedouin Arab, but as a Palestinian from the coast who had married into an 'Ayn al-'Azm family. She never felt socially accepted by her husband's family, and the Naqab felt dry and infertile to her. She remembered the coastal towns being better because of the "freedom, clean air, and . . . pretty nature. There, everything just grows on its own." Creating this private pocket of greenery helped Muna feel at home in a town she viewed as unwelcoming. Other women like Muna, who

Illustration 8. A home garden creates a private pocket of greenery in the township. 2008. Photograph by Author.

had grown up in the north or along the coast before marrying into families in 'Ayn al-'Azm, also contributed to local taskscapes. By recreating personal land-scapes, they carved corners of care into the township's neglected landscapes and brought practices and ideals of landscape beauty from outside the Naqab.

On a more piecemeal level, 'Ayn al-'Azm residents also engaged in task-scapes that reproduced some of the sensory experiences of rural life. Both of my host families ate some store-bought and readymade foods but also cooked large homemade meals. Foods considered to be traditional Bedouin fare were common with the al-'Uwaydis—such as a spiced stew of tomatoes and onions (*mbasala*) poured over a tray of roughly shredded *saaj* bread, and a raisin jam (*nbiy'*) usually eaten with olive oil and bread. In wintertime, women picked armfuls of a wild winter green (*chubeza*) and boiled it into a thick soup. Such dishes were less common in the Abu Assa compound, where Hanin, Mufid's wife, brought northern Palestinian dishes from her home in the Galilee, and Luna avidly watched cooking shows on television and incorporated new in-gredients and dishes. But *saaj*, also referred to as "Bedouin bread" (*chubz bedoui*), was central to both families' diets. This large, very thin, circular bread is baked on a convex piece of metal set over a small fire. The subtle chewiness of the bread becomes rubbery after a day or two, so women in each compound worked together to knead dough and bake the bread every few days.

Because the bread is labor intensive and requires open space for a fire, many people in 'Ayn al-'Azm and other townships have stopped baking it. However, these two families held onto the familiar practice. As a result, whereas many other domestic chores had shifted inside to take advantage of gas ovens and sinks, *saaj*-making continued to mark certain outdoor spaces as domestic. As part of their taskscapes, *saaj*-baking involved social interactions as an extended family, bringing together women from different nuclear family units. It bridged generations, as girls were eager to learn from their mothers and aunts. And in the Abu Assa household, *saaj*-baking in the evening strengthened family rela-tionships, drawing people together to warm by the fire, talk, and sip tea as they ate scraps of fresh bread. Everyday practices of sharing homes and raising or cooking food together form the ties that reproduce families and communities (Carsten 1997).

Motivated by convenience, economic need, and the desire to bring comfort and familiarity into an often alienating landscape, these residents shaped the landscapes of 'Ayn al-'Azm through their dwelling practices. Agropastoralism in-volves not just planting and harvesting crops and raising sheep, but a whole life-style, from cycles of sleeping and waking to the foods people eat and the physical arrangement of their houses. Because many residents kept livestock of some kind, moos, clucks, and manure smells were an integral part of township life. Pens occupied space in families' small courtyards, and trucks rumbled in and out of town with feed. Simple but pervasive practices like bread-baking and the al-'Uwaydis' nightly family gatherings carved social and cultural places into the township's planned grids of efficiency. Building mud-brick houses was more unusual, but Fawzia's and Mufid's projects also constituted the landscape, bringing evidence of unlicensed building and "traditional" Bedouin practices into the skyline.

Negotiating the Politics of Taskscapes

Residents like Um Yunis, Mufid, and Muna did not intend to make political statements with their taskscapes. However, in the Negev where government planners have invested significantly in moving Bedouin Arabs away from agropastoral lifestyles and where they advance a discourse of modernizing Bedouins, even seemingly simple dwelling practices are political acts. As Margaret Jolly noted in observing Trobriand Island women's ostensibly timeless tradition of making banana-leaf bundle skirts, "apparent persistence may be resistance to colonial intervention" (1992:56). Crafted under colonial rule, these skirts became powerful symbols not just of personal creativity, but more broadly of the "regeneration of Trobriand culture in the face of external pressure" (42). Similarly, many elements of agropastoral taskscapes are marked within Israel as Bedouin or Arab—for example, penning animals in the courtyard, saaj-baking, gathering outside in an 'arisha, and sitting on the floor. Such dwelling practices continue rural traditions and contradict elements of 'Ayn al-'Azm's urban planning. These culturally significant taskscapes shape relationships not only among immediate family members, but also between the township and wider Israeli society.

Sometimes residents recognized and voiced the political salience of these practices. While I lived with the Abu Assas, Hanin and I were both learning the art of saaj-making. Family members who gathered to tease our clumsy movements also commented approvingly on how Bedouin we were becoming when we successfully produced the delicate bread without burnt holes. They encouraged the reproduction of explicitly Bedouin practices and social ties.

Some culture workers, like Sarah and Wafiq, actively promoted Bedouin cooking, building, and other practices as part of a movement for cultural revival. The Abu Assas, who had embraced urbanization earlier and more fully than many 'Ayn al-'Azm residents, had recently begun adding agricultural elements into their urban lifestyles. Wafiq's growing environmentalist interests prompted these developments. During work with environmentalist and social justice NGOs, he learned about permaculture (a method of ecological design), the politics of food security, and the environmental ramifications of urbanization.[4] Although he did not speak much with his brothers about his NGO campaigns, he did begin transforming the family compound into a permaculture project. International students planned the layout with family members as part of a service-learning program. Together they dug and reshaped the ground into low footpaths and raised garden beds ready for vegetable seeds. A pit in the middle of the courtyard waited to be filled as a fishpond. The family built a compost bin and a makeshift cage and bought two chicks to become egg-layers. Wafiq explained the pursuit on ideological and educational grounds. He hoped to create a model for strengthening Bedouin Arab communities by combining the authenticity of local Bedouin traditions with the cosmopolitan cachet of permaculture.

Mufid learned his mud-and-tire building techniques through this permaculture experimentation as well. And as the house slowly took form, it became a multivalent symbol to which family members attached very different meanings. In contrast to Mufid's apolitical motivation, Ahmed saw mud-building as a shrewd way of dodging the unfair zoning laws that confined 'Ayn al-'Azm residents. The family did not have permission to build the house, but if "they" came to tear down the house at some point, Ahmed commented, Mufid would have managed to circumvent restrictions temporarily and with very little investment. Wafiq extolled the house as the first mud-and-tire building in 'Ayn al-'Azm, an innovative melding of progress and traditional practices that made a pointed political statement about the limitations that government planners imposed on Bedouin Arabs.

Across town, Sarah interwove her passion for the revival of Bedouin traditions with community-building and business development in even more concerted ways. On the family's 'izbe, which was unlicensed for permanent building, Sarah renovated her brother's former garage primarily using found materials like mud and stone. She created a visitors' center and store for her line of herbal beauty products, which catered to groups of visitors—mostly Israelis but also international tourists. Across the 'izbe was a large herb garden, planted in concentric circles and snaked with black irrigation piping. Even years after the help she received from Bustan to create the garden, Sarah continued cultivating international contacts and occasionally hosted volunteers who weeded and hauled rocks for the paths.

The status of Sarah's venture as tourism gave it more visibility than other agropastoral practices, as well as a more complicated political stance. Unlike other aspects of township life, tourism has been one venue within Israel where

Arab agropastoral taskscapes have been visible and governmentally endorsed. Particularly during the 1990s, when many were optimistic about peace agreements following the Oslo Accords, Ministry of Tourism officials worked with Jewish and Palestinian entrepreneurs to forge "consumer coexistence" (Stein 2008). They codesigned Palestinian Israeli tourist spaces that declare the loyalty of Palestinian citizens and display safe forms of cultural difference, such as "ethnic" food and musical performance (Slyomovics 1998; Stein 2008). At times these spaces offer Palestinians the opportunity to counter their marginalization within Israel, but most often the circumstances of the tourist encounter demand that participants self-censor politically sensitive messages.

In the Negev, images of exotic Bedouin culture and the promise of contact with a relatively untouched "past" have been key marketing tools (Dinero 2002; 2010).[5] Tourists can visit the Museum of Bedouin Culture or book a night of Bedouin camping, enjoying gestures of hospitality like tea and *saaj* bread that give an impression of authentic cultural encounter. Most tourist ventures are not run by Bedouin Arabs themselves and do not occur where they actually live (Dinero 2002). Instead, large-scale tourism operations display carefully formatted cultural elements of Bedouinness (cf. Shryock 2004b). Such enterprises present Bedouins as culturally anachronistic, living today as "exotic" others in a "modern" and "developed" Israeli society. This presentation buttresses a binary opposition between Bedouins and Jews, linking the former with tradition and the latter with modernity (Dinero 2010). Some Bedouin Arab entrepreneurs, however, are joining the business of heritage tourism with the dual goals of creating employment opportunities in their towns and villages and protecting cultural traditions. Sarah counted herself among such entrepreneurs.

When Sarah welcomed visitors, she usually showed them around the herb garden first. Inviting them to smell the wormwood, sage, and other plants, she explained the potency of native desert plants and their medicinal uses. Sarah then led groups through the shop into the large woven tent laid out with carpets and cushions but also with plastic chairs for those not nimble enough to sit on the ground. It was an authentic Bedouin tent, she always stressed to her visitors, which she bought from an old woman in Jordan. "I was born in a tent, . . . but, we are forgetting. . . . These days, one can only find a goat-hair tent like this in Jordan." Several employees, Sarah's sisters and neighbors, served tea. Staging a homelike setting, Sarah provided a taste of the famous Bedouin hospitality, not cynically but nonetheless savvy to its appeal.

Sarah usually told visiting groups the story of her business as they sipped tea or ate a buffet meal of "traditional Bedouin food" consisting of salads, stewed lentils, chickpeas, potatoes and vegetables, and plenty of *saaj* bread. She had long been troubled by the health and social problems experienced by Naqab Bedouin Arabs, she told her guests, and when she went to England to study in college, her time in Europe made her more aware of socioeconomic disparities. Sarah found research showing that chronic diseases like asthma and diabetes that now plague Bedouin Israelis were not widespread forty years ago. She recalled the different eating habits, outdoor lifestyles, and naturopathic remedies her grandmother's generation used, and she saw a connection between worsening health and Bedouin Arabs' "forgetting, losing their culture."

Sarah decided to help her community by combining her college training in business with what she remembered from her grandmothers' botanical practices and with her own research on the Prophet Muhammad's teachings about health. For several years she treated neighbors' ailments with trial batches of herbal products, and then, cobbling together loans from skeptical relatives and neighbors, she bought enough raw materials to begin selling some of these products.[6] Having a place to teach local children about medicinal herbs, desert practices, and environmental stewardship was important to Sarah. After failing to gain land in the township's center from the local council, she settled on converting a portion of her father's *'izbe*. Though many urged her to establish a nonprofit and seek grant money, and though she did welcome help from Bustan to establish her garden, she ultimately embraced the goal of profitability because she wanted "sustainable and independent" projects. In fact, not one for modest goals, Sarah aimed to build "the biggest organic, natural cosmetic line in Israel."

While many other residents individually practiced traditions such as baking *saaj* or raising sheep, Sarah's business venture enabled her on a more collective scale to foster traditions she saw as key to Bedouin culture.[7] Scholars have noted a global trend in recent years shifting "Bedouinness" from a lifestyle descriptor to a shared ethnic or subcultural Arab identity (Cole 2003) and point to the role of heritage tourism in packaging and spreading that identity (Peutz 2011). Sarah's participation in this wider trend influenced visitors' perceptions of Bedouinness, and she was also intent on affecting views and practices among residents of her own neighborhood.

However, the experiential knowledge of landscapes and plants that Sarah wanted to continue had lost its value in the Negev's political and economic shifts, so to make this endeavor financially practicable Sarah put traditions on display. Heritage tourism can revive elements of a fading past, but it also carries risks (Bunten 2008; Kirshenblatt-Gimblett 1998; Slyomovics 1998). These risks arise both from the process of framing certain practices and products as heritage and from the particular sociopolitical context of the Negev. First, tourism may support the continued vitality of certain practices but do so only by commodifying them. Sarah wished to protect and promote agropastoral practices, but heritage tourism risks rendering practices obsolete as they are framed as heritage rather than as everyday practices (Kirshenblatt-Gimblett 1998). For instance, the decision to build an earthen *taboun* oven drew support and participation from Sarah's sisters not because it would bake the family's bread, but because it would display Bedouin traditions to visitors.

Second, in this public venue, her business and the neighborhood outreach projects she initiated maneuvered between positions of defiance and acceptance of Israeli environmental discourses. Tourist enterprises like Sarah's can enlarge the place of Bedouin Arabs in Israeli society. In Sarah's case, teaching children and visitors about a rural Bedouin heritage that is tied to particular desert landscapes conveys a message of fixity that challenges the policy of Iyur HaBedowim as well as underlying narratives of Jews as tied to land and Bedouins as rootless wanderers. By advocating environmentalist stewardship, Sarah countered contemporary discourses of Bedouin Arabs as environmental hazards. However, tourism must also cater to the Israeli market, using a counter-hegemonic practice that is complicit with state power (Bunten 2008; Dinero 2010; Stein 2008). Sarah's Bedouin banquets, herbal remedies, and goat-hair tent are safe displays of cultural difference. These nonthreatening differences fit within liberal Zionist discourses of multiculturalism, which advocate a place for Bedouin Arabs in Israel but one that is carefully bounded off from Jews, reinforcing a dual-society paradigm. At the same time, Sarah's safe elements of difference helped her business grow. She embraced the profit motive and pursued personal goals of success, while channeling much of her earnings into the collectives—neighborhood and family—by which she also defined herself.

Sarah negotiated defiance and acceptance not just with a wider Israeli public, but with fellow township residents too. Though her heritage tourism venture promoted widely appreciated traditions like the use of medicinal herbs and mud-brick building, it simultaneously broke with other traditions. She refused her family's plans for her marriage and started an independent business instead. The ways she moved about in space, both in traveling abroad for college and in the mobility and public interaction necessary to run her business, challenged gender norms within her community. To some extent she also challenged the spatial separation of Jews and Arabs in Israel that has become not just a central feature of Zionist discourse, but also a norm among Bedouin residents. Sarah not only hosted tourists for brief lectures, but also invited volunteers, including Jews, into her family's home for longer periods and incorporated them into the practice of Bedouin lifestyles. Pebbles tossed by neighborhood boys at groups walking to and from the ʿizbe and harsh comments from some adult residents made clear that some in ʿAyn al-ʿAzm felt that these visitors threatened important norms of Jewish-Arab separation, as well as distinctions along family and gender lines.

Sarah thus confronted a particularly fraught context within which to negotiate the dilemmas of heritage tourism. Amid the heightened political salience of everyday taskscapes, she carefully maneuvered between the expectations common among Bedouin Arabs, which frowned on her avoidance of marriage and her public persona, and those more common among Jewish Israelis, which encouraged these behaviors as evidence of a progressive and liberated woman but were wary of serious challenges to a dual-society paradigm. Although some visitors commented on the sociopolitical implications of her business and neighborhood projects, Sarah refrained from public political discussions about her projects. "I think the land is God's land," she explained when I asked if she saw connections between her work and land disputes in the Negev. "My work is inspired more by religion than politics. We come from the earth and return back to the earth. Of course, I can't always avoid it. It's because of the political situation that maybe I can't reach my dream," she said, referring to her dual goals of building her business and strengthening Bedouin Arabs' landed lifestyles. Sarah preferred to keep her efforts apolitical but acknowledged that they had unavoidable political implications.

Dwelling in Neglect

Although Sarah's maneuvering between competing social expectations and the landscape she built on the ʿizbe through these maneuverings were particularly public, residents throughout ʿAyn al-ʿAzm faced similar dilemmas. One morning in January, I visited Amna, who lives on the edge of town. Feeling cramped in a house with four boisterous children, Amna suggested a walk outside. We strolled with her three youngest children along a dirt path to the *wadi*, where we were faced with a thin stream of white-gray water, edged with foam. Amna told me that the dirty water flows from the Jewish settlements in the West Bank (*mustawtaniin*) but also picks up pollution from local dumping along the banks. As we rounded a curve and walked between piles of garbage, Amna shook her head and told me that all this refuse is a disgrace. She wanted this *wadi* to be a place for leisurely walks, but others clearly treated it as a dumping ground. Building materials, household waste, and a bloated sheep carcass lay along the path. Our nostrils filled with the stench of rotting flesh and burnt plastic, and after just a few minutes we turned back to the house. I recalled our earlier interview, when she had described how she reused and recycled items but said with disappointment that most residents she knew did not think about conservation. "They don't have this culture," she explained.[8] As evidence, she spoke of the littered streets and the parks and playgrounds filled with garbage heaps that I had first noticed when visiting the township.

Amna was not the only one concerned about 'Ayn al-'Azm's littered land-scapes; many others noted the trash and rundown public spaces, despite the town's being less than forty years old. Perhaps because litter is highly visible and marks local interpretations of order and disorder, people often use it to read moral statements in landscapes (Alexander and Reno 2012; Argyrou 1997). In the Negev's segregated landscapes, statements about dirt and disorder can be particularly pointed assertions about the people who shaped those places (McKee 2015). In fact, claims about Bedouin Arabs' lack of environmental stewardship have often been used as evidence in arguments against their land rights (Harel 2010; Leibovitz-Dar 2006).[9] 'Ayn al-'Azm residents spoke within this wider conversation about good and bad land uses, but they contested dom-inant assignments of blame.

When faced with the trash-strewn streets and *wadi*, residents assigned re-sponsibility in many directions. Most often they read the littered landscapes as a sign of neglect from *al-hukuma* (the government), an unspecified level of authority that could include the national government and the local council. If pressed for more specificity, residents usually criticized the local council's decision to dump town refuse in the *wadi* running through its center because it had no legal dumpsite. These residents were using a "weapon of the weak," locating responsibility with local actors over whom they might possibly exert some influence (Scott 1985). Some interpreted a wider net of responsibility that included the national government, arguing that budgetary discrimination against Arab municipalities was the root of the problem. They contended that other priorities, such as fixing crumbling and overcrowded schools, providing water and electricity reliably, and finishing the pavement and sewage connec-tions for neighborhoods, quickly used up the local council's tiny budget.

Some saw the litter as evidence of irresponsible neighbors. They spoke of residents' personal responsibility not to litter and invoked the need for better "education." However, perhaps wary of the popular discourse of lazy and ir-responsible Bedouins, they also qualified or elaborated upon such statements.

When I asked one man whether ecological issues were prioritized by 'Ayn al-'Azm residents, he replied defensively, "Yes, it's a priority. But the whole world needs to work on it." After contextualizing the problem within global environmentalism, he averred that "of course, from the house, we should also work on it."

Despite this widespread discomfort with the township's disheveled land-scapes, most residents with whom I spoke felt powerless to change them or pre-occupied with greater problems. According to Hussein, a newly elected member of the 'Ayn al-'Azm local council, many residents visited the council prior to the latest elections to call for a better town environment. Hussein noted, though, that these concerned residents did not come in organized groups, and that their calls for environmental protection were matched by other concerns, such as their children's education, poor health, and persistent unemployment.

Residents' perceptions of 'Ayn al-'Azm, and their ability to change the place, were deeply influenced by the experience of dwelling within what Edward Ar-dener (1989) refers to as a "remote" area. Remote areas are understood by those in a center of power to be geographically and socially distant from the center and in need of development. From the beginning, government planners treated the Negev's townships as tools for various sorts of social development, includ-ing more formal education, liberal gender relations, and decreased tribal af-filiation (Dinero 2010; Horner 1982). These development projects ostensibly aimed to lessen the township's social remoteness.

However, in practice these projects often exacerbated residents' remoteness, both from Israeli society and from their own lifestyle norms. 'Ayn al-'Azm, like other remote areas, was full of the partial remnants of social planning experi-ments (Ardener 1989). Many of those remnants were marks left by initiated but sidelined government projects, like the sidewalks that ended several blocks before the edge of neighborhoods or the trash picked up by the municipal-ity but then dumped in the central *wadi*. In other cases, disheveled landscapes arose where residents' use of space did not match planners' expectation. Hop-ing to teach residents to relinquish tribal ties, planners designed public spaces, such as playgrounds, the main street, and an open market lot, and placed fami-lies from different, sometimes disputing, tribes close together (Dinero 2010; Horner 1982). However, individuals, especially women, avoided spending time in 'Ayn al-'Azm's public spaces. The wide, empty market lot was only occupied on Friday, when it filled with collapsible shade tents and folding tables piled with produce, household supplies, and factory-made clothing. On other days it was mostly deserted, except for a few young men hanging out. Similarly, play-grounds became abandoned lots and quickly accumulated trash.

These public spaces outside the protection of family evoked little sense of belonging, and residents, both men and women, often described them as dangerous. After dark, I was admonished not to walk between neighborhoods alone, and the men in my host families insisted on driving me if I needed to visit other families. Residents perceived the landscapes within which they lived in a bifurcated manner; home and family neighborhood were safe and welcoming spaces, but from the township as a whole residents felt alienated.

Perhaps ironically, residents' reactions to this alienation often created landscapes that seemed to confirm derogatory stereotypes of Bedouin disorder. Residents' attempts to create family cul-de-sacs from planned through-streets looked to visitors like piles of garbage. Residents trying to continue agropastoral taskscapes in the urban township not designed for them displeased some neighbors with the smell of their goats, or slaughtered animals in their courtyards and let blood run into the streets. These residents were resisting the pressures of de-cultural accommodation that push Bedouin Arabs to relinquish cultural practices and conform to state demands that they become urban,

Illustration 9. A public playground becomes a neglected landscape. 2009. Photograph by Author.

wage-earning subjects. But because many of the planned township spaces did not meet residents' expectations, they "made do" in ways that contributed to the township's disheveled landscapes.

Dilapidation was part of the dilemma of dwelling within 'Ayn al-'Azm. When describing their discomfort in the township, residents listed many kinds of dilapidation together—crumbling school buildings, inadequate recreational facilities for the children, and trash-laden streets. They contrasted these flaws with descriptions of Jewish towns, where, residents told me, the government built and maintained parks, schools, and sidewalks. However, other residents blamed fellow residents for the disheveled landscapes and told me of trees planted by an NGO along some sidewalks that died because they were not properly watered or in some cases even vandalized.

David Harvey (1996) notes that people can gain empowerment from places when they work collaboratively to build communities and in so doing, build discursive and emotional attachments too. However, there was no history of shared dwelling in 'Ayn al-'Azm that would make these planned public spaces into places for which residents shared personal responsibility. Instead, numerous development projects had either been initiated in distant government offices and then aborted before completion or thwarted by common dwelling practices. Residents continued to call for development projects, but they felt little power to influence the design of these projects to accommodate their desired lifestyles. The heaps of trash in public spaces suggested a record of abandonment and discrimination. They became signs of neglect that encouraged further neglect. These trash-filled places were to be avoided, not cared for and cleaned up.

Conclusion

These landscapes of neglect made people feel great ambivalence about calling 'Ayn al-'Azm home. I had many conversations with residents about attachments to land and place. None of them expressed a sense of affiliation to the township as a place or group of people. During one conversation, I asked Sarah to identify something good about living in 'Ayn al-'Azm, since she had only mentioned shortcomings. She liked living near all her extended family, she said, but she added no other redeeming feature of life in the township. Similarly, other residents could easily imagine moving elsewhere so long as their family was with them. A number insisted on their attachment to the Naqab, like Amna, who enjoyed walking in the hills by her former home, searching for wildflowers, and teaching her children about native flora. However, none expressed a fondness for the landscapes of 'Ayn al-'Azm.

Bedouin Arab residents throughout the Naqab recount narratives of broken connections to land and lost lifestyles. Many who spoke with me defined Bedouinness in terms of desert lifestyles and mobility and located community in taskscapes that can no longer be fully practiced. Both elders who were expelled and subsequent generations foster "expellee" identities that focus on past losses (Abu-Rabia 2010). In 'Ayn al-'Azm, residents dwelling in the contemporary township also perceived the present absences of their remembered family lands. These attachments to lost places heightened residents' awareness of the landscapes of neglect that they found where they lived. And dilapidated public spaces intensified their alienation from the township.

Residents were building lives in 'Ayn al-'Azm, but their estrangement from public spaces and their affiliation with households and family neighborhoods influenced how they participated in shaping the township's landscapes. While blockading roads exemplified a dwelling practice of deliberate opposition to urban planning, other tasks, such as sowing a kitchen garden or baking *saaj* bread, were less consciously rebellious. Yet each of these practices departed from state planning. As they made do, people engaged in taskscapes that helped to reshape the restrictive and even threatening landscapes of planned 'Ayn al-'Azm into more familiar landscapes. In the dense residential space of the township, this reshaping was not always a comfortable process, as one person's tasks could negatively affect her neighbor's. At times this led to violent confrontation, such as the blood revenge recounted earlier. More often it aroused simmering resentment, directed either at neighbors or at the state agencies that required residents to live in close quarters.

Not all residents embraced rebellious taskscapes, even in their less defiant forms. Some accepted the power of state institutions to shape people in and through their landscapes. Just as the elder Abu Assa brothers initially wanted to move into modern Israeli society through residence in the planned township, some residents continued to strive for inclusion through cooperative participation in the taskscapes encouraged by Iyur HaBedowim. They built and lived exclusively in houses rather than tents, accepted the growing independence of nuclear families, and often frowned on the nuisance of neighbors raising animals in their courtyards. These "more modern" neighbors (cf. Kanaaneh 2002), as well as the imagined gaze of a Jewish majority, brought dominant discourses of nature and human nature to bear within the township, judging whether households' practices were sufficiently modern and Israeli. These real and imagined judgments, paired with the material constraints of restricted land plots and small municipal budgets, pressed Zionist discourses upon many everyday endeavors.

Thus, residents in 'Ayn al-'Azm were caught in a dilemma. On the one hand, they could act in ways that felt consistent with their memories of landscapes and taskscapes past, but these practices are marked as backward and deviant within Israeli society, and their practice often builds the stigmatized landscapes that opponents of Bedouin land rights use to justify their opposition. If they do not care for the places in which they live, such people argued in casual conversations and newspaper editorials, why should they be allowed to spread over more areas? (Harel 2010; Leibovitz-Dar 2006). On the other hand, residents could accede to the demands of de-cultural accommodation and try to play by the rules of Jewish Israeli society to improve their financial and social standing. This would involve renouncing claims to family lands and silencing their counter-narratives of Naqab history. The disparate taskscapes that Bedouin Arab residents and government planners take up in response to this dilemma continue to shape and reshape residential landscapes across the Negev, often in ways not fully controlled or anticipated by either party.

4 Reforming Community

"IT'S A BIT FUNNY TO ME, THIS RESEARCH, because we're not Bedouin or something, living off the land [*ha'adama*]." This was Pnina's first reaction when I explained my study as being about connections between land and people in the Negev. Pnina lives in Moshav Dganim, and though she helped on her family's farming plot (*meshek*) as a child, I met her when she worked as a guide in the community's heritage center and no longer practiced agriculture. Her statement simultaneously signaled several important features of the dwelling practices and environmental discourses prominent in Dganim. Most obviously, she asserted a distinction between *moshav* members and Bedouins that drew from the association, which is common in Israel, of Bedouins with nature and Jewish Israelis with society (Zerubavel 2008). She thought it logical for me to research relationships between people and landscapes among the Bedouin, but not among her community of Jews. In fact, though, the imperative to establish deep ties between Jews and "the land" drove the founding of her *moshav* and others throughout Israel. Thus, on another level her statement points to the profound changes that have come with the countrywide decline of cooperative agriculture. Taskscapes were profoundly shaped by agriculture just fifteen years ago, but Pnina's daily life had come to feel disconnected from the land by the time we sat talking in 2009.

In this initial confusion of our first meeting, Pnina began teaching me about the environmental discourses that shape Dganim residents' senses of group identity and belonging to place. As in 'Ayn al-'Azm, *moshav* residents lived in a community created to fit the central government's plans, and like residents of 'Ayn al-'Azm, these residents grappled with a shift away from agricultural taskscapes. However, residents of these two communities reacted very differently to government interventions and to their postagricultural circumstances. The meeting with Pnina was during my first week living in a small apartment in the *moshav*. Over the next four months as I joined families for meals and weekend afternoons, spent time in the elder care center, and took part in community yoga and volleyball sessions, I learned more about this planned community and realized some unexpected comparisons with the Bedouin Arab planned community across the *wadi*.

In Dganim, residents had a history of investment in making place through physical labor and told affectionate narratives of this past. As most Dganim residents were members of a Jewish ethnic minority from India who arrived after statehood, there was also strong pressure for them to participate in this place-making and display its importance to Zionist nation-building. As they paved roads, created a garden and hosting tent to expand their visitors' center, built fences, and spoke about these practices, residents demonstrated the importance of a sense of group identity and belonging. These residents' interpretations of the *moshav*'s past and their relationship as immigrants to wider Israeli society and government officials shaped their contemporary dwelling practices and in turn influenced the Negev's ongoing conflict.

Planting Eden

When I asked residents about contemporary life on the *moshav*, they often began by explaining their role in founding the community. Moshav Dganim was originally founded in 1946 by a group of immigrants from Eastern Europe as part of the Zionist movement's frontier-settling endeavors, but those settlers deserted the site within a few years. Dganim's current incarnation began in 1953, when a group of two dozen families immigrating from the state of Kerala, India, agreed to settle a few kilometers from the original site. The *moshav* has since grown to approximately seven hundred residents.

Dganim, like many other immigrant settlements in the Negev during the first decades of Israeli statehood, was founded as a *moshav olim* and guided closely as an "administered community" (Kushner 1973). Arriving from such an "exotic" place as coastal India (Blady 2000), these Cochini immigrants were viewed paternalistically by the mainly Ashkenazi absorption officials in charge of their settlement. Disdain for purportedly primitive practices like dress and hygiene, which faced these immigrants, resembled attitudes of the time toward Bedouins, but immigrants were pushed to assimilate. Advisors urged them to meet the demands of cooperative farming through physical strengthening, train in punctuality and appropriate child-rearing practices, and curtail religious observance to encourage economic productivity (Kushner 1973; Mandelbaum 1975). However, while im-migrants who settled in Dganim could be viewed like other Mizrahi immigrants of the 1950s as the "Jewish victims" of Zionism (Shohat 1988), they recounted agentive stories of their arrival to and building of Dganim. Faced with negative views of Mizrahim in Israeli society, Dganim residents presented themselves not as part of a larger category of Mizrahim, but as Cochinim, a label derived from the primary city in Kerala, and as proactive participants in the Zionist project.[1]

Contemporary *moshav* residents told me proudly that they were unlike other immigrants to Israel of their era because they had not come as refugees escap-ing persecution. On the contrary, they spoke of Cochin as a cosmopolitan place of trade and amicable interactions between Jews and people of other religions.[2] One resident, Yaron, recalled two of his recent return visits to Cochin. The non-Jewish Cochin residents had received him kindly and asked tearfully why the Jews had deserted them in the 1950s. Jews were business leaders in Cochin, he said, and well respected. "No," Yaron assured me, "there wasn't anti-Semitism, not at all," either during his recent trips or before his parents' emigration.[3]

Further, he added, the Cochini Jewish community immigrated to Israel with their own money, not relying on the Jewish Agency (JA) for aid. Cochini synagogues in India had been centers of financial redistribution, and the JA used these synagogues' funds to finance members' transportation to Israel (Katz and Goldberg 2005; Kushner 1973). Whole congregations, including wealthier and less wealthy families, undertook *aliyah* together, they told me. A few residents recollected poverty and hunger in India, but escaping hardship was not put forth as a reason for emigrating. In fact, they said, the new immi-grants faced similar hardships and hunger during their early years at Dganim.

Rather than being driven by need, Dganim residents insisted, Cochini Jews had come to Israel motivated by Zionist zeal to build the Jewish state. They had agreed to settle in the Negev because of its holy connection to forefathers in the Bible (Tanakh). As my landlord, a middle-aged man named Chaim, told me over dinner one evening:

> Back in the 1950s, when all the Cochini Jews came, we were staying at Sha'ar Ha-Olim, near Haifa. And someone from the Jewish Agency came and brought a group down to check out this place and see if the larger group would move down.... My brother likes to tell me how he asked my mother, "Why here, of all places (*lama davka po*)! Were there really no better options for you, up in the greenery of Haifa, or someplace else?" And my mother responded, "Do you know what was here? This is Beersheba! This is where our father Abraham came, and Isaac! And you want someplace else?"

This assertion of biblical ties depicts Dganim's place as a landscape linking ancient Israelites and contemporary Jews. It also asserts Dganim residents' rightful place in an Israeli mainstream by countering ideologies of them as less dedicated to Zionism than earlier Ashkenazi immigrants.

This recollection of agency in choosing their location departs from more common narratives of Mizrahi immigration in the 1950s (Shohat 1988). According to both scholarly literature and recollections shared by residents elsewhere in the Negev, Zionist leaders in the JA simply assigned immigrants to settlement sites. Immigrants from Algeria and Morocco living in other *moshavim* near Dganim recalled being brought in large trucks to desolate sites in the desert and deposited, alone amid "the sand and birds," and some even reported being tricked into moving to empty sites (see also Weingrod 1966). In contrast, all residents with whom I spoke in Dganim affirmed having chosen their location.

Other accounts of and by Indian Jews describe considerable discrimination in Israel. "Colour prejudice" was strong enough to prompt a different group of Jews from India, the Bene Israel, to return to India in the 1950s soon after making *aliyah* (Weil 1986:20). In her 1995 memoirs, a Cochini woman living in a northern Israeli *kibbutz* notes that while she was prepared for the physical hardships of moving to Israel in its earliest years, she was surprised by the treatment she and fellow Cochini immigrants received from Ashkenazi Jews: "They thought we have come from some jungle. . . . Everywhere we felt discrimination, and I still do" (Daniel and Johnson 1995:105).[4]

Dganim residents did not share tales of prejudice from Ashkenazi Jews. Instead, their narratives of *moshav*-building took part in a common storytelling practice in Israel, what Virginia Domínguez (1989) describes as a script of integration, in which the wide diversity of Jewish *edot* (ethnic groups) in the Diaspora integrate after *aliyah* into a unified group.[5] *Edot* categories mark variegated distinctions that avoid the politically contested binary division of Ashkenazi and Mizrahi and are more widely celebrated in Israel's contemporary climate of Jewish multiculturalism. If asked directly, most Dganim residents would acknowledge that they and other non-Ashkenazi Jewish immigrants have been treated similarly by government authorities and are rarely differentiated from Mizrahim in an Israeli popular imaginary. But "Mizrahi" was never the label residents chose to specify their ethnic identity to me or in publicity about the *moshav*. Rather, they were part of the Cochini *eda* (singular of *edot*).[6]

Dganim residents agreed with dominant accounts of new immigrants settling the Negev on one important point, though. They too painted the Negev as barren. And they took this as a particular point of pride. Many residents contrasted the barren landscape of the Negev to the verdant, tropical climes of India. Cochin was surrounded by water, located on a sheltered bay at the mouth of the Piriyar River and just three miles from the Arabian Sea. Kerala, named after the coconut palm (*kera*) that grew so plentifully there, was a place of lush vegetation, where fish, fruits, and vegetables were abundant and relatively cheap (Daniel and Johnson 1995).

In contrast, Dganim residents spoke of the Negev to which they arrived as an empty wilderness (*shmama*). Ephram, who arrived in 1954 as a child, recalled this emptiness, narrating the past in the present tense: "There aren't showers, there aren't toilets." He paused to reflect and then added, "And there was sand, just sand." Remember, several interviewees born in Dganim emphasized, our parents came from the tropics of India and lived in cities and towns there. For these immigrants, the *moshav* site they found, with only the basic structures initiated by the Settlement Department, looked empty. Most immigrants were merchants and some were craftsmen; they did not have experience farming or living in such a rural setting.

This contrast between the Negev and their former homes, along with Zionist depictions of the Negev's remoteness, made the Zionist call to "conquer the wilderness" (*kibush et ha-shmama*) seem all the more necessary. That the *moshav* had previously been inhabited and then abandoned added to residents' sense of achievement, because they succeeded where others had failed. In this context, the narrative of Cochin's social harmony and lush tropical climate serves as an important contrast. If life in India was good, then coming to Israel and enduring the ordeals of *aliyah* in the 1950s renders immigrants' contribution to the nation that much stronger. Their initial alienation from Negev landscapes serves as further justification for their claim to the land.

The emptiness residents described in these earlier landscapes was not only ecological, but also social. Chaim, also from Ephram's generation, stressed many times that the settlers were on their own since there were no other rural Jewish communities between Dganim and the nearest cities. Such accounts ignored the Bedouin Arabs who had already settled the place. In part this was because these immigrants arrived in the 1950s, after nearly nine-tenths of the Bedouin Arabs who once dwelled in the Negev had either been expelled or fled (Abu-Rabia 1994). These residents' accounts also exhibit a "dichotomized conception of space" that is fundamental to Zionist environmental discourses, which perceives Jewish settlement as civilization and that which surrounds it as wilderness (Zerubavel 2008:202). Dganim residents narratively erased Arab sociality from the landscape. Such reiterations in community-building stories draw from and reinforce a binary framing of Jew/culture/progress versus Arab/nature/tradition.

Indeed, an idea of progress from wilderness to civilization was central to Dganim residents' senses of place. Like many *moshavim*, Dganim went through different agricultural phases as it sought to make profits in changing agricultural markets. Beginning with vegetable farming, the residents then shifted to growing fruit trees, then chickens, and finally flowers. Agricultural guides from the JA led each shift and government agencies contributed substantial loans, infrastructure, and equipment. Anthropologist Gilbert Kushner (1973) outlines a pattern of dependency and apathy that grew from such pervasive external management, and such intensive governmental involvement would seem to contradict Dganim residents' accounts of independent agency. However, although residents did also refer to the JA and agricultural guides, or more vaguely to "them," as sources of loans and advice, residents focused on the first few families who switched to each new agricultural branch as trailblazers. If they enjoyed some success, others followed suit.

Residents' stories of the *moshav's* early years highlighted their agency in navigating these difficult transitions and turning this empty place into a lasting community. As Ephram told me with pride while we drank tea and discussed the *moshav's* history: "Nobody believed that this desert would transform into an oasis. Nobody. Even our agricultural guides! It was we, the driven ones, who did it." Residents' labor finished the houses, plowed the fields, planted orchards, and built greenhouses. Ephram reveled in his generation's success in achieving their dreams "to plow [*l-hafeakh*] the land, to expel the wilderness."[7] They turned the *moshav* into such lush farmland, he exclaimed, that "it was a garden of Eden!"

Residents' success in overcoming past hardships lived on in the present through storytelling. For example, one Friday evening when I joined Chaim and his family for dinner, the winds were kicking up a sandstorm. We sat together at a large dining table set with cloth napkins and matching tableware, sipping grape juice from wine glasses and savoring spiced rice and broiled chicken. The house's open-plan architecture, similar to many in the United States and Western Europe, gave a clear view of the kitchen and living room from the table. A particularly strong gust of wind against the windows prompted Chaim to recount the *moshav's* early days. Directing his comments to me and his grown children, he described the harsh climate and frugal lifestyles they had endured. He gestured to the nice furnishings around us and lamented that today's young people do not understand the sacrifices of early residents. Chaim echoed Zionist leaders such as A. D. Gordon, asserting that sacrifices like these rendered even stronger the Jews' claims to lands in the Negev and throughout Israel. The importance of suffering for bonding Jews together as a group has been demonstrated in many contexts (e.g., Cohen 1997; Markowitz 2006; Rubin-Dorsky and Fishkin 1996). But Chaim's point was more particular, asserting a history of Jewish suffering in this place as grounds for stronger land claims (see also Moore 2005). I surmised from his daughter's subtle smile that she had heard this story many times. Such stories told by parents to their children are lessons in the progress that comes with national loyalty and collective sacrifice to build up a place.[8]

Agriculture's Absence

Recent developments, however, were challenging residents' perceptions of Dganim as a progressively civilizing place. By 2009, this Eden was wilting. In the 1990s, when prices for Dganim farmers' most recent product, flowers, had begun plummeting, the government's priorities had shifted and aid had dried up. The JA withdrew the last of its direct financial assistance and advising for collective farming, and farmers in this marginally fertile land could not compete on the open market without such aid. Racking up debts, family after family quit agriculture and began searching out other livelihoods. Ephram lamented, "Today, because the farmers aren't working . . . the desert is beginning to enter the *moshav*." The green *moshav* is turning brown, Ephram told me, and sandstorms hit with more force because no orchards buffer the winds.

Such historical shifts marked Dganim's contemporary landscapes. The fields, houses, gardens, and public areas revealed evidence of the *moshav*'s four waves of agriculture, as well as the disappearance of agricultural guides and government loans. Just as 'Ayn al-'Azm residents drew meaning from the landscapes around them to interpret their own position in the order of things, so too Dganim residents used the *moshav*'s landscapes to interpret their place in Israeli society. Evidence of decline and of the encroachment of wilderness on the *moshav* challenged perceptions of progress through agricultural settlement and raised debates about cooperative responsibilities in the present.

Contemporary Dganim emptied out each weekday. Beginning at 7:00 in the morning, the *moshav* had what passed for a rush hour, when most residents left their homes in private cars to drive to work in other towns and cities, and children left for school. After this, most yards and streets were quiet. Former sites of cooperative agricultural production stood present but disused. A large building in the *moshav*'s center had housed the agricultural cooperative where people from around the *moshav* once gathered to chat and socialize as they packaged produce for sale. Now it lay empty. A corner store, which had been the only business on the *moshav* serving residents rather than producing goods for export, was also empty. It lost customers when so many began leaving the *moshav* for jobs and doing their shopping at the supermarkets around Beer-sheba. At first this slack in customers was offset by Bedouin Arab residents of the nearby unrecognized settlements. However, when a tall perimeter fence was erected around the *moshav* in the late 1990s, this flow of customers dwindled too and the corner store eventually closed.

Paved streets wound in gentle arcs through the *moshav*, with houses lined neatly along the streets and families' former agricultural plots lying in long, thin strips behind each house. During weekday walks about the *moshav*, I often crossed these abandoned fields to shorten my way. Rough, narrow footpaths of hard-packed dirt cut through fields of dry soil and weeds. Though these lay at the center of the community, I never met anyone else walking through the fields. Rusting piles of discarded farming equipment lay here and there, and the tall skeletons of former greenhouses leaned against the sky. Only small copses of lemon and pomelo trees remained of the large orchards that once included apricots, apples, and plums. And in a few places, the formerly plowed ridges of vegetable plots were still evident as petrified crusts of mounded earth.

Though most farming plots stood empty, a few families managed to stay in agriculture by enlarging and intensifying their operations. Half a dozen ware-

Illustration 10. Former greenhouses in Dganim. 2009. Photograph by Author.

house-like chicken coops hummed with activity, relying on high volume and fast turnover (raising chicks to two-kilo chickens in forty-five days) to make profits. Two men headed flower-growing operations. Amnon used mechanization and synthetic breeding and employed several wage laborers to grow bundles of flowers for export. These workers included Bedouins, who worked each day "by the unit" and were paid for each package of flowers they bundled, and foreign workers from Thailand, who lived on the *moshav* for the length of their temporary visas. Pushing their businesses to raise larger quantities, use the latest chemical inputs, and even hire foreign workers, these residents attempted to keep up with an agricultural industry that they saw as running away from them.

Ephram, the other flower grower, seemed the exception that proved the rule of *moshav* agriculture: scale up or cease production. Identified by a friend as "the last dinosaur of farming," he grew a single greenhouse of expensive, high-quality roses for the local market. Several other residents commented regretfully to me that they thought Ephram's business would not last much longer. His approach was not their vision of modern agriculture and appeared doomed by the inevitable decline of prices. Ephram insisted, though, that his approach met his priorities

> to work as a family, to make a living on the farm, not to grow too big, so that you also have time for other things, to enjoy life. . . . I tell myself that I want, first of all, health for me and for my family, that we will be healthy. After that, that we have clothes to wear, bread to eat, and a little recreation.

In addition to his farming practices, these priorities helped Ephram earn his "dinosaur" label because they were associated with the outdated discourses of collective agriculture and a pioneer's frugal lifestyle.

Although a few individuals continued to earn a living from agriculture, and foreign workers could be seen driving tractors along the streets between greenhouses, these examples did not constitute the collective taskscapes of agriculture that residents like Dani remembered. Dani, who was born in Dganim and grew up working on his family's allotment, fondly recalled the tasks of harvesting that periodically brought farmers from across the *moshav* together. Now, he told me, nobody had time for socializing, since they all left the *moshav* to work in different markets and careers. In fact, many residents dismissed remaining farming taskscapes and spoke of agriculture as having ended on the *moshav*.

Success in agriculture once held not just economic importance, but also individual and collective implications for moral character, as residents' agentive stories of arrival and building made clear. Ceasing these agricultural taskscapes held similar implications. As among 'Ayn al-'Azm residents, the different ways Dganim residents read changes in the *moshav*'s landscapes revealed debates about responsibilities, rights, and belonging in Israel. Though most residents lamented elements of these changing taskscapes, they also held multifaceted opinions about what or who caused agriculture's demise and what implications this had for the future of the *moshav* and the wider country.

On a sensory level, many residents lamented the lost experiences of a *moshav* formerly filled with bountiful greenery and delicious produce. Esther, an elderly resident who had emigrated from Ernakulum as a young woman, recalled the rich tastes of Dganim's past. "In the market, they always used to search out our apricots. The most tasty," she declared with pride. "In the earlier years," she continued, "[we had] potatoes, cucumbers, tomatoes. Do you know how tasty they could be?!" she exclaimed. She brought her fingers to her lips and breathed a sigh as she recalled that succulence. But now, she said, the vegetables have no taste.

For Ephram this lost agricultural landscape represented a reversal of the unity and high moral standards that had helped create the State of Israel. Losing a base of agricultural workers was "a terrible hardship" because "we, all of us who were farmers, used to be the kings of the country. Proud people. Good people." Think of David Ben-Gurion and Yitzhak Rabin, he continued. "All of our leaders grew out of working the land, [whether] it's shepherding, or [farming], because he who works the land loves this country." Ephram worried that Israel's shift away from agriculture would rob future generations of the collective work and contact with soil that strongly attached his generation to Israel as a place and a national body of people. Once land is simply traded by real estate agents, Ephram reasoned, people become less attached to places, are more willing to move for conveniences like higher-paying jobs, and are less willing to defend particular places within Israel. Ephram's concerns echoed Labor Zionism's discourse of redemption through agriculture, which set individual responsibility to the nation as the cornerstone of its institution-building.

Some former farmers in Dganim, including Esther and Ephram, read the *moshav*'s empty fields as reminders of state neglect. Esther narrated the series of challenges she and her fellow farmers faced in adjusting to their new desert home and the state-directed model of collective labor. Dganim's residents built this *moshav* for the good of the country, she explained, as a key point of Jewish settlement amid Arab squatters. But when the *moshav* encountered financial difficulties, she said, "the state didn't care for us at all!" Similarly, Ephram expressed disappointment in the state's recent treatment of himself and his generation. He listed the wars in which he had fought, describing the traumas he and his fellow soldiers had endured as their contribution to the Israeli state. "My generation," he said, pausing to gaze past me into middle space for a moment, "I don't know if it was our good fortune or our bad fortune, but we delivered the country on our shoulders." However, the state demonstrated it was not "with us," he lamented, when agencies withdrew financial aid during the *moshav*'s economic crisis.

Both Ephram's and Esther's disappointment with "the state" rested on an understanding of reciprocity that recognizes suffering and labor as contributions that deserve reciprocation (Moore 2005), regardless of market conditions. Though they shared with many 'Ayn al-'Azm residents a complaint about state neglect, these Dganim members differed from 'Ayn al-'Azm residents in understanding this neglect as a reversal of earlier state care. Their complaints accuse the Israeli government of "cutting the network" (Strathern 1996) of reciprocity that had previously bound together workers and government leaders. *Moshav* residents had attended agricultural schools, participated in the army, and followed the guidance of JA agricultural advisors. Such experiences taught the redeeming power of physical labor in nature and the centrality of agriculture to national strength (Zerubavel 1995), while *moshav* participation taught that independent work should be framed within mutual aid (Zusman 1988). With the decline of agriculture and the collapse of the collective economy, many residents worried about the disappearance of reciprocity *within* the *moshav* as well. They described feeling that Dganim's *kehilatiut* (community spirit and activity) was slipping away.

Illustration 11. In honor of fallen soldiers on Israel's Memorial Day, the flaming letters spell "remembrance." 2009. Photograph by Author.

Other residents disagreed with these evaluations of state neglect, shrugging off these concerns and contending that the failure of collective agriculture demonstrated the greater power of the individual profit motive. Those who referred to Ephram as a "dinosaur" and predicted the collapse of the *moshav*'s other remaining farmers emphasized the value of adapting. The global agricultural markets had simply changed too much, they said; prices had fallen and collective agriculture in the Negev could not compete (Sherman and Schwartz 1995). Chaim, who had gained a degree in agronomy and directed Dganim's export flower growing for several years, explained how he had learned in the early 1980s that Dganim's flowers were being undersold by Kenyan exports. He traveled to research their growing methods and found European-run companies holding usufruct rights to thousands of *dunams* of land "without problems" (that is, with no competing claims of ownership), free and plentiful lake water, and abundant low-wage laborers to tend the flowers by hand. Dganim did not have these assets. "We didn't have a chance," he said flatly. "In another couple years, we would fall." Looking at agriculture as a practical business venture rather than as character- and nation-building endeavors, as did Ephram, Chaim began urging his fellow residents to leave agriculture for other trades.

Chaim and others sharing his view saw Dganim's landscapes as evidence that individualism and neoliberalism were the *moshav*'s best path to success. Agriculture and collective work simply were not feasible, these people felt. Chaim frequently expressed territorial Zionist views equally as strong as, if not stronger than Ephram's, but he saw Zionism's movement of *moshavim* and *kibbutzim* as a touchingly naïve dream. Human nature, he explained, prompts self-interest first. Chaim offered Dganim's housing as a case in point. In contrast to the *moshav*'s landscapes of abandonment in fields and public spaces, the individuation of Dganim's houses suggested considerable investment. A few homes were still the uniform, frugal structures erected in the 1950s by the JA. But Dganim's houses had come to exhibit significant variation in size, style, and apparent expense. Some families had built entirely new structures with curving contours and tall windows. Most had enlarged and embellished their houses in some way during more profitable years, though the small structures of the original JA houses were still visible underneath these additions (see Ill. 12).

Chaim spoke proudly of his own home improvements. Beginning with the "small box" provided by the JA, he had built additions on either side for bedrooms and a spacious master suite, a large covered porch in back for shaded summer relaxation, and a small porch in front. He had worked for many years both within and outside the *moshav*. For Chaim, his home was solid evidence

Illustration 12. A renovated home in Dganim. Photograph by Author.

of his success in taming the wilderness that he and his parents had encountered when they first reached this harsh place, and of his industriousness in business. He was also proud of the community's success, which he saw proven in the many neighbors who had completed similar renovations. But this house was a personal achievement, built through his own initiative and finances and meeting his own desires.

Like the individual attention evident in houses, the lush gardens surrounding many homes signaled residents' shifting focus of economic activity and leisure time from a *moshav* community to nuclear families. Many homes were surrounded by thick gardens of greenery and bright, water-thirsty flowers. Residents who had once cared for large fields of fruits and vegetables contracted their focus to the yards around their homes. Esther, for example, who had spent decades working in agriculture, spoke proudly of the care she devoted, despite the expense of water and the limitations of her aging body, to the flowerbeds and cluster of fruit trees in her yard. Residents sometimes criticized those few families who did not share this investment in home gardens. Esther acknowledged that with the growing income disparities in the *moshav* not everyone could afford this sort of gardening, but she was disappointed with those who simply chose not to maintain their properties.

Many others in Dganim shared Esther's concern with the *moshav*'s appearance and were ashamed of the ramshackle former agricultural fields in its center. However, residents generally avoided these plots and resisted taking personal responsibility for cleaning out old equipment, stating that the local council should handle this. The fields were no longer a place of shared responsibility. Like public spaces in 'Ayn al-'Azm that did not belong to places in residents' taskscapes, these fields gathered rubbish and weeds. As in 'Ayn al-'Azm, shifting away from agricultural lifestyles had eroded formerly wider webs of cooperative work. And workers departing each day for employment in Israel's commuter economy drove the nuclearization of families in both communities. In Dganim, the striking juxtaposition of renovated homes with tended gardens and the rusting equipment and original JA houses that were still visible only displayed more starkly the *moshav*'s departure from its once egalitarian and cooperative practices.

Moshav residents' contradictory interpretations of the departure from past taskscapes mirror splinters in Zionist discourse nationwide. These debates were neither new nor limited to Dganim, as residents of veteran *moshavim* were already questioning cooperation as a basis of social and economic life in the 1960s and 1970s (Baldwin 1972), and social analysts have shown the individual and factional competition that often pervaded these purportedly cooperative settlements (Mars 1980; Zusman 1988). However, by the 2000s, neoliberal norms dominated economic practices. By this time, even steadfast Labor Zionists like Ephram conceded that although collectivism helped build the country, perhaps it was not viable in the long term.

Corners of *kehilatiut*

Owing to crucial differences between Dganim and 'Ayn al-'Azm, however, cooperative taskscapes were not entirely absent from Dganim. First, whereas 'Ayn al-'Azm residents experienced state intervention in the townships' taskscapes primarily in negative terms, as the restriction of past lifestyles, Dganim residents described more ambivalent relationships with government agents. Second, residents in each community experienced different sorts of nostalgia. 'Ayn al-'Azm residents located their lost social ties primarily in landscapes outside the township, but Dganim residents fondly recalled the *moshav* landscapes as socially vibrant places. Prompted by these different perceptions of place, Dganim residents continued to see their *moshav* as a site for the potential revival of *kehilatiut*, and to consider government agencies as potential allies for this revival.

Two notable exceptions to the contraction of daily activities around the nuclear family were spaces that catered to either end of the age spectrum. Near the *moshav*'s center, wisps of children's voices could be heard each day from the community preschool and kindergarten. Next door, a building hosted the elders' club (*moadon ha-kashishim*) each day, and occasional community events such as bridge games and Torah (Hebrew Bible) readings in the evenings.

With funding assistance from the regional council and directed by a social worker, the elders' club was open to elderly residents each weekday morning through lunchtime. The director, Adina, commuted daily from a nearby town to run the club and pay house calls to less mobile residents; her assistant, Chava, was a *moshav* resident. As a rare site of social activity during the week, the elders' club drew me to help each day with activities. Though it is unusual for such a small community to have their own elders' day center, Adina told me, caring for the elderly was particularly important for "this community." Many residents affirmed this in explicitly ethnic terms, describing elder care as a central value of Cochini culture.

Elderly attendees socialized through a program of exercise, arts and crafts, Hebrew language practice, and current events organized by Adina and Chava. A rabbi came each Sunday to explain Torah passages and lead discussion. After organized activities each day, attendees gathered in the dining room for tea, often chatting with each other in Malayalam, their south Indian language.[9] A few older women still dressed in sarong skirts, though all wore sweaters and polyester tops rather than the thin cotton blouses they had donned in India. Elder men, like the younger generation, wore distinctive boxlike skullcaps (*kipot*) typical of

Illustration 13. Doing arts and crafts at the elders' club. 2009. Photograph by Author.

Cochinim. The most mobile attendees helped to prepare salads with lunch each day. After lunch, a hired van driver transported attendees back to their homes.

Not all elderly residents attended the elders' club. Like discussions about the end of agriculture, residents' decisions to attend or avoid the club demonstrated varying interpretations of the *moshav*'s socially contracted landscape. Between ten and twenty residents attended regularly. While chatting over tea, several regulars described the care and activities provided at the club as their due after many years of hard work building this *moshav*. Other elderly residents stayed at home by themselves. Adina explained the stigma that kept them away: they saw this as a place for poor people who could not take care of themselves. Elderly residents' different interpretations of the elders' club highlighted disagreements about independence and reciprocal obligations with which Dganim, like Israel's other *moshavim* and *kibbutzim*, struggle. Both groups of residents emphasized the importance of individual work, but some held strict expectations for self-sufficiency while others saw an ongoing need for cooperative care.

Each afternoon, those of working age returned to the *moshav*, joining the young and elderly. Many men attended synagogue regularly, gathering in this communal space each evening before returning to their homes for dinner. Because Dganim had been settled primarily by a few large families, many residents had cousins, aunts, and uncles within the *moshav*. Extended family members did visit each other frequently, and I was sometimes invited to homes for tea or a meal on weekday evenings. However, nuclear families spent most of their time in Dganim in their houses, and I spent most of my evenings in the small apartment unit I rented behind Chaim's house.

During the weekend, a combination of religious observance and leisure time brought more of Dganim's residents into social contact. Cochini Jews have been characterized through the 1960s as a predominantly Orthodox community (Katz and Goldberg 2005; Kushner 1973; Segal 1993), but contemporary Dganim residents' adherence to religious laws varied. Still, on Friday afternoons most women busied themselves preparing for the holy day, Shabbat, by cooking an assortment of dishes for large family meals. For its social and religious significance marking the beginning of Shabbat, the Friday night meal served as a meaningful time to recall Cochini cultural origins and express a syncretic Cochini-Israeli identity (cf. Bahloul 1999). Foods considered traditional to Cochini cuisine, such as fish with a strong cilantro sauce and cardamom-infused rice, featured prominently along with non-Cochini Israeli inclusions, like fluffy white challah bread. Shabbat eve meals often focused on the nuclear family, seeing the return of grown sons and daughters who had moved away from the *moshav*. But the meal was also an opportunity to visit extended family and invite guests. Even as a temporary resident without family ties, I never spent Shabbat eve alone. At some Shabbat meals, as at Chaim's house, parents recited prayers and the best flatware was set out, but other families forewent prayers and treated the meal primarily as a social gathering.

On Saturday mornings, some residents, especially men and older women, walked to synagogue services. The ornate building reproduced the style of one of the large synagogues in Kerala. To understand the community, many residents told me, I needed to visit this synagogue. On the first Shabbat that I attended services, I followed my host, Einat, through the side door and climbed to the women's balcony. We sat viewing the main room below, where the men recited segments of the Torah in unison. Though the balcony was plain and functional, with beige carpeting and stackable chairs, the main hall was vibrantly colored in blue, red, silver, and gold. Elaborate floor-to-ceiling silver molding surrounded the ark housing the Torah scrolls, and many chandeliers—electric but styled like oil lamps—hung from the ceiling. A few key pieces of architecture, such as gold posts ringing the lower cantor's stand, had been brought from Cochin, and the rest was constructed in Israel to duplicate the synagogue the immigrants had left behind.

Residents had made significant financial contributions to build this synagogue, and they pointed to it proudly as the defining feature of Dganim. It marked the *moshav's* landscape as distinctly Cochini. Attendance was light that morning, my host told me, because the fiercely cold winds that buffeted us on our walk had kept many in their homes. However, elderly residents told me that overall attendance had declined through the years. The synagogue mattered to residents as a marker of their communal identity and continued to be a main gathering place on high holidays, but it was not a place for shared practices that united everyone in the *moshav*.

That Shabbat after services, I walked home with Einat and spent the day with her and her family. As was common on Saturdays, we lounged on the couch in her tiny living room to chat and play board games with her four children. At midday, we added leaves to a small kitchen table to make room for bowls of pre-prepared food and share a meal with her husband and aging father. On Saturdays with pleasant weather, Einat's children rode bikes and played sports, and many residents went for walks and visited neighbors. Those observing Shabbat in a less orthodox fashion drove to nearby towns or nature reserves.

One Saturday toward the end of my time in Dganim, a new addition appeared in the community that demonstrated residents' shared hopes for a communal revival. The community garden, which had required fund-raising and months of construction, was finally completed, including an artful pond stocked with fish. Einat eagerly led the family to the *moshav*'s center, and we met other families, all walking to the fishpond. As we mingled by the pond, comments about this unusual public gathering peppered conversation. One resident referred to the new pond as bringing back the old days of more frequent social gatherings when everyone in the community farmed. "Look," I heard another man comment more sarcastically, "it takes fish to bring out the people here," as if rueful that fellow residents were not enough to prompt gatherings. Notwithstanding the sarcasm, the pond's planners and fund-raisers had indeed hoped the fish would "bring out the people," both from within Dganim and from outside. Community leaders had raised the funds for this garden through a tourism initiative they hoped would revive Dganim economically and socially. They and a large portion of Dganim's residents had come to see Cochini tourism as the *moshav*'s hope for cooperative success within Israel's new economic climate.

Envisioning Cochini Tourism

Signs at Moshav Dganim's entrance gate welcome visitors and announce the Heritage Center of Cochin Jews, as well as the horseback riding school, an artist's gallery, and several other businesses. These signs declare the mix of tourism and Cochini heritage that most residents saw as Dganim's most promising new socioeconomic basis. Seeing "the writing on the wall," that the *moshav* could no longer be successful in agriculture, Chaim and a group of charismatic leaders had begun pushing fellow residents to shift to a community economy of tourism in the 1990s. Chaim had since served as head of the local council many times and had recently been reelected for another term. Having served in several governmental and semigovernmental positions before his retirement, Chaim was savvy to bureaucracy and skilled in garnering financial support for community projects. Several other Dganim residents had gained positions in the regional government too. During the 1990s, when Chaim worked for the JA, the Israeli Ministry of Agriculture developed a plan called "Village of 2000" (Kfar Alpayim). This plan recognized that the agriculture of *moshavim* was collapsing but sought to maintain these communities as viable villages in order to continue dispersing Jews across Israel's rural spaces. The plan advocated initial financing to train residents and construct infrastructure for more diversified economies, followed by a gradual reduction in governmental assistance to leave the villages financially independent. In this way, privatization and the individual profit motive could be harnessed to continue socializing rural lands as Jewish.

Chaim and other Dganim leaders embraced the Village of 2000 model, looking to bed-and-breakfast ventures in Europe as examples, along with some early experiments in rural tourism in the Galilee. However, land-use regulations allowed *moshavim* to use open areas of land only for agricultural purposes, not to build tourism facilities. Chaim began lobbying Dganim's regional council to change these regulations, and he began developing plans with former colleagues in the Ministry of Agriculture to run Dganim as a "tourist village" rather than an "agricultural *moshav*." Regulatory change happens slowly, however, and Chaim and many fellow residents knew that "for every green track there is also a bypass," or for every authorized route, a back door. The handful of residents running tourism ventures during my fieldwork had built first and then sought temporary permission, hoping their land uses would be approved retroactively.[10]

Most commonly, residents described Dganim's future not just as a tourist village, but specifically a Cochini tourist village. As members of a minority ethnic group in Israel, residents in Dganim, as in 'Ayn al-'Azm, faced challenges in negotiating displays of similarity with and distinction from other Israelis. However, Cochini identity offered an opportunity for multicultural belonging in mainstream Israeli society that was unavailable to Bedouin Arabs. In particular, Dganim residents foregrounded their "authentic" Cochini synagogue and the Heritage Center of Cochin Jews.

These plans build on Israel's growing embrace of the global trend of multiculturalism (Kymlicka and Banting 2006; Taylor and Gutmann 1992) among its Jewish *edot*. Whereas the *moshav*'s settlers were initially urged to shed their "Oriental" traits and assimilate to the Ashkenazi-dominated Israeli norms, widespread multicultural ideals have since softened this assimilationist pressure. Since the late 1980s, non-Ashkenazi Jews have made real economic, educational, and status gains (Ben-Rafael 2007). Politicians and government ministries commonly refer to the Jewish "mosaic" rather than the "melting pot," and certain forms of Jewish otherness are celebrated in tourism and festival settings (Domínguez 1989). Heritage centers and immigration programs encourage immigrants from rural Ethiopia to revive pottery traditions and continue gardening in their urban housing blocks. The Mimuna festival at the end of Passover, a Moroccan Jewish tradition that was suppressed in earlier decades because of its associations with "Oriental" religious practice, is now celebrated as a national holiday.

However, great inequalities still exist and constrain the kinds of identity expressions Mizrahim can make without stigma (Mizrachi and Herzog 2012).

The "trope of tribalism" that Arjun Appadurai (1996) found in the United States, whereby unspecified America is understood to be white and multicultural America is "the black, the brown, and the yellow," is expressed in Israel along Ashkenazi-Mizrahi lines. Virginia Domínguez's (1989) observation from fieldwork in the 1980s that Ashkenazi norms prevailed as "culture" (*tarbut*) while the "heritage" (*moreshet*) of non-European Jews provided sources of diversity remained true in 2009. The heritage that a Mizrahi group displays must be carefully chosen so as not to challenge the group's Israeliness.

This dynamic was clear in Dganim residents' efforts to attract tourists to the *moshav* by displaying their heritage. The heritage center was a small museum housing artifacts from Jewish communities in Kerala, India. Large pots, metal molds for shaping dumplings, and wooden utensils; Torah cases and Hanukkah lamps; and the canopy bed, dowry box, and white clothing of a wedding were clustered in cases around a large room. Plaques next to cotton blouses, long wrap-skirts, and skullcaps (*kipot*) explained men's and women's daily habits of dress, and signs describing festive occasions flanked elaborately embroidered vests and kerchiefs. Displays conveyed a narrative of cyclical continuity, grouping artifacts by life cycle events such as weddings, births, and holidays (cf. Kirshenblatt-Gimblett 1998).

These artifacts were donated by Cochini immigrants throughout Israel, and they displayed the elements of culture deemed most uniquely Cochini and, significantly, least connected to the everyday lives of immigrants and their children in Israel. This preservation of Cochini heritage was important for Dganim residents because, as Pnina, a tour guide at the center, put it, many young Cochinim are marrying outside their ethnicity (*eda*) and "just want to be Israelis." In Pnina's and other residents' eyes, the future of Cochini culture was uncertain. These objects were important "to preserve and bequeath the culture," Pnina asserted. Other *moshav* residents also expressed the responsibility they felt to safeguard Cochini culture by preserving these artifacts.

Yet most visitors to the heritage center were not the children and grandchildren of Cochini immigrants, but rather other Israeli visitors stopping by during tours of the Negev. Indeed, community leaders sought to put the *moshav* as a whole on display (see Kirshenblatt-Gimblett 1998). In addition to the heritage center, several bed-and-breakfasts and "authentic Cochini cuisine" restaurants run out of families' homes aimed to entertain and educate these visiting Jewish Israelis. Brochures and websites were written in Hebrew, and *moshav* council members and entrepreneurs referred to visitors from Tel Aviv and Jerusalem and nearby Jewish towns as their intended customers.

As in Sarah's tourist venture, Dganim residents strove to establish Cochini tourism for its potential profits but also to preserve a cultural tradition. Yet as with Sarah's Bedouin heritage venture, identifying Cochini heritage presupposes the foreclosure of the past that constituted it (Kirshenblatt-Gimblett 1998). In this case, *moshav* residents' assimilation into Israeli society had already led to a more complete cessation of Cochini cultural practices than Iyur HaBedowim had prompted for Bedouin Arabs. The lamps, clothing, and cooking utensils on display in the museum were already heritage objects without any daily utility. Instead, their display made them useful for establishing Dganim residents as ethnically Cochini but culturally assimilated Israelis.

Whereas Sarah's venture was thoroughly infused with the landscapes of the Negev (from the stories she told to the raw materials for her products and the Bedouin taskscapes she continued), Dganim's tourism invoked faraway tropical landscapes. If left unbalanced by other indicators of their Israeliness, this turn toward Cochin could paint Dganim residents as outsiders to Israeli society, something the early immigrants fought hard to prevent. But none of Dganim's residents expressed concern over this possibility in 2009. Their pursuit of heritage tourism through the framework of the "Village of 2000" plan actually demonstrated their sense of belonging within Israel, because it depicted Cochini difference in terms of the tools and clothes that had become disused artifacts of past lifeways. It told a story of incorporation from many diasporas to "one people" that is common in Jewish heritage museums throughout Israel (Fenichel 2005).

The contrast between methods pursued in Dganim to use land in ways contrary to governmental plans and those in 'Ayn al-'Azm is striking and points to residents' differential positions vis-à-vis state power (Li 2005). Living in the Negev and no longer enfolded in national economic plans through agricultural subsidies, Dganim also became a more remote place. They had large fields they could not afford to farm and wanted to use these fields for other, unlicensed purposes. However, unlike in 'Ayn al-'Azm, Dganim residents engaged in resistance through participation by working to position themselves closer to centers of power. In Dganim, residents had had cooperative relationships with governmental bodies and told agentive stories of building their *moshav*. They had been historically administered as less civilized people in need of reeducation, but through government-savvy community members like Chaim, with his personal relationships with government decision-makers, they now knew how to change laws and regulations to fit their needs. In contrast, 'Ayn al-'Azm residents had been the objects of development plans but had not had opportunities to work as real partners with government agencies in designing the policies and budgets that shaped their living spaces. They spoke of "the state" as a powerful agent imposing its will from afar and recalled histories of impersonal pressure and coercion in which the government suppressed their dwelling practices in order to benefit Jewish Israelis. As a result, residents engaged in alternative taskscapes with which they were comfortable but which neither directly confronted state sources of power nor positioned residents closer to centers of influence—for example, using alternative building materials to remain outside the attention of the local council or blocking neighborhood streets with debris.

The approach in Dganim also contrasted with that in 'Ayn al-'Azm because it built on a history of cooperative taskscapes during the *moshav*'s early years. Like the *moshav*'s agricultural model, which combined individual initiative for production with cooperation for building infrastructure and distributing produce, *moshav* residents described a vision of tourism that would also combine independence and cooperation. As a *moshav* council member elaborated, the *moshav* was already collaborating to create infrastructure conducive to tourism by laying down water and sewage pipes, paving roads, and building facilities like the community garden and an events pavilion in the *moshav*'s center. Individual residents should then create small businesses to draw tourists in, she said.

Without the governmental guidance and financial support of Dganim's agricultural past, some residents balked at the financial risk of these new ventures. However, others saw the approach as the best way to hold Dganim together in Israel's increasingly neoliberal economy. Many residents were driven not only by a fondness for fellow residents, but also by their commitment to the Zionist project of settling the desert. Pnina, the heritage center guide, narrated the *moshav*'s different economic periods as she insisted on the continuous goal of remaining settled in this remote but important area of Israel:

> There are the grandmothers and grandfathers. After that, there are our parents, who continued the work. And their children, which is us, who continue to help. Until agriculture was destroyed. And then, [we] go out to work, but [we] don't leave the place where you grew up and came to in order to grow this state of ours.

Slipping between first- and second-person pronouns and past and present tenses, Pnina drew a narrative line joining this settling mission across generations, despite changing economic practices. Pnina leaned in as she finished this statement, adding staccato emphasis that stressed "not leaving," "growing up," and the "state of ours."

As Tania Li (2005) notes, the interests of a ruling regime can be achieved through shifting assemblages that include not just government agencies, but also others such as experts, local elites, and social groups seeking greater inclusion. In this case, the same goals of settling Jews in the desert and "civilizing the wilderness" can be served as the community shifts from government-directed agriculture to a more individualist combination of some residents seeking external employment and others, like Pnina, building the *moshav*'s Cochini tourism.

Drawing Lines, Policing Boundaries

Dganim residents seek to define their community through welcoming features such as the synagogue and heritage center, but for their closest neighbors, Bedouin Arab residents of unrecognized villages, the *moshav* constitutes a sharp boundary in the landscape. The *moshav*'s perimeter fence is a particularly clear division, but renovated homes and tourism development also facilitate boundary drawing. Just as 'Ayn al-'Azm residents like Um Yunis and Mufid may not have intended to make political statements through their dwelling practices, so too Dganim residents like Pnina and Chaim may not have viewed their community development tasks as politically contentious. However, because they lived in the midst of competing land claims and social segregation, such tasks became the everyday means of drawing lines and policing boundaries, along with more stark acts like fence-building. Understanding how and why Dganim residents reshape landscapes in and around the *moshav* as they do requires attention to the perceptions, judgments, and actions that make up these boundary-drawing tasks.

Place-making and dwelling in a place involve acts of inclusion and exclusion, acts that define what kind of place this is, who belongs, and who must not be allowed in. During my research, Dganim continued to be identified by both residents and nonresidents as a "Cochini community." It has grown more diverse since its settling in the 1950s, though, as young residents have married partners from other *edot* and a few Ashkenazi couples from Beersheba and elsewhere have bought homes in the *moshav*. However, the efforts of one couple, the Kafnis, to rent their home to friends several years before my fieldwork demonstrated the limits of this expanded sense of community. The Kafnis' friends were a Bedouin Arab family, and their attempt to rent a house in Dganim raised a furor in the community. When the local council learned that the prospective renters were Bedouin Arabs, they refused. The event spawned legal battles, and the Kafnis faced ostracism, taunts of "Arab lover," and property damage from some within Dganim. Ill feelings linger between the Kafnis and those who opposed Arab residents. Since then, there have been no Arab residents or attempts by Arabs to rent.

The local council's exclusionary housing policy and the retaliatory behavior of community members against the Kafnis effectively policed a boundary between "us" and "them." This episode did not result from state housing policies being imposed on local communities, but from the voluntary policing of residential space by residents. Like the Kafnis, others in Dganim viewed Arabs as potential friends and neighbors, but the stance voiced by officials and the vast majority of residents during my fieldwork excluded Arabs. The willingness to include Jews of other *edot* but not Arabs reinforced an Arab-Jewish division as the line between acceptable and unacceptable otherness. Defense of this line socialized the landscapes of Dganim as Jewish through the active participation of residents, a process repeated throughout Israel (Rabinowitz 1997; Slyomovics 1998; Sufian and LeVine 2007).

In addition to policing community membership, Dganim residents drew discursive and material boundaries across the landscape to define the place of the *moshav*. Residents perceived a variety of threats in the desert landscapes surrounding the *moshav*. Consistent with the ethos of development that pervaded Zionist discourse at their time of arrival, immigrants described their early years as a struggle to civilize a Negev environment that was harsh and inhospitable. In these descriptions, sandstorms blew piles of sand through every crack in the houses and coated one's mouth with grit whenever one tried to eat or speak. Swarms of "black crickets" from Sinai landed in the fields and decimated the crops. One particularly frequent anecdote from elderly residents told of the special work teams formed on the *moshav* to combat scorpions and snakes. As Ephram summarized a common sentiment, his parents and other immigrants arrived in Israel thinking that it was a land of milk and honey but found it to be "a land that eats" its inhabitants. Residents tamed many of these threats through technological mastery, such as spraying pesticide and pumping water to grow crops and fix soil. But even during the successful farming years, the dry climate and powerful windstorms challenged farmers each season.

Added to and sometimes melding with these "natural" threats, residents perceived a Bedouin threat to be part of these landscapes. Dganim residents' comments suggest that the association of Bedouins with nature, in contrast to Jewish civilization, often held sway in their minds. When describing "the Bedouin problem," Ofra told me that the Bedouin just "multiply" and "spread all over" the lands surrounding the *moshav*. Using a term like "multiply" to describe Bedouins' procreation associates Bedouins with animals and challenges their status as fully human, social members of the landscape. With their spread, Ofra asserted, theft and violence increases. Similarly, other residents worried about theft that was "in their blood" or "just their way of life," describing a Bedouin problem that grew naturally and uncontrollably. As residents naturalized Bedouins' reproduction and behaviors, "the Bedouin problem" became part of a threatening landscape. Unlike the harsh desert climate, which could be held at bay with air conditioners and chemicals, residents perceived "the Bedouin problem" only to grow worse. As a result, many residents felt surrounded, encroached upon, and spoke with dismay of the *pzura*, the unplanned "dispersal" of Bedouin settlements that grew around them unchecked. These same residents pointed out that *Dganim* was alone because it was the only "settlement" (*yishuv*) in the area, a seeming paradox explained by a perspective that continues to associate Jews with civilization and Bedouins with nature.

The threat Dganim residents interpreted from the Bedouin Arabs around them was associated not purely with nature, but also with a social order believed to be dysfunctional. Although few Dganim residents had spent significant time in Bedouin settlements, many constructed ideas of the internal landscapes of these settlements based on occasional visits, depictions in news media, and views from the highway. Dganim residents described Bedouin living spaces, either governmentally approved or unrecognized, as shacks built on the median strips of roads, litter, and an uncivilized mixture of people and animals in the same space. This lack of order was not interpreted as simply a matter of circumstances, but rather as a reflection of residents' marred character. When describing disheveled Bedouin landscapes, Ephram explained, "*ayn l'hem elohim*; they don't care about the environment." The phrase, translating literally as "they don't have a god," identifies extreme disregard and a lack of any reasonable limits.

Linking immorality with dirt and disorder is neither new nor unique to Israel. From caste relationships that draw on exposure to "dirty" jobs to justify social separation, to judgments of the physical state of immigrant neighborhoods as measures of moral decrepitude, to common linguistic slippage between waste as a lack of efficiency and waste as degradation and shame, people often make moral judgments based on a person's association with dirt (Alexander and Reno 2012; Rome 2008). And people often stubbornly assign responsibility for maintaining order and cleanliness at the individual level (Graeber 2012) rather than recognizing mitigating factors like poverty or the inability to attain building permits. Such associations of dirt and disorder with particular social groups often justify discrimination and paternalistic interventions by asserting a moral divide between the orderly and the disorderly (Argyrou 1997; Davis 2005).

Some residents described Bedouins' disheveled disregard as being tied to socioeconomic status and educational opportunities, and thus changeable. For instance, Ephram suggested that Bedouins could learn respect for their surroundings and responsibility to society, given the right education. This paternalistic notion associated disorder with Bedouins but deemed them capable of progress. However, many asserted disorder as an inherently unchanging characteristic of Bedouins. Miri, a Dganim resident and regional government leader, spoke of the area's rising rates of theft as coming from the great increase of "spontaneous" Bedouin settlements. She remembered only a few clusters of families around Dganim in the past. But, she said, "you know how it is. Nomads. They build the tent, and around it, instantly, a big village. Israelis, Jews, can't do that." Jews respect government, she explained, and limit themselves to legal settlement, but Bedouins do not respect laws. And just as they built without permission, she lamented, so too they stole without qualms.

In particular, Dganim residents worried about the younger generation of Bedouins, who they asserted were more violent, unchecked by respect for either Israeli law or the tribal law followed by their parents' generation. As evidence of this growing violence, many residents repeated the story of an elderly woman who had been hit over the head during a recent home robbery. During discussions at the elders' club, residents assumed the invasion to have been committed by Bedouins and cited it as evidence of a wider social pathology.

Not all residents held such negative views of all Bedouins. A few contextualized these thefts within the wide socioeconomic disparities between Jews and Bedouin Arabs in the Negev, identifying the thefts as an expression of the growing frustration spawned by inequality. Others explained a distinction between the Bedouins "around here," some of whom had been *moshav* employees in the past, and those who lived farther away. For example, when precious artifacts were stolen from the synagogue, heated, emotional debate arose among residents about the culprits. All suspected Bedouin perpetrators, but some carefully specified that the neighboring Bedouin would not commit such a betrayal.

In fact, Bedouin Arabs had once been frequent participants in the *moshav*'s taskscapes. In the 1980s, Dganim families who farmed their own plots were pressed to produce greater quantities to compete in increasingly globalized markets. They began hiring Bedouin Arab laborers from 'Ayn al-'Azm and the surrounding unrecognized villages, as well as Palestinians from Gaza and the West Bank. With the outbreak of the Palestinian Intifada in the 1990s, the Israeli military restricted border crossings, slowing the flow of wage-seekers from the Palestinian Territories. Meanwhile, the government began issuing permits for migrant workers, which shifted the position of Bedouin Arab workers again. Being vulnerable to deportation, migrant workers labored for lower wages and longer hours than most Palestinian citizens of Israel. Most farmers who remained in business through the economic storms of the 1990s shifted to hiring these foreign workers, and working relationships with Arabs dwindled. Dganim residents recalled these relationships with conflicting emotions. Some, like the gate watchman, Nehemiah, recalled some of his former workers fondly as having been "like part of the family, coming to share meals at my house, and everything," though he had not heard from them in years. Others recalled the interaction as more burdensome because, they said, the Arabs were always stealing. Only one Dganim resident I knew maintained semiregular contact with a family from 'Ayn al-'Azm that had once worked guarding his fields.

In the 1990s, in an effort to prevent thefts and incursions into the *moshav*, residents erected a barbed-wire fence around the center of the *moshav*, leaving outside the outlying fields that fewer and fewer of them were using to grow field crops and orchards. Several years later, residents reinforced this fence with electrification and buried concrete tubes. Once built, this fence became not just an effect of the segregation and mistrust between Dganim residents and the Bedouin Arab residents around them, but a cause as well. The fence bars entrance into the *moshav* from any of the surrounding Bedouin Arab villages and cuts off *moshav* residents from the *wadi* and surrounding landscapes. Bedouin residents from surrounding settlements stopped visiting the *moshav*'s corner store, and Dganim residents rarely ventured into the landscapes surrounding the fence. In this sense, the fence is a striking example of the materialization of environmental discourses. The *wadi* became a dangerous place to be avoided. When I mentioned plans to walk into the *wadi* to meet my friend from 'Ayn al-'Azm and her group of children, the couple I was visiting for tea warned me against such a risky outing. Later, when Gil led me on a tour of the territory outside the fence, he brought along his gun and drove us rather than having us walk.

As the fence redirected residents' taskscapes and Dganim residents withdrew from landscapes beyond the *moshav*, the *wadi* reverted to the wild and contested territory that it had been before the place-making of cooperative agricultural taskscapes. The Bedouin Arabs who lived in or traveled through those lands outside the fence were no longer employees; tentative social ties were cut with the cessation of agriculture and the raising of the fence. Like the warnings I received not to walk the streets of 'Ayn al-'Azm that lay outside known families' neighborhoods, the couple's warning over tea steered me away from lands that lay outside the socialized place of Dganim.

The fence also fed resentment for those outside the *moshav*. Yousef, a resident of the unrecognized village across the highway from Dganim, explained the moral meaning the fence held for him by pointing out an area of his family's land that lay under several rows of crumbling former greenhouses inside Dganim's fence. He had been denied use of those lands for many decades, but the *moshav*'s erecting of the perimeter fence was a more forceful and insulting denial of his claim to these lands that were "taken, not bought" by Dganim. By its physical presence and the interpretations it prompted, the fence reinforced conflictive relations between increasingly reluctant neighbors. It cut off personal interactions between them, leaving only the circulation of frightful rumors to characterize the landscape and its people.

Conclusion

Building fences, enforcing selective residential policies, and telling stories of threatening differences are all part and parcel of Negev land conflict. So too, many Dganim residents would argue, are Bedouins' home-building without permission and their acts of theft. Such acts are not predetermined by hegemonic discourses and institutions that direct residents' thoughts and behaviors. Neither are they simply the angry acts of individuals. Individuals negotiate group responsibilities, government mandates, social norms, and personal interpretations as they participate in these antagonistic taskscapes.

This portrait of Dganim, alongside the account of 'Ayn al-'Azm, highlights clear differences in dwelling practices and interpretations of rightful land use and ownership, as well as some striking similarities, which illuminate the dynamics of contemporary Negev land conflict. The comparison shows how two very different versions of socially relevant "place," with divergent notions of shared ethical life, exist in this single geographical piece of the Negev.

Residents of both towns share experiences of upheaval, as governmental planning experiments came and went in this formerly frontier, now peripheral region within Israel. These modernization interventions, however, were executed and experienced differently in each locale, and residents have thus developed very different senses of place and different understandings of their own power to shape place.

Whereas 'Ayn al-'Azm residents denounced government policies that restricted their lifestyles for the good of Jewish Israelis, Dganim residents complained of Bedouins flaunting Israeli laws and failing to "modernize" in ways that would accommodate Israeli norms. Fears and criticisms about Bedouins expressed in Dganim contribute to a wider moral narrative that demands dramatic cultural disruption and accommodation from Bedouins, while blaming them for the results of this chaotic transition. On its surface, this moral narrative is similar to that applied by Ashkenazi Zionist leaders to non-Ashkenazi immigrants. And this similarity likely explains some of the harshness with which *moshav* residents spoke of Bedouins. For the good of Israel, Dganim residents went through the upheaval of *aliyah* from a radically different ecology, culture, economy, and social status. Why shouldn't Bedouins do the same? Indeed, this group of immigrants who were settled by the Israeli government on these formerly Bedouin-claimed lands, and who created this *moshav* as a collective place, have come to feel and express a sense of connection to and ownership over the land because of their struggles. However, while Dganim's Cochini residents faced the demands of assimilation, they also gained material support from the state through loans, advising, and regulatory assistance, as well as the promise of social belonging. Bedouin Arabs have been asked to accommodate without the option of truly joining Jewish Israeli society.

As is clear in these community portraits, both governmental plans and residents' dwelling practices have proven influential in the shaping of Arab-Jewish relations. Often residents create or intensify material barriers that solidify these groups. However, a single act can have multiple effects, which may go beyond the intent of its actor. Even seemingly mundane dwelling practices can hold significant political implications within the Negev's fraught context of segregation and mistrust. As they dwell, residents engage with extralocal participants in their taskscapes—government agencies, environmental NGOs, and international markets—in complex combinations of resistance and cooperation. Can these taskscapes break down segregation rather than buttressing it? Dwelling in 'Ayn al-'Azm and Dganim was not always so spatially separated, and the *wadi* was once more of a meeting zone than an avoided buffer. Can everyday interactions be amended to create a different sense of the local that has space for both Jews and Arabs? And can organized activism play a role in such a shift?

Challenging Boundaries

NESTLED AMONG THE SMALL TIN-AND-CONCRETE-BLOCK HOUSES of one neighborhood in the unrecognized village of Wadi al-Naʿam stands an innovatively designed straw-bale health-care clinic. The thick walls of straw and mud keep the clinic cool even in the desert's summer heat. A double-slanted roof channels precious rainwater to plants, and solar panels can power lights, computers, and medical equipment. This building, surrounded by a wall and several fanciful animal sculptures made of mud, tires, and trash, resulted from a "direct action protest" led by the environmental justice group Bustan.

By 2001, Wadi al-Naʿam residents, members of the al-ʿAzazme tribe, had been appealing for nine years through Israeli courts to be included in the national health-care system but had made no progress. Bustan, led by Devorah Brous, offered to help. Bustan recruited Jewish Israeli permaculture specialists to design a clinic in consultation with an ʿashira in the village and worked for two years to raise funds. Then, during a week-long work camp, an eclectic mix of Americans and Israelis, which included hippies, conservative Jews and Muslims, travelers and locals, built the Medwed Clinic. At a basic level, clinic builders sought to materially improve residents' lives. As an intervention in the region's land conflict, the project aimed to shame the national government for neglecting village residents and banning new buildings in unrecognized villages. Once staffed by local doctors, its builders also hoped the clinic would ease the pressure on residents to leave their village and move to a government township by making routine health care more accessible, particularly for women and children.

The Medwed Clinic, however, never opened to patients. Al-ʿAzazme leaders and then Bustan struggled to staff the clinic. National health-care physicians

Illustration 14. Medwed Clinic in the village of Wadi al-Naʿam. 2005. Photograph provided by Bustan.

avoided the unauthorized clinic to protect their government jobs, and private physicians who were then hired quit due to death threats.[1] By 2008, the clinic stood empty, its windows boarded up against vandals. The Medwed project seemed to have failed. However, just a year after the clinic's completion, the government opened an official clinic in Wadi al-Naʿam. Bustan members contend that their insurgent building and transnational advocacy had successfully pressured the government to act (cf. Keck and Sikkink 1998).

Bustan's work is a demonstration of innovative attempts to mobilize everyday dwelling practices in service of an activist cause. In particular, Bustan's activities focused on boundary softening rather than seeking fast and radical change. They worked at an interpersonal scale to change attitudes by adding new connotations to familiar environmental discourses and to chip away at lines of segregation through shifts in individuals' dwelling practices. Though members then experimented with ways of scaling up these individual shifts to prompt national change, they also encountered the challenging discontinuities that often face activists trying to work at multiple scales (Silverstein 2013). This chapter follows three of Bustan's projects to explore the potential and pitfalls of a politics of boundary softening. It shows both the transformative power of such activism to shift stubbornly entrenched discourses and their material manifestations, and also the constraining power of societal norms and existing power inequalities on such activism (Hallward 2011).

Building Bustan

Devorah founded Bustan in 1999 hoping to transform Israeli attitudes about Jewish-Arab conflict. She had grown up in New Jersey in an "upper middle-class family" of "assimilated American Jews," as she put it, and became involved in social diversity activism during college in Vermont. These activities were a turning point for Devorah because they "made me look within and realize I don't really have much of a connection at all with my own heritage and culture." In 1993, Devorah traveled to Israel searching for this connection. She fell in love with the landscapes and people she met, but was heartbroken that both were being torn apart and degraded by conflict. She became galvanized toward social justice activism. Devorah first joined coexistence campaigns in the Occupied Palestinian Territories, but like many left-wing activists of this period she became disillusioned with these "cosmetic dialogue projects" (Brous, in Johal 2008) and the superficial provisioning of aid supplies. "We were racing around and putting out fires," she told me, referring to the Palestinian-Israeli conflict, "while people were throwing buckets, gallons of fuel onto these little fires that were being set all around the country. And . . . we were coming with a little spoon of water to pour on the fires."

Then, in a tactical move, Devorah shifted her focus to the Negev. She hoped that although many Jewish Israelis saw Palestinians in the West Bank and Gaza as purely external enemies, they would be more disturbed by how unjustly Arabs in the Negev were treated, despite being Israeli citizens.[2] A call for multicultural citizenship that recognizes both Arabs and Jews has been at the core of Bustan's work from its founding.

Beginning as a small group of Jewish Israeli activists, Bustan aimed to become jointly run by Jews and Arabs. In the early years, they initiated practical projects with Bedouin communities, including creating gardens, running workshops, giving tours, and organizing a festival, and issued public critiques of governmental policy regarding Bedouin Arabs. In more recent years, they have established a series of "Negev Unplugged Tours"; a set of solar energy installations for medical equipment in unrecognized villages; and environmental sustainability courses.

The Medwed Clinic was Bustan's largest project in its early years, and it became central to organizational lore and pedagogy. Even members who were not involved at the time evaluated new projects five years later with the Medwed Clinic in mind. Bustan members praised the project's ability to bring together diverse participants to work toward practical goals, which became a founding principle of Bustan's approach. As Devorah explained the origins of the clinic project:

> We don't want to have just a homogenous group of activists that have already converted so we can sit down and sing songs like we're part of a choir. We didn't want to work in that way. We wanted to try to forge new ground with

this project. So, we were looking for people that had never been inside a Bedouin village to get involved. We were looking for people with different skill sets that could take on some responsibility, that could actually be involved with the planning.

This collaborative and practically oriented approach came to characterize much of Bustan's work. Its projects consistently opened interactions between scholars and activists, and theoretical innovations and practical work came from both sides. From reading technical reports on new green technologies or studying environmental justice campaigns in Australia and the United States to initiating trial-and-error experiments in community collaboration, Bustan members were investigators.

Because sociopolitical contexts profoundly impact how activists frame their arguments and mobilize support, the avenues and obstacles facing Bustan's work as a small, socioenvironmental NGO have been shaped by historical practices of environmentalist and social activism in Israel. From the Jewish National Fund's use of afforestation to claim and hold land beginning in the early 1900s to the professed motivations of Israel's most vocal environmentalists since then to uphold Zionism and strengthen the Jewish state, environmentalism in Israel has drawn heavily on Zionist discourses and nationalist priorities (Braverman 2009; Glazer and Glazer 1998; Tal 2002). Early environmentalists in the 1950s strove to temper the young state's rapid industrialization and called for legislation and citizens' participation to protect nature. The Society for the Protection of Nature in Israel (SPNI), founded in 1953 and now the largest environmental preservation organization in Israel, has strong ties to the Israeli military and state government. It emerged from the *Palmach* (a prestate Jewish paramilitary organization), and service as one of its park rangers satisfies Israel's mandatory military service requirement (Ben-David 1997). During the 1960s and 1970s, popular movements to protect flora and fauna continued to grow.

Though dominated by Zionism, this mainstream environmentalism is avowedly "biocentric" and "apolitical" (Benstein 2005). Activities have political consequences, but organizations avoid explicit discussion of political issues. In this context, calls for conservation euphemize (often violent) power relations by masking the systematic costs they exact from Palestinian citizens of Israel, such as the expropriation of their lands to create national parks. Such an approach has alienated Palestinian citizens of Israel from mainstream environmentalism (Tal 2002). During the 1980s, a more inclusive paradigm arose among Israeli environmentalists that addressed environmental quality as a matter of citizens' rights and advocated the fair distribution of state resources (Benstein 2005). Some Palestinian Israelis became active in environmentalism in Israel's north in organizations such as the Galilee Society and LINK for the Environment. In the Negev, no similar socioenvironmental campaigns had begun before Bustan's founding, but the variety of social justice groups like the Negev Coexistence Forum, Bimkom, AJEEC–Negev Institute for Strategies of Peace and Development, and the Laqiya Women's Association has been growing.

Within this context of activism, Bustan's work challenges the boundaries of dominant environmental discourses in Israel in two main ways. First, it blurs the binaries that enframe land conflict by identifying interconnections between purportedly natural and social factors and by depicting both Jews and Arabs as social and natural beings. Bustan advocates a holistic definition of environment, which includes all the inhabitants of a landscape, regardless of ethnic affiliation, and urges them toward collective stewardship. Second, Bustan's campaigns propose replacing Jewish-Arab conflict with joint opposition to a new threat: the destructiveness of overconsumption and distortedly short-sighted notions of "progress."

Bustan's valuing of past dwelling practices challenges dominant notions of progress and reverses negative Israeli images of Bedouins. At times this challenge was explicit, as when Communications Director Rebecca Manski responded to a newspaper article listing Bedouin settlements as among Israel's top ten environmental threats (Leibovitz-Dar 2006):

> The "enemy" is not Arab. . . . The depiction of Bedouin as environmental hazards represents the most insidious kind of greenwashing. It casts the very persistence of the Bedouin way of life as intrinsically harmful to the sanctity of the land. And it presents the Bedouin among the chief obstacles in the way of the Zionist dream of "making the desert bloom" . . . when in actuality the Bedouin presence mainly represents a threat to the Zionist reality of sprawling Jewish-only development. It goes without saying that the true "hazard" is not the Bedouin, but factories and toxic waste dumps, and their efforts to keep a burgeoning environmental health crisis under raps [sic]. (Manski 2006)

Rather than striving for idealized modern solutions to problems of the present, Manski suggests that striving toward modernity is part of the problem and that some solutions lie in what I heard referred to as "progress through tradition," that is, drawing on practices of the past to solve modern problems. Recognizing "true hazards," Bustan members contended, can help Jews and non-Jews find common solutions.

Despite the broadening of environmentalism that came with the rise of a civil-egalitarian paradigm, positions such as these confused standard categories of activism in Israel. Bustan members realized that they did not quite fit fellow Israelis' notions of either a social justice group or an environmentalist group. Their concern with the implications of insecure land tenure and their criticism of Bedouin Arabs' greater exposure to environmental hazards aligns Bustan more closely with environmental movements in the global South (Guha and Martinez-Alier 1997) and environmental justice movements in the United States (Bullard 1994; Checker 2005) than with Israeli environmentalism. Some projects that are environmentally mainstream elsewhere remain "too political" in Israel. Because of public concern about national security, environmentalists in Israel avoid challenging Zionist tenets like securing land through settlement (*hityashvut*) and the demographic majority of Jews over Arabs (Glazer and Glazer 1998). Few environmentalist groups dare to suggest curbing new settlement in rural areas or promote smaller families, and those that campaign to protect "open spaces" tread gingerly and ignore military use of these spaces (Oren 2007; Tal 2002). Public fears can particularly limit campaigns dealing with Palestinian Israelis, who are often suspected of being a "fifth column" in Israeli society.

Both Bustan insiders and external commentators told me their uncertain social-environmentalist identity was a strength and a weakness. Members drew creatively from the language and tactics of both social and environmentalist frames. This boundary blurring helped their projects highlight the political implications that residents often took for granted in their relationships with environmental resources. When addressing different Israeli audiences, members also could choose which identity to highlight, helping them negotiate the tense political climate. This ideological flexibility also helped Bustan seek funding from a spectrum of donors. Bustan drew on contributions from environmentally concerned American Jews in its early years and later won grants from more socially concerned European foundations such as Forum ZFD (in Germany) and the World Social Forum. However, members sometimes felt stretched thin between competing priorities, and potential partners in Israeli environmentalist NGOs wondered if Bustan was "environmental enough," while social justice NGO members wondered if it was "political enough."

Using this joint social-environmentalist identity, Bustan is part of a minority of activist groups that explicitly challenge Israel's redline political issues. However, these activists are also members of Israeli society and must operate within the discursive fields that are inseparable from their social worlds. Rather than creating new discourses from scratch, Bustan members engaged in what I refer to as discursive bricolage. *Bricolage* is the French term for a process of appropriation and reassembly, which Claude Lévi-Strauss (1966) discusses in relation to both material building and myth creation. It is a hands-on, commonsense approach, like the practical knowledge James Scott (1998) refers to as *mētis*. The *bricoleur* proceeds by resourcefully reappropriating what is at hand, retooling or resignifying these secondhand materials, and creating something new. Bricolage is a retrospective approach because *bricoleurs* find existing tools and materials and consider how to resignify them for the project at hand. Bustan assembled existing ideas, practices, and rhetoric about Bedouins and Jews, sustainability, citizenship, and nature into environmental discourses that were new in the internal disposition of their parts, though not in their raw materials or the tools of their making. These environmental discourses reframed traditional Bedouin pastoralism as modern environmental sustainability, proposed multicultural citizenship as a set of substantive rights that includes ties to land, and defined sustainability as a holistic socioenvironmental goal.

Of course, this bricolage is constrained. Sometimes activists tailor the tone and political vigor of their messages for mundane reasons, like reaching a broader Israeli public or meeting the perceived preferences of funding agencies; at other times, for fear of reprisal. For these reasons, NGOs, like individuals engaged in insurgent planting and building, often reinforce the very structures of knowledge and power they try to resist (Rabinow 2002).[3] Likewise, Bustan is led by individuals living within Israel's social segregation and power imbalances, and their campaigns rely on many of the dominant environmental discourses that undergird the land conflict and social exclusion against which they struggle.

Such constraints drove the collapse of relations between Wadi al-Naʿam residents and Bustan following the Medwed Clinic's construction. Village residents complained that Bustan demonstrated no long-term commitment, leaving the clinic empty as they moved on to projects in other communities. Bustan members complained that residents failed to maintain the clinic and protect it from vandals. Commentators from both positions agreed that Bustan's status as a Jewish group entering a Bedouin village made truly equitable partnership difficult.

In 2007, Bustan underwent two structural changes in an attempt to ease these constraints. First, the organization inaugurated its Green Center. This apartment in Beersheba, they hoped, would be a neutral space where Jews and Bedouin Arabs could come together for workshops, movie screenings, gardening events, and a permaculture course. The group planned to gradually retrofit this apartment cum community center to demonstrate environmentally sustainable practices. For the next year and a half, the Green Center served as Bustan's office, volunteer housing, and activity space.

Second, and even more significantly, Devorah handed leadership of Bustan to a Bedouin Arab Negev resident named Ra'ed al-Mickawi. Ra'ed first learned of Bustan while working for the internet television station he had created with his brothers. Bustan partnered with a woman in his town to host a sustainability workshop based on Bedouins' "traditional knowledge" of farming, herbal remedies, and biofuels, and Ra'ed covered the story. "And at that day," he exclaimed to me during our first interview, "I opened my eyes, and I said, 'Okay, here's the place that's reminding me of the way I used to be.'" Since moving from his family's rural lands to a government-planned township, Ra'ed felt that he had lost something important. He was unhappy and unhealthy in his little town plot and troubled by the Jewish-Arab hostilities around him, but he did not see a way to change these things. Finding Bustan was "the point I change my life," he told me, because he began "realizing that the development the government is offering my community is not development. It's really a disaster and is not a sustainable way of living." Combining Bedouin "traditions" with "green technologies" became Ra'ed's driving mission.

During his early months of leadership, Ra'ed spoke of refocusing Bustan's limited resources on a few initiatives based on long-term partnerships, a decision that pointedly addressed critiques of the Medwed project. At this time, Bustan had a fluctuating staff of four to six people, including a grant writer in Tel Aviv, a financial manager in Jerusalem, and the director, Green Center coordinator, and community coordinators living in the Negev. Bustan also engaged long-term interns from Israel and abroad in addition to several consultants in permaculture design, desert ecology, architecture, and solar energy on individual projects.[4] Though Bustan struggled over the following year to adapt to its new leadership and its new base in the Green Center, the group succeeded in focusing on three main projects: the Negev Unplugged Tours, the Children's Power Project, and a permaculture class. Each project faced different challenges in the effort to soften boundaries that divided Israeli society and compartmentalized issues as either political or environmental.

Displaying Dwelling

Noga stood at the front of a tour bus, microphone in hand, introducing the work of Bustan to a group of about fifty American and Israeli college students. Most of the students directed their gazes toward Noga and removed the earphones connecting them to iPods as Noga explained that Bustan is an environmentalist organization, but not part of an environmentalism that seeks to conserve pristine nature by protecting it *from* human influence. Humans are part of the environment, she said in a firm tone, so protecting an environment means also helping the people living there. It is for this kind of green thinking, she explained as we rolled along in the bus, that we at Bustan do this tour with Bedouins in the Negev.

These students were on one of Bustan's Negev Unplugged Tours, which have long been one of Bustan's primary activities. Noga, a Jewish Israeli university student majoring in Israeli and Middle Eastern Studies, had completed Bustan's Green Guides training course in order to lead tours like this one. In that course, she had learned about the impact of economic development on Negev residents and environments, new and old techniques for sustainable desert living, and the social inequalities faced by Bedouin Arab residents. Now she hoped to pass some of these lessons along to these Negev visitors.

For the benefit of the American visitors, she began with basic information. "Does anyone know what the Negev is?" Noga asked the group as we rode out of Beersheba and passed by the rows of warehouses and malls that line the city's southern edge. She waited and then repeated a student's answer: "The Negev is the desert at the bottom of Israel, that's right. . . . And before the state of Israel, in the Negev, there were Bedouins living here," she added, moving toward more controversial ground. "*Bedouin*, does anyone know what this means?" This time, there was a longer pause before students called out: "A group of people that travels by the needs of the group." "Muslims."

Noga smiled wryly and responded, "Okay, so I can talk a lot because you don't know much." At this gentle challenge, several Israeli students piped up in Hebrew, and Noga translated to English for the American students. "People say they steal cars. They say this in Hebrew and only very quietly, but they say this." Noga responded with a brief description of Bedouin dwelling practices as they had been before Israeli statehood and after. She explained the former mobility of Bedouin Arabs within tribal territories and the ways some Bedouins had "helped Jews against the British, sneaking in goods" and providing water to remote *kibbutzim*. In 1948, Noga continued, the new state "wanted to plan things, rather than allowing the Bedouin to live in the desert on their own," so they took away the Bedouins' black goat herds and cracked down on smuggling.

As we neared the tour's first stop, a home in the unrecognized village of Um Batin, the bus turned off the highway and onto a pitted sand and stone path. A student raised her hand and asked Noga why there was so much garbage scattered about. And if Bustan is an environmentalist organization, why doesn't it clean up the litter? Noga responded that the village had no garbage pickup service because the government withholds municipal services from unrecognized villages. Many residents cope by burning garbage, she added, but this causes health problems.

As Noga demonstrated in response to these students' comments, Bustan led these tours to put Negev dwelling practices on display, and specifically to assert and comment on the political implications of Bedouin Arabs' dwelling practices. As with Noga's response to comments about thieving Bedouins and a littered landscape, the tours aimed to dispel stereotypes by introducing visitors to the politicized everyday lives of Bedouin Arabs. According to Bustan's publicity:

> By going beyond the standard "Camels, Carpets and Coffee" we expose students, human rights activists, journalists, medical workers, and residents from the Negev, all of Israel and international visitors to the reality of life and the ecology of the region, and the interplay between development and sustainability. We visit unrecognized villages, chemical plants, development towns, farms, and forests and through a process of critical questioning, led by local guides, look at divides between environment and industry, tradition and modernity, and ethnicity/religion/class divides in the region.[5]

The tours focused on moving visitors not just through landscapes, but through inhabited, sociocultural landscapes. Coordinated by Bustan's Green Guides, the tours revolved around visits with multiple paid local experts, such as unrecognized-village residents and Bedouin Arabs who were also community organizers and small-business owners.

The group tour is a familiar tool of territorial contention in Israeli society with a long history of use for bolstering land claims between particular groups of people and landscapes. From the youth movement–led hikes of the British Mandate era, when Jews of the *yishuv* hiked through Palestine to learn and claim its landscapes as part of their Jewish heritage, to contemporary Taglit-Birthright tours that bring young Jews from around the world to travel the country, tours in Israel have been imbued with nationalist significance (Almog 2000; Kelner 2010; Kirshenblatt-Gimblett 2002; Zerubavel 1995). In recent decades, the SPNI has been a main provider of environmental tours. Subsidized largely by the Ministry of Education and requiring past army service of all its trained guides, the SPNI's nature tours work "to strengthen the link of the Jewish people to their land" (Ben-David 1997:143) and "omit" Arab presences (Selwyn 1995).[6] More recently still, Palestinians have begun using hiking tours of the West Bank as opportunities to convey their own emplaced national narratives (Szepesi 2012).

Bustan used this familiar practice of connecting visitors to landscapes but reappropriated it for a new purpose: to assert an environmental justice critique of Arabs' status within Israel. Whereas the SPNI's nature tours concentrated on physical exertion in "nature," Unplugged tours focused on peopled landscapes. Buses shuttled participants from place to place to spend time with Negev residents in their homes, gardens, and community centers. These visits provided interpersonal encounters across lines of cultural and ethnic difference and highlighted provocative juxtapositions in the dwelling practices of different Negev residents. Israel's claimed status as "the only democracy in the Middle East" and as a multicultural society including Jews from England to Ethiopia are important elements of Israeli nationalism. Bustan's projects pointed out the differential citizenship that actually discriminates between Jewish and non-Jewish citizens and challenged Israelis to align stated ideals with practice.

On the tour with Noga, students visited Um Batin to meet Anwar, a village resident. Disembarking from the bus, we walked past houses made of concrete and tin. To our right, sheep in pens bleated against the wind. From a raised point, Anwar explained his village's relationship with the surrounding area. Like many Unplugged tours, this one had passed by Omer, one of Israel's wealthiest towns, to reach Um Batin, an unrecognized village with no electricity or paved roads. As we stood with Anwar, looking back toward Omer, he commented on the forest beside that town in contrast to the barren land around Um Batin: "If we had the conditions of Omer, we would have a forest, too," he told us. "They have internet; we don't have electricity or water." Noga often supplemented these narrated landscapes of inequality by making the link to citizenship explicit. When Anwar pointed out the dirt path to his village's elementary school, Noga added that although the state government did not recognize this village's land claims, the High Court ruled that Bedouins, as citizens, have certain rights, including state-provided primary education. One of Noga's primary goals in guiding tours, she told me, was for participants to understand and speak of Bedouins as citizens, because many arrive to her tours unaware of this legal status. During tours, she repeatedly used the incongruence between equal juridical rights and actual disparities in social services to make this point.

The tour, as an activist tactic, entails risks and benefits. Displaying injustice with the goal of instigating sociopolitical action can bleed into voyeurism, depending on participants' intentions (Abbink 2000; Hoskins 2002). Some critics dismiss tours such as Bustan's as "voluntourism" that only commoditizes suffering by selling a "pain and poverty" narrative, which "not . . . many Negev bedouin willingly embrace" (Dinero 2010:178). Furthermore, gaining a nuanced view of dwelling practices and land conflict is difficult within the limited scope of a single tour. Unplugged tour visits to Wadi al-Na'am, for example, displayed the village's social neglect, but did not offer the extended experience I had found necessary to understand its appeal for residents. The tours also struggled to convey the complexity of Bustan's socioenvironmental vision, as when Noga explained Bedouin culture as "a whole way of life that involves great respect for the earth." She was attempting to dispel negative environmental images of Bedouins, but this familiar "noble savage" trope also romanticizes Bedouins as closer to nature than Jews.

Despite these criticisms, local experts and Bustan's two Bedouin Arab guides expressed satisfaction in being able to educate people about the Negev's social problems and their aspirations. During our visit in Um Batin, after our overview of the area, we sheltered from the wind on Anwar's patio and drank tea as we discussed Anwar's hopes for his children's generation, the difficulties young people from the community face, and whether they are dedicated to living in these villages or if they move out to cities. Conversation flowed easily as Anwar answered questions from students in the group. And tour participants later stated their appreciation for a normal conversation with someone they would have been unlikely to meet otherwise. Local experts also benefited directly from the tours. Each was paid, and some gained visibility for their own projects and small businesses across what would otherwise have been stubborn social barriers. For instance, many of Sarah's early visitors to her 'izbe in 'Ayn al-'Azm were Jewish participants on Unplugged tours, and some returned as volunteers to weed and build.

These tours worked to broaden participants' perspectives both through discursive bricolage and by moving people physically through landscapes. Itineraries placed participants in striking juxtapositions of comfortable Jewish landscapes and uncomfortable Bedouin landscapes, and guides offered explanations of lifestyles radically altered by the creation of Israel. In so doing, Bustan's tours attempted to make participants reflect on taken-for-granted discursive associations between Jews and civilization versus Bedouins and wildness, and between rootless nomads versus rooted agriculturalists. Buses took individuals across the normally rigid boundaries between Jewish and Bedouin Arab social spaces. Through their small scale and intimacy, the tours worked to humanize and personalize participants in land conflict who are typically subsumed in a simplified portrait of radical difference. Some Unplugged participants were already aware of these discrepancies and eager enough to learn more that they had signed up for individual seats on tours. But because Bustan offered the convenience of a prearranged excursion, large companies, including Taglit-Birthright, also booked group tours for first-time visitors to Israel. In bringing uninformed outsiders to learn from Bedouin residents positioned as local experts, the tours also attempted to upend norms of interpersonal power dynamics by valuing the knowledge of these long-time residents. They displayed ties that non-Jewish citizens of Israel have to its landscapes, conveying the political message that these residents' attachments to place are just as strong as Jewish Israelis' attachments.

Conducting Power

Bustan members valued the Negev Unplugged Tours for their ability to spread the group's socioenvironmental perspective on the Negev's problems in a participatory way and reach a wide range of people, from international tourists to Israeli high school students. They also exercised considerable control over the tours' messages and framing. However, tours reached only small groups of people willing to pay to cover their costs. Bustan struggled to balance its drive to challenge boundaries and visitors' stereotypes with the need to attract these visitors. With the Children's Power Project (CPP), Bustan attempted to sidestep this dilemma.

The CPP provided solar-powered equipment to families who lived in unrecognized villages, without access to electricity, but whose children needed electricity for medical reasons. The initiative began as a onetime project to help Inas al-Atrash, a three-year-old with cancer. To bring her home from the hospital, her family needed a refrigerator to store her medicine, but living in an unrecognized village, they had access to electricity only through a diesel generator for a few hours each night. Inas's parents petitioned the High Court to be connected to the electricity grid, but their petition was denied because the "parents chose to live in an unrecognized village knowing they will have no electricity."[7] Bustan raised funds to install a solar-powered refrigerator in the al-Atrash home. When Inas's cancer went into remission, they passed the solar equipment to a child with sleep apnea to power an oxygen machine. Funded by an anonymous donation, Bustan's leaders then decided to extend this project by installing ten more photovoltaic systems. They would create an awareness campaign with the Israeli public by seeking media coverage of the installations. This focus on media coverage as a central tactic was new for Bustan. Previously, newspaper op-eds and radio interviews had merely supplemented more tangible collaborative projects with residents, but had not been the group's focus.

In extending the project, Bustan leaders aimed to challenge stubborn sociopolitical boundaries and reach a national audience in two ways. First, the project called Israelis to take responsibility for these children who, whether Bedouin or Jewish, were citizens. Second, as Bustan's director, Ra'ed, explained, these parents faced an excruciating choice:

> Because they wanted their children to survive, [parents] will do one of two things. [One possibility is] to move and to relocate themselves inside a Bedouin township, and that means they are giving up all their lands. . . . The other thing is to keep their home at their land and to rent a house in a different place and just to pay the [extra] rent and the costs, all these things just because of the electricity. [This] is not sustainable for these families because they are coming from a very . . . hard socioeconomic background.

Bustan ran the CPP, Ra'ed continued, "because we really want you to stay and keep your land because this is the real connection between the earth and the people." Government authorities aimed to compel residents to move away from their rural villages by providing basic services only to planned townships. Bustan's campaign attempted to weaken that strategy by demonstrating one way families could remain steadfast on their lands. By using solar energy, these Bedouin families could also set an example for other Israelis, another staff member explained to me during a meeting. The CPP would demonstrate that citizens' needs could be met with clean energy rather than by extending "the polluting grid." Recognition of cultural rights in land could coincide with socioenvironmental sustainability.

Thus, the CPP aimed to foster a notion of multicultural citizenship that recognized the protection of all citizens' cultural and historical connections to landscapes as being equally integral to their citizenship rights as their rights to basic municipal services. Such a message resists de-cultural accommodation pressures on Bedouin Arabs. It contends that achieving multicultural citizenship requires also embracing landscapes as multicultural rather than claiming and cordoning land as either Jewish or Bedouin. Tactically, the project engaged in discursive bricolage by drawing upon discourses of multiculturalism and citizenship widely associated with Jewish Israelis and applying them to Arabs as well. However, as Bustan's members soon found, this sort of discursive bricolage had limits.

As I arrived to work with Bustan, the extended phase of the CPP project was commencing. Two coordinators from Bustan accompanied social workers at Soroka Hospital in Beersheba to learn about children who could benefit from the solar installations and to meet interested parents. One Bustan coordinator traveled to the families' villages with a solar equipment expert to examine the technical requirements of their homes and begin installation. Meanwhile, Bustan staff members planned a public launch of the CPP project. They arranged a five-hour tour and invited reporters from Israeli and international news outlets.

During planning for the press tour, it became clear that Bustan faced two main dilemmas by relying on media coverage to convey their discursive bricolage at a national scale. Staffers were most worried that reporters would portray the CPP as a "humanitarian" project, missing the "political" message they wished to convey. They worried that if press coverage portrayed the project as charity to Bedouin Arabs, this would neglect their right to expect municipal services as citizens and would reinforce their second-class citizenship status in Israel. They had good reason to be concerned. As social researchers have shown in other contexts, becoming visibly vulnerable may get governmental attention and care (Zeiderman 2013), but when substituted for political rights, humanitarianism can actually be exclusionary (Feldman 2007; Ticktin 2006; Willen 2012). Like de-cultural accommodation, a humanitarian justification addresses people as living beings, but not as citizens or members of a cultural group.

A second concern, which more implicitly shaped the CPP, was how to convince and not simply antagonize a wide Israeli audience. If reporters did set aside humanitarian interpretations to focus on the more substantive issues of Bedouin inclusion in Israeli society, equal citizenship, and land rights, how could the project encourage Israelis caught up in a zero-sum conflict over land to listen rather than react defensively? Early planning discussions centered on which CPP families the reporters would meet and what to do with reporters in each village. In these debates, Bustan members strategized ways to expand discursive limits. Which dwelling practices and their associated landscapes would display the inequalities faced by Israel's Bedouin citizens but also allow audiences to relate to Bedouin residents as fellow Israelis? And what kind of Bedouin persons would be sympathetic to a primarily Jewish Israeli audience?

For many Israelis, unrecognized villages are wild, dangerous landscapes. Even one of Bustan's Jewish staff members expressed fear during a planning meeting about visiting these villages after dark. She cited their unlit roads and an unspecified anxiety about their "danger." Other staff members quickly censured what they interpreted as a stereotype of Bedouins and a retrenchment of Jewish-Arab separation, insisting instead that Bedouin villages were no less safe than Jewish towns. I observed as voices rose in argument until one staff member proposed that we begin the tour earlier and finish before dark. This argument demonstrated that deconstructing frames of opposition in which Bustan members had grown up and assembling a new understanding of "Bedouin" was an ongoing task with which they struggled. This was a politics in process, not an already enlightened group spreading its message to the masses.

On the day of the tour, Bustan staff and volunteers gathered with a dozen reporters on a bus in Beersheba. We drove to the village of Um Batin, where we sat on cushions in the shade to hear opening remarks from a citizens' rights activist and guide of Negev Unplugged Tours (Sliman Abu Zaedi), Bustan's director (Ra'ed al-Mickawi), the dean of the Faculty of Health Sciences at Ben-Gurion University (Shaul Sofer), the installer of the CPP's solar equipment, and two fathers of children receiving equipment. Reporters viewed a solar installation and conducted interviews. Next, we drove to Wadi al-Na'am. As we stood underneath the high-voltage electrical lines of the power plant and viewed the industrial waste facilities across the road, Sliman and a village leader spoke about the elevated rates of cancer, asthma, and miscarriages afflicting this unrecognized village. Finally, the group rode to the village of Qasr Assir to have lunch with another family receiving CPP solar equipment at their humble, tin-roofed home and to listen to closing remarks.

The press tour aimed to familiarize the Israeli public with these villages through the eyes of reporters by emphasizing both the hardships they face and their place within Israeli society. Poverty was evident in the villages, and speakers explicitly decried Bedouins' unequal treatment. But Bustan organizers also carefully scheduled time for reporters to mingle and talk with residents, including over a leisurely lunch. At this last stop, the hospitality so strongly associated with Bedouin culture was on display, but it was choreographed to show Israeliness. Foods served could just as easily have been found in a Jewish or Arab home: pita bread, hummus, sliced cucumbers and tomatoes, olives, French fries, fruit soda and Coca Cola. The people and landscapes of the tour depicted Israeli citizens seeking equal treatment from the state.

CPP organizers were also careful to foreground Bedouin Arabs they thought would be sympathetic representatives to the Israeli public: primarily children and military servicemen. Bustan leaders hoped that the needs of sick children would inspire empathy that would "break through some of those stereotypes about Bedouins," as a Jewish staff member named Karen put it, and "open" people to hearing about the issues. She continued, "It really brings out what it means to not have electricity, what it means to be an unrecognized villager, how that affects your life in profound ways and also the most superficial ways." The children were put forward as innocents who suffered because of their status as Bedouins in Israel rather than any wrongdoing of their own.

Bedouin volunteers in the Israeli military represent a different notion of citizenship, one based on the reciprocity of services and loyalties, which could disassociate the CPP from charity. As a duty of Jewish citizens, military service usually divides Jews from Arabs, but enlistment by some Bedouin volunteers troubles this division. When during one staff meeting a CPP coordinator mentioned that the father of one family receiving a solar unit was an officer in the army, Karen responded excitedly. "Really, the father's in the army? That's perfect." This was ideal for publicizing the project's political message, she elaborated, because it foregrounded the irony of a man volunteering his life for the state, then being denied access to electricity from the state to care for his children. Bedouin servicemen are visible but contested figures within national debates about citizenship, Palestinians, and compulsory service (Kanaaneh 2009). The father was wary of being a representative in this political way, but reluctantly agreed. At the tour's first stop, another father revealed that he "served a long time in the IDF and am partially disabled as a result." By presenting sympathetic beneficiaries, the tour encouraged empathy with fellow citizens and urged action from the government through the moral leverage of shame (cf. Keck and Sikkink 1998).

Media coverage of the project met some of Bustan's goals, but it also demonstrated limits in promoting new environmental discourses and doing so at a national scale. Both empathy and shame were included in broadcasts and newspaper coverage from a variety of sources in Hebrew, Arabic, and English. Articles included Professor Shaul Sofer's assertion that he was "embarrassed because of the lack of basic infrastructure in the unrecognized villages" (Almadar 2008) and his declaration that the state must provide these residents with infrastructure because they are "citizens of the state and they live here!" (Yahav 2008). At least one newspaper report discussed the military father's "simple and eloquent" address (Waldoks 2008). Another sympathetically quoted a different father who invoked an unspecified collective "we" to assign blame: "We are disappointed by the authorities and angry at the government [because] they left us out to dry" (Yahav 2008).

Bustan staff members were initially pleased with this media coverage, but as time passed they wondered about the efficacy of the CPP. Media coverage lasted only a few days, and there was no evidence of its having widened Bustan's reach within Israeli society. Though coverage included basic calls for empathy or praise for solar technology, it did not link these issues to assert Bustan's more fundamental message about landscapes and belonging. I later interviewed two reporters who had participated in the CPP tour, asking what they learned from the day and how they evaluated the project. Both recognized the sociopolitical message that Bustan attempted to convey but acknowledged only partially including it in their articles. One who had portrayed the project as an innovative use of solar technology explained that the political message was "very obvious, which is one of the main points that I got, but which, to a certain extent I ignored. My thing is not fighting the fight for the unrecognized Bedouins and improving their rights. . . . To be perfectly blunt, that's not my beat. My beat is . . . environmental stuff." Though this reporter appreciated CPP's social justice message on a personal level, he felt compelled to keep sociopolitical and environmental issues compartmentalized. Indeed, his and other newspapers running "environmental" stories generally steer clear of threatening political issues like Jewish-Arab inequalities or land claims. Israeli media outlets were guided by discursive norms that constrained Bustan's efforts to promote a hybrid socio-environmental discourse. Among the staff, enthusiasm for the CPP faded, and no similarly media-focused projects have since been initiated.

As an experiment in scaling up activism, the CPP campaign offers insight into the politics of scale embedded in Bustan's activism. Political realists define power in terms of competing state interests and brute force, and critiques from this perspective argue that while small grassroots NGOs may be effective in alleviating poverty and providing social services, they are neither large nor powerful enough to push states or multinational corporations toward meaningful change (Fisher 1997; Luong and Weinthal 1999). However, other scholars suggest a different measure of power. Small NGOs can influence society on the level of identity representation, "legitimacy wars," and the diffusion of cultural norms (De Cesari 2010; Escobar 2008; Gibson-Graham 2006; Hallward 2011).

Bustan has always been small in staff size and operating budget and local in its geographical focus, and most members noted its small size as a strength. Although I witnessed complaints during staff meetings about being pushed around in partnerships with larger organizations and debates about how to raise a larger budget and whether to hire more staff, such discussions usually ended with members noting the importance of intimacy and adaptability for Bustan's particular goals. Projects at different scales involve different kinds of relationships (Harvey 1996; Swyngedouw and Heynen 2003). While larger groups sought more sweeping reforms in governance structures, legal rights, and territorial claims, Bustan leaders sought to improve life in the Negev by modifying interpersonal relationships. As Devorah explained:

> I believe that that kind of . . . organic and visceral loving connection with the land is what opens us to want to care for it. Whereas a more rights-based kind of ownership, [a] possession kind of argument, like, "this is mine by right, because of my blood, because of my bloodline" . . . leads us to a place of wanting

to grab it and hold it and fight over it, and even divide it and exploit it in order to make sure that it's still mine at the end of the day.

This focus on intimate engagement places Bustan within a wider trend of scholars and activists criticizing the romance of the global (Appadurai 1996) and revaluing the local (Escobar 2001). Local and slow food movements (Wilk 2006); a renewed interest in cooperative stores and economies (Gibson-Graham 2006); and New Urbanism, ecovillages, and intentional communities (Peters, Fudge, and Jackson 2010) all share this small-scale focus on the politics of everyday practices.

Of course, local dynamics, particularly for social movements, are not isolated from forces at other scales (Choy 2005; Nonini 2013; Silverstein 2013). Indeed, members of Bustan, as in many NGOs in Israel-Palestine (Hallward 2011), felt compelled to prove their power in more forceful terms, to prompt significant, national change. The magnitude of social inequalities and environmental degradation in the Negev, as well as the volatile political climate created by the wider Palestinian-Israeli conflict, seemed to demand more than local interventions. However, the attempt to scale up the CPP to a national scale revealed challenging differences in priorities and kinds of accountability at the larger scale (Silverstein 2013), which Bustan was not prepared to handle. The group was ultimately unable to control the project's public messaging. In 2009, Ra'ed announced,

> we came to the realization that the expense of each solar-system makes it impracticable. To continue making an impact, it would have to either grow enormously and become a humanitarian alternative to the lack of electricity in unrecognized villages, or turn towards advocacy in the Knesset to change these conditions, neither of which fall within our area of expertise. (email communication)

During meetings, Bustan members had stressed their desire to pressure the Israeli government to take responsibility for its Bedouin citizens, not reduce this pressure by replacing the state in providing electricity. Staff members decided to return to a small-scale and long-term approach, partnering with particular communities to garner more meaningful, if geographically limited, improvements than they could through public advocacy.[8]

Designing Dwelling

Permaculture education, which had already been an element in several of Bustan's past projects, met this aim of returning to Bustan's previous approach, fostering discourses and subjectivities on a more intimate level. Permaculture is an approach to sustainable living that draws design principles from patterns observed in ecosystems and applies them to many human endeavors, including food provision, building, transportation, and economic networks (Mollison and Holmgren 1987).[9] Since its initiation in Australia in the 1990s, permaculture has become a worldwide movement, and the concepts and practices first developed for rural farming have been extended to urban and suburban settings and adapted to various climates. Contemporary permaculturists engage in projects ranging from designing home gardens to consulting with city planners and establishing new farming communities.

In 2008, Bustan undertook its long-standing goal of hosting a course in permaculture design. Permaculture had already been gaining popularity among small pockets of Jewish Israelis before 2008. These enthusiasts often used permaculture apolitically, but Bustan staff members aimed to apply permaculture's analytic and practical tools directly to politically vexed socioenvironmental challenges. Advertisements for the course announced:

> As in other trainings, participants in this three-month course will meet weekly to learn the principles and application of permaculture through theory and hands-on practice. However, the course is unique in being the first of its kind to be undertaken within the Bedouin community in Israel. The course will be attuned to both the desert ecology and the current political context of the Negev, so that participants will gain tools of analysis and planning to respond to local issues.

Organizers hoped these tools would help Negev residents, particularly those in unrecognized villages, to create better lives by narrowing the large gap in living standards between Jews and Bedouins without creating the long-term problems they identified in typical development efforts (for example, pollution, overconsumption, and disconnected communities). The goal was not to make do with less and be satisfied, Devorah clarified, but to help those in Israeli society with the least to "make themselves strong and gain more resources."

With its first three-month class, Bustan hoped to train a core group of permaculture experts in the Negev. During phase two, students would undertake permaculture projects, with Bustan's financial assistance and supervision from course instructors, which would earn them an internationally recognized certificate of training. These "model 'green' projects" within Bedouin communities could later be replicated throughout the region. Bustan hoped these projects would tap into existing agropastoral dwelling practices in places like 'Ayn al-'Azm and make them more sustainable and communal through systematic permaculture planning.

While engaged as a volunteer staff member, my main duty with Bustan was to coordinate this permaculture initiative. I participated in staff meetings where we established the goals of the course and the strategy for recruiting funding and participants, met with the three coinstructors as they designed the class and drew up a budget, and drafted and edited advertisements and a newsletter article. I worked with the community organizer who was recruiting participants, gathered materials, and prepared the class space. Eventually, I participated in classes and workshops with the students.

Beginning in late spring, the class gathered each Tuesday night in the Green Center. Guided by three coinstructors who took turns traveling by train from northern Israel, we listened to explanations of the complex ecology of trees, permaculture's planning system of zones and sectors, and chemical-free solutions to household needs such as cleaning and pest control. We discussed the consumption of energy and material goods in our homes and did group exercises in household design. In the garden, we gathered to practice observation skills, dig irrigation channels, and try our hands at several green building techniques. All class participants were adults with busy lives of work and family, and though

Illustration 15. Learning environmental interconnections in Bustan's Permaculture Course. 2008. Photograph from Author archive.

a core group of participants arrived regularly, class attendance and homework completion never reached the consistency that instructors hoped for. Core participants included four Bedouin Arab men, two Bedouin Arab women, and three Jewish women; an additional six participants attended classes less regularly.

Like the CPP and Unplugged tours, the permaculture course sought to reconfigure Israeli discourses of progress and sustainability. More than other projects, it combined discursive and material bricolage. Exercises ranging from thought experiments to bench building promoted Bustan's notion of progress through tradition and of dwelling in rather than dominating landscapes. In the process, instructors modeled the practices and aesthetic sensibilities of bricolage and engaged students physically in bricolage as well. Students reacted with varying levels of enthusiasm or reluctance.

Class discussions about designing living spaces demonstrated students' mixed reactions to Bustan's efforts to challenge the boundaries of binary Jewish/culture/progress versus Bedouin/nature/tradition discourse. One Tuesday evening in June, an instructor, Talia, began the class by discussing "green building" and showing slides of environmentally responsible architecture around the world. Talia described how international certification schemes like LEED (Leadership in Energy and Environmental Design) promote green building. This was already familiar material for several class participants who were also studying architecture at the local college, but Talia then brought Bedouins into this discussion of environmental leadership. Today's "alternative building" draws from the principles common to all "traditional building," she told the class, using the Bedouin tent as a prime example. The tent relied on locally available resources—goat and camel hair—rather than transporting special building materials. Today we have been caught up in ideas of progress that push us constantly to seek out the new and different, she lamented, and this notion of progress brings problems such as pollution and global warming. Talia cast traditional builders such as Bedouins as the forerunners and inspiration for progressive contemporary environmental practices like LEED certification.

The link Talia drew between Bedouin tent-making and green building was just one example of a common practice within Bustan: promoting a discourse of the ecologically progressive Bedouin. Bustan's earlier projects promoting Bedouins' ecological savvy included their "Waste-to-Energy: Biofuel" initiative of biogas digesters that use animal dung as fuel and their partnership with Sarah in 'Ayn al-'Azm to teach visitors about "organic farming and traditional herbs." Permaculture instructors drew participants into this discourse, as when

Eitan guided a discussion about how Israelis could reduce their carbon foot-prints by learning about traditional Bedouin practices. One participant de-scribed his grandmother's use of every part of a slaughtered sheep, and another discussed former practices of olive production that were more sustainable and less polluting than current methods. However, both lamented, the rural lifestyle of which these practices were a part is no longer feasible for Bedouin Arabs in Israel. No specific solutions to this dilemma were offered that night, but Eitan suggested that training in permaculture could help participants address them by combining "traditional Bedouin knowledge" with "the good [aspects] of new technology."

Some participants appreciated the course's progress-through-tradition dis-course. Faris, a young Bedouin man who had participated in past Bustan proj-ects, often spoke proudly of Bedouin traditions as wise and environmentally responsible. For example, during one class, Hava, a third instructor, introduced the importance of observation before building on a plot, and Faris elaborated on several methods Bedouins used to choose tent locations, including prevail-ing winds and the location of anthills. When I spoke with Hiba, a young Bed-ouin Arab woman from Rahat, five months after the class finished, I asked if anything from the course continued to be relevant to her daily life. She replied, "Today we live like we're trying to be developed, or modern. . . . When I took this class, they told us that we must return to long ago [*min zamaan*]." Bedouin heritage had already been important to Hiba before the permaculture class, and she appreciated the new vocabulary she learned from Bustan's discourse of the ecologically progressive Bedouin. As we sat sipping lemonade in her well-appointed living room with the television on, Hiba said that she likes the "Bed-ouin lifestyle" of eating healthy foods and living more simply but also enjoys the conveniences of hot showers, electricity, and television. She wants "to put some pieces of that life together with the modern," she explained, giving the mud oven (*tanour*) as an example. She planned to build such an oven beside her house because it did not require expensive electricity.

Not everyone was comfortable with this focus on Bedouin traditions, though. Early in the course, Hava was explaining the importance of carefully observing both natural and cultural factors before planning changes to a new setting. "For example," she asked the class, "what mistake could a planner who comes to plan a Bedouin area make if he doesn't know the Bedouin culture?" When Faris began to respond, "Let's say we're talking about a tent," another Bedouin man, Samad, immediately interrupted. "No, we're not talking about a tent!" he declared, as a small chorus of other voices agreed. "We'll talk about a house, a proper stone house." A third Bedouin participant then referred to such a house to respond to the original question, suggesting that a kitchen must be separated from the living room so that women can work out of view of visitors.

Samad's objection to the tent example seemed to stem from his aversion to pigeonholing Bedouin Arabs as traditional, not modern like other Israelis. Participants like Samad were accustomed to frequent derogatory references to Bedouin backwardness within the Israeli public sphere. These perma-culture lessons could easily be interpreted as a threat to Bedouins' status as modern because they seemed to some participants to value only Bedouin practices that have largely been lost. Samad and another participant, Bashir, were quick to correct instructors or other participants if they spoke of past practices as if they were still common among Bedouin Arabs today. Though their reactions softened as the course went on, a dichotomy of traditional and backward versus modern and valuable remained influential for these participants, and they resisted the discursive bricolage of the ecologically progressive Bedouin.

The bricolage work that the permaculture course attempted to accomplish was not just about cerebral interpretations and vocabulary. The intimate en-gagement Bustan wished to foster among Negev residents, of knowing and lov-ing rather than claiming and exploiting land, also required a particular type of sensorial knowledge. Permaculture design calls to integrate universal principles with the gradually accrued lessons of long-term experience in a place. These two ways of knowing correspond closely with another contrasting pair: *mētis*, piecemeal and situational knowledge, and *techne*, rigorous application of sci-entific principles (Scott 1998). By integrating the two, permaculture planning attempts to "use small and slow solutions" and avoid the follies that come with large-scale social engineering.[10]

To meld these two types of knowledge, students engaged in learning bodily. During one class in May, the group stepped outside to the Green Center's gar-den for a lesson on building with cob, which is a mixture of sand, soil, water, and straw. We decided to build a garden bench. To begin, we needed to deter-mine the correct ratio of sand and soil. Because grain size and moisture content vary from place to place, this ratio must be determined at each building site. In a small bucket, two students mixed sand, soil, and water. Then Talia scooped a glob of the mud and let it hang from her hand. When the glob stayed stuck to her hand for ten seconds, the proportions of sand and dirt were right. Several students began using these proportions to mix a larger batch in a plastic bath-tub found in a pile of abandoned articles at the edge of the garden, while Bashir and Amir found an old rabbit cage from this pile and used it to sift the sand free of rocks. Throughout, students engaged in the creative reapportioning of objects that is valued in permaculture.

Talia told us that often this mixing is done by foot. I volunteered, took off my sandals, rolled up my pants, and hopped in. A few students giggled at first as I, a grown woman, began mucking about in the mud with my bare feet, but others chided them, saying this approach made sense. Talia supported the method in technical terms; my body weight helped me put more force on the mud with less effort than if I used my hands. The rest of the class joked and suggested singing as my feet squished through the mud. Once the water seemed well mixed, Talia picked up a ball of mud to demonstrate another test. While squeezing and releasing the ball, one hears the squelching sound of water and the raspiness of sand. If you hear both, she told us, and one does not block out the other, the mixture is ready for straw to be added. Our mixture passed this test, and classmates began tossing in handfuls of straw as I continued stomping. I leaned into my steps as the treading got harder, and my shirt lifted to reveal the notebook tucked into my back pocket. Yael laughed and pointed to the notebook. "Ah," said Talia, "she thought she was going to come out and learn some theoretical things to write down. But she's learning more this way."

Indeed, embodied learning was a mainstay of the permaculture class. In exercises, instructors asked students to use every sense to observe the environmental forces affecting a house plot and implement their plans while staying attentive to these forces. This style of learning brought together *mētis* and *techne*. Rather than identifying an ideal blend of sand and soil that could be standardized and brought from elsewhere, Talia taught students practical experiments to find ideal materials in the field. Rather than reducing the complexity of a multivariable situation, as in scientific agriculture or standard planning practices, *mētis* makes the most of instability and contingency because it includes an intimate (and largely implicit) knowledge of how these variables interact. Yet course materials included universally applicable knowledge, such as ideal soil pH and nitrogen levels, which promoted the value of *techne* as well.

While permaculture aimed for tangible outcomes, the particular aesthetics and sensibilities of its bricolage practice are also important. Full of creatively reappropriated objects, permaculture projects like our garden bench often share a particular aesthetic. In contrast to a modernist aesthetic of sleek lines and unobtrusive seams, bricolage products are often less polished, and with the outlines of original components still visible. The permaculture class sought to

Illustration 16. Embodied learning: permaculture students build with recycled paper. 2008. Photograph by Author.

raise the prestige of this aesthetic. During visits to permaculture farms or slide viewings of gardens and homes made through permaculture design, instructors praised the "organic" appearance of these products. Perhaps even more importantly, Bustan valued the subjectivities engendered through bricolage. Creative reappropriation and comfort with multiple variables and ambiguity were crucial to the sort of socioenvironmental change the group sought.

Bustan leaders had great hopes for this course. They envisioned it building a cohesive group of permaculture experts residing in the Negev. But the course did not go as they planned. After sparse attendance and tight funding, students did not complete community projects, but only gave final group presentations proposing permaculture refurbishment projects for their homes. Students have not become public leaders in permaculture. Several students told me later that they were disappointed Bustan had not raised more money or laid more groundwork to make the projects happen, and Bustan staff members were frustrated that class participants had not shown more initiative in classes or their projects. Both complaints echoed critiques of the Medwed Clinic, suggesting similar social interactions within Bustan's projects despite the structural changes of Ra'ed's leadership and the opening of the Green Center.

Conclusion

Socioenvironmental change of the type toward which Bustan strives takes time, and even if this research covered a long enough period to record such change, causes and effects could not be isolated enough to determine the societal impact of one NGO. Rather, this investigation of Bustan's practices illuminates the promise and challenges of activism aiming to soften boundaries through personal engagement with people and their dwelling practices.

First, dominant environmental discourses were the resources for Bustan's bricolage activism, but the rigidity of certain binary oppositions imposed limitations on reappropriation and resignification. Bustan members themselves struggled to escape the stereotypes and aversions shaped by their experiences in Israel's divided landscapes, as became clear in planning meetings for the CPP tour and occasional "noble savage" implications in Unplugged tour guides' talks. The conventional contrast between modern orderliness and primitive disorder made the sensibilities of permaculture difficult for some participants to embrace. When visiting permaculture farms or viewing slides, class members objected to their cobbled-together and eclectic appearance. And for architecture students trained in conventional methods of planning that began with the blank space of a computer screen or piece of paper, permaculture's approach of slow observation and incorporation into landscapes was intriguing but difficult to fully adopt. The real and imagined audiences of Bustan's projects also guided its discursive work, as in permaculture students' resistance to the ecologically progressive Bedouin and Bustan's tailoring of the CPP to be acceptable to a broad public audience.

Second, political-material realities, reinforced by these stubborn discursive binaries, intervened in Bustan's efforts to cultivate new relationships between people and landscapes. Insecure land rights limited village residents' participation in permaculture projects. Permaculture practices entail long-term residence and investment in a place, requiring great initial labor and capital to build homes and gardens that eventually return that investment. However, many Negev residents, especially those whom Bustan most wished to reach—residents of unrecognized villages—do not possess secure, long-term ties to land. The Negev's divided landscapes also made cooperation between Jews and Arabs on neutral ground nearly impossible. Participants' homes were always socially marked places, and the Green Center never became the hub of Jewish-Arab interaction for which Bustan had hoped. Standing in a Beersheba neighborhood of only Jewish residents, it remained a Jewish place for many of the Bedouin Arabs who did venture there, and this likely deterred many others from visiting.

Nonetheless, Bustan did continue running these and other activist projects in the face of abundant cause for pessimism, and this offers a lesson in the politics of possibility. Scholar activists Gibson-Graham (2006) proposed a politics of possibility as a way to move forward from the negativity and despair that had characterized radical sociopolitical critiques, including their own. Nourished by feminist theory and based on analysis of small-scale social movements, a politics of possibility recognizes individual subjectivities as both the sites and sources of political action. Struggling along the way, sometimes stumbling and adjusting course, Bustan did realize some of its goals at the level of individual subjectivities.

At a basic level, their continued activities contributed to the sparse but dedicated work of activist groups in Israel and Palestine that not only soften Jewish-Arab barriers by crossing them, but show that it can be done with mutual respect (Hallward 2011). Negev Unplugged Tours showed desert landscapes shaped by Jews and Bedouin Arabs to tourists who are typically shown wilderness or Jewish towns, and they asserted the integral place of land in social relations. The CPP showed journalists and some of their readers a portrait of Bedouin families as co-citizens who suffered physically from their low social status in Israel, and it materially improved the lives of a handful of these families.

At a deeper interpersonal level, the permaculture course ran for seven months and fostered new possibilities of interaction—between Jews and Arabs and between people and their landscapes. Participants experienced a comfortably interacting group of Jews and Arabs in a setting that included discussions of social justice. The course encouraged new associations for existing environmental discourses, namely an approach to progress that incorporates long-standing traditions, and an openness to Bedouin Arabs as environmental stewards rather than hazards. Some participants found this association troublingly anachronistic, like Samad, who resisted consistent association of Bedouins with tents. Others, like Hiba, appreciated these associations and discussed them with friends outside the class. Students who embraced permaculture's bricolage practices fostered the aesthetic, practical, and intellectual sensibilities that have been aspirational in much of Bustan's work. Attention to long-term sustainability, comfort with mess and improvisation, and appreciation of the *mētis* gained through dwelling all suit the alternative socioenvironmental relations for which Bustan has been striving.

Attempting to build on these successes, yet also learn from the project's setbacks, Bustan continued its permaculture focus, this time in partnership with a single village, Qasr al-Sir. They began creating a permanent ecotourism site and permaculture school called the Eco-Khan. Ra'ed told me excitedly in 2010 that residents of the village, which had recently been granted provisional governmental recognition as part of the Abu Basma Regional Council but had not yet seen substantive changes in infrastructure, were eager to work with Bustan in creating an "ecovillage." Ra'ed reported that between villagers' historical and emotional attachment to the landscapes of Qasr al-Sir and the new promise of permanence offered by recognition, the village seemed an ideal site for the material realization of social and environmental sustainability. Two years later, the first class of students completed PermaNegev, a six-week course in permaculture and Middle East studies, and the Eco-Khan was receiving a small trickle of guests.[11]

Finally, close examination of one NGO's activities reveals how organized activism is part of a larger social context of such practices. Social activism is in many ways a privileged practice. For those able to take part, it facilitates access to transnational networks of funding, political backing, and expertise. As a collective endeavor, it can also cultivate affective stances and new languages that help reveal the taken-for-granted and even naturalized elements of one's social world (Gibson-Graham 2006). Indeed, campaigns that drew links between the availability of medical care and a family's ability to stay on their land, or between permaculture training and community development, helped me formulate the political dwelling perspective that continues to inform my research.

Activists live in larger communities. They mutually learn from efforts outside their own campaigns and nurture (and sometimes compete with) these outside efforts. Researching across social realms and traveling through relationships linked to NGO work, I saw similarities and direct interconnections between Bustan's projects, 'Ayn al-'Azm's culture workers, and those unrecognized village residents engaging NGO networks. Many Negev residents are working out their own life projects in association with activist groups. Sarah constructed her herb garden, and Twail Abu Jarwal villagers held their public planting with the help of NGO financing and volunteer labor. These and other collaborations between residents and organized activist groups contain their own limitations and potential for conflicting priorities, but many residents have sought them out for the expansion of resources they provide. Conversely, Bustan leaders learn lessons from some Negev residents' dwelling practices, such as the use of animal waste as biofuel or healing through herbal medicine. Bustan projects drew upon these practices in their discursive bricolage, framing them as modern traditions of desert living worth emulating, and promoted them to both Arab and Jewish residents. Using their access to funding, media contacts, and networks of other organizations, NGOs that are focused on the politics of dwelling, like Bustan, can amplify these everyday acts of boundary crossing.

This study, along with studies of other small grassroots NGOs in Israel-Palestine, suggests that in Israel's sociopolitical milieu such NGOs hold potential for change, but not in terms of large policy shifts or the removal of structural economic disparities (Hallward 2011; Svirsky 2013). Rather, they can foster more civil, egalitarian modes of everyday interpersonal relations and keep challenging issues, like Jewish-Arab relations, substantive citizenship, and environmental rights and responsibilities, in public view. This is no small feat when elites and power brokers hold vested interests in maintaining a status quo of Jewish-Arab separation, Zionist territorialism, and simmering conflict, and when many residents respond to my queries about resolving land conflict by saying simply, "I think it's not possible."

Of course, not all efforts to challenge dominant discourses are explicitly political and formulated as activism. In their own ways, many residents who are "making do" (de Certeau 1984) with nonconforming dwelling practices are also participating in efforts to soften social divisions. Bedouin residents of 'Ayn al-'Azm, like Mufid with his mud-and-tire house, engaged materially in bricolage as they experimented with new possibilities for improving their lives within the uncomfortable structures imposed on their landscapes by state planning. Sarah, with her desert botanicals venture of education, marketing, and heritage tourism, used the resourceful reappropriation and retrospective building typical of bricolage. Some residents also engaged in discursive bricolage. Through innovative juxtapositions, insurgent planters in Twail Abu Jarwal creatively reappropriated and added new connotations to existing symbols of farming, Bedouin traditions, and rootedness. In so doing, they worked to reposition themselves as landowners, producers, and citizens—as farmers who could "green the desert," like other Israelis.

In fact, bricolage is what many disadvantaged members of society do precisely because it makes something new out of a limited set of materials or choices. There was a shade of insurgence in many of these social projects, but none of them was simply resisting "the State" or opposing Israeli society. Rather, they were selectively invoking and seeking admission to this powerful imagined community. While their actions challenge the legitimacy of the discriminatory practices that favor Jewish residents over Bedouin Arabs, they also hail the state for help. Whether striving for recognition of land rights or more socially and ecologically sustainable practices, these boundary challengers generally engaged a politics of softening.

Conclusion

ON A SUMMER AFTERNOON IN 2013, angry voices clashed during a community meeting in a stuffy lecture hall at Beersheba's Etgar Community College. Packed in every seat, squatting on stairs, and standing in the aisles, residents of the Negev had gathered to debate a recently announced government plan to establish ten new settlements for Jewish residents in the northern Negev. Maxim Oknin, advocate of the plan and a deputy mayor of Arad, another city in the Negev, promised that the new communities would strengthen the struggling peripheral city by "bring[ing] order to Bedouin settlement" and bringing "strong residents from the center [of Israel]" who would build up Arad's schools and business sector. Many audience members criticized the project's price tag and its condescending assumption that residents needed guidance from Tel Avivans. "Zionism costs money, my friends," Maxim responded. "In the Negev, it is clear that it is one large Wild West. Someone has to put an end to this Wild West." The Negev was still a frontier, in Maxim's response, which reinforced the call on Zionism to tame the wilderness through association with the United States' historic frontier mission.

Meanwhile, a government proposal to "regularize" Bedouin settlement in the Negev, known as the Prawer Plan, had passed a first reading in the Knesset and awaited the second and third readings that would determine if it became law. The plan would recognize some existing Bedouin villages, use law enforcement to move residents of other villages to planned townships, and establish a final offer of resettlement and partial compensation for unresolved land ownership claims (Begin 2013). Bedouin residents of unrecognized villages and their advocates contended that the bill violated the civil and human rights of Bedouin citizens by planning to forcibly relocate thirty thousand or more from their current homes. Advocates of Zionist settlement in the Negev, on the other hand, opposed the bill for "giving away" state land to illegal Bedouin squatters.

At the community meeting, some speakers contrasted these two plans, describing the simultaneous expulsion of rural Bedouin residents and the incentives for Jewish residents to create new rural communities on the same plots of land as racist and insulting to Bedouin citizens. Samir explained how his family was uprooted from their lands in 1956 and moved by the military to a plot of land where they had lived since then and knew as the village of 'Atir. But then the government planned a new town (*yishuv*) "on my house!" he shouted angrily. "Why do they uproot a town just because they're all Arabs? Why!"[1] The meeting's emcee joined in to ask Maxim, "Let's say there is a need for ten towns between Beersheba and Arad. If there is a town already, why not just recognize it?" Maxim resisted Samir's frame of fairness and evaluated 'Atir in terms of legality. "The word 'town' [*yishuv*] is the problem. . . . What is called a 'town,' I say unequivocally . . . that it is an illegal, partisan settlement, from the Wild West; it needs to be evacuated. Period." The phrasing was all too familiar to Bedouin land-rights activists, who have long struggled against such references to legality that ignore how laws are socially constructed to benefit particular groups and how socioenvironmental assumptions undergird this social construction.

Others addressed the contrast with irony. Ra'ed, Bustan's director, stated, "I think Zionism is the solution, really. . . . Like the residents who don't want to join Arad . . . the Bedouins will also be Zionists and stay in their own [rural] place . . . and the government should finance them." As he trailed off, searching for the right words, several panelists joined in agreement: "I wanted to ask, if a Bedouin contractor builds a single-family home in Dimona [a Jewish development town], is he a Zionist?" Erez, a panelist and Jewish Israeli academic, predicted wryly at the end of the discussion that all this worry about the effects of the ten new settlements was pointless, because the government did not actually plan to build towns. They only wanted to create "a planning reality," he predicted, to block any efforts to recognize Bedouin villages in the area.

This all happened four years after I completed the primary fieldwork for this book. Well-worn binary oppositions between Jew and Arab, progress and tradition, and culture and nature wove through the discussion in implicit and explicit ways. These same oppositions were powerful in shaping the early Zionist movement, in justifying the *siyag* and subsequent land laws attenuating Bedouin Arabs' holds on land, and in creating the planned communities for Jewish immigrants of the 1950s. They continued to be powerfully evident in these more recent development plans and in residents' reactions to them. As I drove with a Bedouin colleague back to 'Ayn al-'Azm from the meeting, we discussed how "the more things change, the more they stay the same."

Integrated Planning

Land claims have become the focal point for a panoply of social conflicts in Israel. This meeting in 2013 demonstrated the tenacity of entrenched social and spatial divisions that I observed from 2007 to 2009, and which have been developing over many decades. This book has explored how such divisions are reinforced through historically constructed environmental discourses that manifest themselves in words, residential patterns, and government structures. Within these discourses, nested binary oppositions guide how Negev residents think, talk, interact with one another, build homes, govern, and are governed. As a result, Dganim and 'Ayn al-'Azm became very different places to live, and residents developed divergent relationships with the Israeli government and with each other. To the extent that individuals' understandings of these places and their people are shaped within the context of these discourses and the physical landscapes of segregation they have built, these same oppositions also place blinders on how people understand the world, limiting the possibilities they can imagine for other, less conflictive social and environmental relations. Knesset members, for example, understood residents of unrecognized Bedouin settlements and residents of Jewish single-family farmsteads as fundamentally different kinds of people who required distinct solutions.

But the ethnography and analysis in this book also point to useful tools for moving past such stubborn entrenchment. On a procedural level, this study suggests that integrating planning and development decisions for Jewish and Bedouin communities in the Negev would be useful in troubling these persistent binaries. The goal of such integration would not be to create a one-size-fits-all solution, but to distinguish between differences in planning that stem from residents' priorities and desired dwelling practices and those created by political marginalization or by naturalized but anachronistic assumptions of difference. Recent Negev development efforts demonstrate both the difficulty and necessity of such an approach.

Contemporary efforts to solve the Negev's social problems and land claims continue to reveal the widespread understanding that it is only "natural" to do so through segregation. All proposals with government or popular backing, including the Prawer Plan and the proposal to strengthen Arad with new Jewish communities, assume the continued residential segregation of Jews and

Arabs. Plans for Bedouin and Jewish settlement in the Negev continue to be compartmentalized in different government agencies and different Knesset debates. Government spokespeople promise that Jewish settlement in the Negev will strengthen civil society. In contrast, whether in the heated words of Maxim describing Bedouin residents as making the Negev a "Wild West" or in the more measured statements of the Prawer Plan's public consultant, Ze'ev Begin (2013), government representatives frame Bedouins as backward and in need of plans like Prawer to help them "leap through time into the 21st century."

This kind of binary thinking about social groups, when laid onto contested land, melds binaries that are not necessarily parallel, thus hardening lines of contestation. Social separations become taken for granted and naturalized into the divided landscapes. This nested binary thinking, which has solidified Arab-Jewish divisions in the Negev, has similarly petrified land and resource conflicts around the world. This is the case in contexts with a colonial history, such as Zimbabwe, where agrarian livelihoods, land ownership, and structures of local and national governance continue to be shaped by the racialized oppositions drawn during the colonial era (Moore 2005). Social divisions of race and ethnicity often initiate these spatial separations (Kosek 2006; Merlan 1998), but class divisions also become naturalized into segregated landscapes (Escobar 2008; Holston 2008). In Israel, both directly through segregated towns and indirectly through strategic planning and zoning for construction, the driving motivations of Zionist settlement have carved divisions between Jews and Arabs and between purportedly modern and traditional cultures into the material environment.

At the 2013 public meeting in Beersheba, a handful of panelists and vocal audience members challenged the binary framing that separates modern Jews from traditional Arabs. But the suggestion for combined Bedouin-Jewish communities was aired more as a provocation than as a serious suggestion. The representative for the urban planning group, Bimkom, finished his remarks by asking: "Why shouldn't a town be established with Bedouins and Jews together? Why not? What would happen? What is forbidden?" No other panelists or audience members addressed his queries. This refusal to engage with Arab-Jewish social issues in an integrated manner echoed the 2009 Knesset debates of the Negev Development Authority amendments, when several participants called for a joint legislative solution to the plights of both unrecognized village residents and single-family farmstead residents, but the Knesset majority quickly sidelined those calls.

Such integrated planning for Jewish and Bedouin Arab citizens would indeed be difficult to manage, but it would acknowledge the reality that supposedly parallel "dual societies" of Arabs and Jews are in fact intertwined, despite spatial and social segregation. Joining debate, legislation, and policy formation for all the Negev's residents within integrated Knesset committees, land-use planning bodies, and governmental social service agencies would more starkly reveal the inequalities and double standards that are partially masked by bureaucratic boundaries. This would certainly create more friction in the short term, but as Anna Tsing (2005) has suggested, such friction can be used productively for forward momentum.

To create an atmosphere in which sociopolitical friction can be productive, two important truths about experiences of dwelling would need to frame proceedings. First, senses of place matter. Though government officials often claim that plans like Prawer are dispassionate bureaucratic necessities designed simply to bring order to the Negev landscape, these plans are in fact just as emotionally, socially, and politically motivated as the Bedouin "dispersal" (*pzura*) they seek to rein in. Negev residents, both Jewish and Bedouin, have demonstrated that their ties to landscapes, in addition to being of economic use, fulfill emotional, ethical, and legal needs and support collective, cultural identities. This is as true for Jewish residents of single-family farmsteads and Bedouin Arab residents of unrecognized villages as it is for residents of planned settlements like Dganim or 'Ayn al-'Azm. Attending to senses of place matters for the humanistic endeavor of understanding and empathizing with a wider arc of the human experience in this conflict zone. Examining the micropolitics of dwelling in conflictive landscapes illuminates what it is like to live in such places, to dwell in politics. This kind of ethnographic insight can open paths for empathy, if neighbors across fences and *wadis* can understand how each sees contested landscapes and why.

Senses of place also matter for the practical goal of understanding how and why residents react to changes in the taskscapes and landscapes in which they live. This can be seen clearly in the case studies of Dganim and 'Ayn al-'Azm, where very different senses of belonging shaped residents' reactions to the involvement of state agencies in each town. In Dganim, even when the government employed top-down and paternalistic means (as in administration approaches for *moshvei olim*), residents felt like participants in place-building, and they acted accordingly. In contrast, 'Ayn al-'Azm residents felt alienated from their town; they viewed governmental interventions with suspicion and often resisted zoning and regulations through a variety of mostly nonconfrontational means. Planning and legislation that take account of these senses of place will be more attentive to how residents are already shaping—and trying to shape—their landscapes through their dwelling practices, and therefore more likely to implement feasible plans.

The second recognition that can help to make sociopolitical friction constructive is a corollary of the understanding that place matters: history matters. This study has shown the paradoxical invisibility and hypervisibility of historical forces and events in land contestations. Viewers of a landscape selectively see taskscapes. In cases of land conflict, ignoring large-scale, institutional participants in local taskscapes can have profound consequences. This selective sight and its ramifications are clear in the comparative analysis of two sets of "illegal" settlements in the Negev. A partial history of the Bedouin villages that highlighted their lack of historic farming but ignored the role of Israeli military forces in moving and resettling residents in the 1950s facilitated unswerving declarations in the courts of their illegality, whereas a reframing of Jewish farmsteaders as Zionist pioneers facilitating long-term government priorities allowed them to achieve legality. Some individuals, like Bedouin Arab residents narrating a richly historical Naqab, and advocacy NGOs, like Bustan, with its Negev Unplugged Tours, attempt to highlight the state and military taskscapes that have shaped the Negev. But these alternative historical accounts are rarely well amplified.

Instead, many Jewish Israelis, particularly voters and government officials not living in the Negev, see a contemporary problem there of sudden and illegal settling. The labels common in governmental discourse, "spontaneous settlements" (*hityashvut spontanit*) or "dispersal" (*pzura*), assert their recency and erase the social history that built them. Such ahistorical framing ignores the roles of government policies like the relocation of Bedouin Arabs to the *siyag* and the exclusion of Bedouins from small Jewish communities. It makes the Negev's current segregation seem natural. Viewing each unrecognized house solely as the result of a resident's unlicensed actions allows commentators like Maxim to assert its unequivocal illegality. In fact, as this study has demonstrated, a long chain of institutional, extralocal actors has participated in these processes, along with local residents. Keeping this historical construction of landscapes in view is necessary for assigning responsibility more fairly and for seeing current landscapes of segregation not as natural, but rather as socially constructed.

At the same time, the selective hypervisibility of history serves as a tool of contention, as land claimants compete to assert longer-term historical ties to place. Selectively acknowledging or denying landscape histories is a common tactic of land conflict (Heatherington 2010; Nadasdy 2003). Jake Kosek's observation in the American Southwest that "the past is a vibrant but volatile site for contemporary land and forest politics" (2006:34) also holds true in the Negev, as residents' oppositional historical narratives attest. Participants on opposing sides of land conflict claim historical attachments that predate recent contestations. However, as the comparison of unrecognized villages and single-family farmsteads demonstrates, some historical land uses are more valued than others, and identity politics strongly shape whose dwelling practices are interpreted as contributions to the nation-state and whose as obstacles. Audience members at the 2013 public meeting saw this pattern continue. Bedouin commenters repeatedly asserted their status as "citizens," as participants in Israel's military defense, and as those who "support the economy [of Arad]." Jewish residents' basis for belonging is not questioned, however, and so they do not need to make a case for it in debates like these. Any discussion of contemporary land use must negotiate the contradictory time depths and historical narratives that assert the belonging of some citizens and deny the belonging of others.

Softening Boundaries

While these shifts in governmental perspectives and practices would shake up the chronic segregation of the status quo in potentially beneficial ways, they are not likely to occur in the near future because conflictive binaries remain so deeply seated in the debates and landscapes of the Negev. Before national land-use policies can be nonconflictive cooperative endeavors, it must be conceivable for Bedouin Arabs and Jews to be coparticipants not only in a regional economy, but also in place-making and even nation-building. For this reason, the work of Bustan, other NGOs, and Negev residents who have been working to change the status quo of simmering conflict and repressive inequalities is crucial.

Unlike other sorts of land conflicts, such as struggles over wildlife parks or mining operations (Heatherington 2010; Kirsch 2014; Tsing 2005; West 2006), which pit international actors against local residents, people on all sides of this land conflict are claiming home. The emotional attachments forged while building homes and communities, whether over fifty or five hundred years, can escalate land competition. However, the home ties of opponents in the Negev's divided landscape can also open the way for the more intimate engagements of social change agents like Sarah in 'Ayn al-'Azm or Bustan. Addressing Jewish and Bedouin residents as neighbors, these efforts seek the change not of radical revolutions, but of incremental modification. They offer unexpected juxtapositions of and small additions to dominant discourses. These are attempts to soften boundaries, not tear them apart.

Hints of this boundary-softening work were also evident in public debate about the Prawer Plan and establishing new settlements. The 2013 public meeting was cooperatively hosted by eight NGOs that take very different approaches to working on social justice, civil rights, and environmental issues. They share the desire to get more Negev residents involved in the discussion of governmental land-use plans. While much of the discussion reinforced binary oppositions, the event also highlighted the potential of activism to cultivate new language and affective stances (e.g., Gibson-Graham 2006). Some audience members and panelists brought attention to the social construction of social and physical boundaries that binary enframing typically obscures. Several speakers repeatedly corrected statements about spontaneous settlement and squatting by pointing out the state's role in displacing Bedouins from their previous homes. One Jewish immigrant from Argentina brought sociolinguistic analysis to the debate: "The Bedouin residents in the Negev, they are not the 'Bedouin problem,'" he began, and then compared this labeling to the alienating treatment of Jews in Argentina that prompted him to emigrate. Noting shared experiences of discrimination as a basis for cooperation, the speaker suggested that "if we embrace the Negev, the Negev will embrace us."

Both emotional appeals, like this Argentine immigrant's, and ironic comparisons, like Ra'ed's and Erez's above, present troubling juxtapositions that highlight not just the existence of binary divisions, but their "unnaturalness." This Argentine speaker pushes us to ask, Why should ethnicity be more important than shared suffering in determining social belonging? And Ra'ed, in his comments, implicitly inquires, Why should ethnicity trump the hard work of establishing homes and communities, which Zionism recognizes among Jewish pioneers?

This ethnography's journey through organized activism and the less formal social projects of making do, *sumud* (steadfastness), and insurgent building and planting suggests that small-scale politics and boundary softening play an important role in Israeli social change. By striving to unsettle binary oppositions between nature and culture, tradition and progress, Arab and Jew, the people engaged in these projects seek not to erase difference but to multiply it and open possibilities for exchange and learning across what are currently rigid social boundaries. Activists elsewhere, like the indigenous and black Colombians with whom Arturo Escobar (2008) has worked and the Indonesian participants in community forestry whom Anna Tsing (2005) describes, have shown how social difference can be used as a basis of dialogue and coalition-building rather than distancing. In Colombia, the consolidation and governmental recognition of black communities as groups with a distinctive cultural background facilitated their inclusion in land-use decision making aimed at the shared national goal of protecting Colombia's unique biodiversity. In Indonesia, participants with disparate sociopolitical and ethnic backgrounds and very different views of a forest and its meanings managed to protect the forest from corporate destruction.

Can boundary-softening social action succeed in establishing enough commonality among Negev residents to allow for productive, equitable cooperation? For brief moments at the 2013 public meeting, Jewish and Bedouin residents found common cause in their peripheral status as Negev residents. Panelists and audience members protested this new settlement plan as an example of the occasional, misguided impositions that punctuate the national government's general neglect of the Negev. Bustan's struggles to build lasting coalitions and senses of affiliation, however, demonstrate the difficulty of sustaining such commonality.

In divided and unequal social contexts like Israel's, a politics of softening may actually be more radical and harder to sustain than a seemingly more rebellious combative politics. Efforts to soften binary oppositions between Jews and Arabs are far from superficial because these oppositions currently frame Negev social relations so firmly. Yet such a politics faces critics arguing that any efforts not actively aimed at overthrowing a system are, in effect, working to sustain it. In addition, without strong ideological barriers of its own, such a politics risks losing its direction, sliding from the incremental softening of fundamental social divisions to incremental amelioration on a more superficial level. This was the concern that led Bustan not to continue its CPP campaign. Leaders worried that their intended lesson about unequal citizenship would become just another temporary aid program.

However, social change efforts in a context where conflict is already so embedded in the norms of social relations cannot achieve their goals if they simply become part of the ongoing combative process by which Israeli society defines itself. Both the government's proposal of the Prawer Plan and opponents' responses to it exhibit the same old oppositions and divisiveness that have characterized social relations for decades. Unless the nested binaries underlying this conflict can be transcended by a significant portion of the Israeli public and government, developments like the Prawer Plan will only be further blips in ongoing conflict.

Creative projects like Sarah's herb garden and visitors' center, Mufid's mud-and-tire house, and insurgent building and planting in unrecognized villages are taking a step in this process by dwelling in ways that challenge the Negev's typical binary divisions. Grassroots organizations such as Bustan amplify such steps by asking the difficult questions prompted by these projects more loudly. Why should Bedouin Arabs' lifestyles not be considered constructive elements of modern Israeli society? Is ownership the only way we can think about land relations? What if we embed stewardship more deeply in our thinking?

These are difficult questions that reach to the heart of Zionism and Israeli national identity. They raise uncomfortable questions about privilege and injustice and highlight the negative implications of taking Arab-Jewish difference, the primacy of agricultural attachments to land, and territorialism for granted. But projects like Bustan's also show that familiar environmental discourses can be creatively reappropriated to new ends. While parallel questions of belonging, control, and land use trouble every nation-state, they cannot be answered in the abstract. For any resolution of land conflict to be more than an uneasy détente, the difficult, often discriminatory implications of Israel's dominant environmental discourses must be faced. The politics of boundary softening examined here is still only a possibility on the Negev's social fringes. For it to become part of a groundswell of change, this difficult conversation and embodied experiments in new lifestyles must grow to include more of the Negev's—and Israel's—residents.

Glossary

adama   "land" or "soil," as well as "land" as an observable area; the word is semantically distinct from but often politically and socioculturally linked to *aretz* (*see below*) (Hebrew, or H.)

aliyah   "ascent," commonly refers to Jewish immigration to Israel (H.)

aretz   "land" or "country"; *ha-aretz*, "the land" (and also "earth," as in *cadur ha-aretz*, "the globe/Earth") (H.)

'arisha   a gathering space for the women of the household and their visitors (Arabic, or A.)

'ashira   tribe or extended family (A.)

Ashkenazi   a Jewish person identifying with European ancestry (plural, Ashkenazim); also an adjective (e.g., Ashkenazi Jew) (H.)

bedaawa   Bedouinness (A.)

chalutz   pioneer, especially referring to an early Zionist pioneer farmer (plural, *chalutzim*) (H.)

dira   a well-defined territory within which a tribe or group migrates (A.)

dunam   area of land, approximately one-quarter acre (originally Turkish, now A./H.)

eda   ethnic group, generally used to distinguish between Jewish ethnic groups (plural, *edot*) (H.)

Eretz Israel   "The Land of Israel," a biblical name for a geographical area wider than but including present-day Israel

fallah   (Palestinian peasant) farmer (plural, *fallahin*) (A.)

Iyur HaBedowim   "Urbanization of the Bedouin," an Israeli governmental policy initiated in the 1960s (H.)

'izbe   camp or retreat (*see Chapter 3 for a more specific usage*) (A.)

kehilatiut   community spirit and activity, a sense of community (H.)

kibbutz   a collective or formerly collective agricultural community (H.)

Mizrahi   a Jewish person identifying with Middle Eastern or North African ancestry (plural, Mizrahim); also an adjective (e.g., Mizrahi Jew) (H.)

moshav   a type of cooperative agricultural community, less economically and socially collective than a *kibbutz* (plural, *moshavim*) (H.)

moshav olim   immigrants' *moshav* (plural, *moshvei olim*) (H.)

pzura   dispersal, used by some to refer to Bedouin settlement outside recognized townships (H.)

saaj   large, flat bread baked on a convex piece of metal over a fire (A.)

sabr   patience (A.)

sabra   a Jew who was born in Palestine during the *yishuv* period (*see below*), especially during the 1930s and through the end of World War II (H.)

Shabbat   Saturday, the Jewish day of rest (H.)

siyag   fence, enclosure; a specific area of enclosure in the northern Negev (H./A.)

sumud   steadfastness, also political resistance (A.)

Tabo   deed of ownership, from the Ottoman-era Turkish word for "deed" (A./H.)

Tanakh   Hebrew Bible

wadi   seasonal stream bed (A.)

yishuv   time period beginning with the initiation of Zionist immigration to Palestine (1890s) and ending with the establishment of the Israeli state; also designates the society of Jews living in Palestine at this time (H.)

Notes

Introduction

Map created by Steve Charlton, based on source materials from Diva-GIS (www.diva
-gis.org), MapCruzin (www.mapcruzin.com/free-israel-country-city-place-gis-shapefiles
.htm), Natural Earth (www.naturalearthdata.com), and The Arab Bedouin Villages in
the Negev-Naqab (www.dukium.org/map/).

1. The region, "Naqab" in Arabic and "Negev" in Hebrew, is most often referred to
in English as Negev.

2. See Swirski and Hasson (2006). In addition to seven existing townships, nine
other communities gained statutory recognition under the Abu Basma Regional Council (formed in 2005), but little integration through municipal services, infrastructure, or
local elections has occurred.

3. A growing literature addresses unrecognized villages in terms of historical land
use (Falah 1985; Abu-Saad 2008; Swirski and Hasson 2006); citizenship, nationalism,
and human rights (Gottlieb 2008; Kressel 2003; Schechla 2001; Yiftachel 2009a); and
practical and legal effects of these unrecognized settlements on Israeli society (Abu-
Bader and Gottlieb 2008; Shamir 1996; Yiftachel 2009b).

4. Legal suits have pressured the government to provide some services in unrecognized villages—several primary schools, wellness clinics, and "minimum water"—by asserting basic rights to education and health care that Israel acknowledges for all citizens
(HC 4671/98, Abu-Frech, et al. v. The Education Authority for the Bedouin in the Negev, et
al. [1998]; HC 7116/97, Adalah v. The Health Ministry [1999]; CA 9535/06, Abdullah Abu
Musa'ed, et al. v. The Water Commissioner and the Israel Lands Administration [2011]).

5. For example, one of the first two Israeli civilians killed during the 2014 battles
between Hamas and Israel was a Bedouin Arab man from an unrecognized Negev village. None of these villages are protected by the sirens, bomb shelters, or Iron Dome
missile defense system that protect Jewish municipalities, and news reports and NGO
campaigns took up this man's death as a symbol of the unequal treatment of Palestinian
citizens of Israel, including a lawsuit by the Association of Civil Rights in Israel against
the state to provide protective shelters (Aljazeera 2014; Maan 2014).

6. Other influential "new historians" include Tom Segev (2000), Ilan Pappé (2004), and Hillel Cohen (2010).

7. The term *yishuv* describes the society of Jews living in Palestine between the initiation of Zionist immigration to Palestine and the establishment of the State of Israel, as well as this time period itself.

8. Eretz Israel, the Land of Israel, is a biblical name for a geographical area broader than, but including present-day Israel.

9. Mainstream histories of Zionism focus on these agricultural settlements, bolstering Zionism's image as an agricultural movement greening the desert. But as other scholars have shown, urban immigrants have been more numerous (Kellerman 1993), and labor competition in factory and construction work, as well as on farms, significantly shaped the *yishuv* society and Jewish-Arab relations (Shafir 1996).

10. Debates were strongest between "practical" Zionists, who sought immediate settlement on whatever portions of Palestine were available, and "political" Zionists, who advocated careful diplomacy to secure a charter from the Ottomans for larger-scale settlement (Kornberg 1993; Laqueur 1989).

11. During the decades immediately following 1948, the newly dispersed Palestinian communities in Israel, Lebanon, Jordan, and elsewhere used different terms for the war (Allan 2007). The term "al-Nakba" became more widespread following the 1967 War (Sa'di and Abu-Lughod 2007).

12. Estimates of the number of Palestinians who left or were driven from their homes range widely, from approximately 500,000 by an "observer sympathetic to Israel" to 940,000 by UN figures, and higher according to a number of Arab sources (Tessler 1994:279). Reasonable estimates for the number of Palestinians remaining resident after hostilities ended range from 125,000 to 150,000 (Tessler 1994).

13. While historians, other scholars, and public leaders aligned with either side initially explained the war through starkly contradictory analyses as the result of either Zionist aggression or the refusal of Arab leaders to accept reasonable compromise, scholars began offering more nuanced, evidence-based analyses by the 1990s. These accounts recognize the importance of interwoven class and ethnic conflicts that had been created and exacerbated during the decades prior to 1948 (Shlaim 1995).

14. By 2013, desalinated seawater was beginning to replace the Negev's Kinneret-drawn water.

15. These plans include the "Southern Project" (1975), the "National Industrial-Zone in the Negev" (1972), the "Southern District Outline Plan" (1981), "The Negev in 2000" (1986), "Negev Progress" (1991) (Teschner 2007), and most recently, "Negev 2015."

16. Military bases and training zones now occupy more than 60% of the region's territory (Teschner, Garb, and Tal 2010). Mining facilities, a nuclear reactor, and the country's only hazardous-waste processing facility were also built in the Negev, extracting the region's natural resources and taking advantage of areas with few Jewish residents.

17. Environmental discourses address the broad question of how people perceive, categorize, and act in the environments around them. Evaluating environmental-*ist* dis-

courses, other authors have taken up the pressing but separate and more specific question of whether noninstrumental and conservationist environmental norms have taken hold in Palestine-Israel (Benstein 2005; Cohen 2011; Schoenfeld 2005).

18. As accounts in the book will demonstrate, this naturalized Jewish-Arab opposition is bound up with broader Orientalist discourses (Said 1978), but is also more specific and more recently entrenched.

19. This treatment of tasks is similar to Bourdieu's (1977) discussion of *habitus*, though with less emphasis on shared class norms and more explicit attention to how tasks shape us and our landscapes.

20. As in English, "landscape" in Arabic (*manzar*, from the verb "to view, gaze") and Hebrew (*nof*, meaning also "high place") is primarily a visual term, with the connotation of a distant observer.

21. Timothy Mitchell describes "enframing" as a variety of practices that "seem to resolve the world's shifting complexity into two simple and distinct dimensions" (1990:566). Though I draw on Mitchell's notion of enframing, I am not concerned specifically with his material/ideological distinction. The binaries I describe defy categorization as either material or ideological, being treated as both in different contexts.

22. The total research period of twenty months included four months of preliminary work in northern Israeli locales.

23. Both place names are pseudonyms. See "A Note on Language" in the front of the book.

24. For example, anthropological works address nation-building and ethnic minorities (Ashkenazi and Weingrod 1987; Deshen and Shokeid 1974; Goldberg 1972) and collective communities (Kushner 1973; Schwartz, Lees, and Kressel 1995; Shepher 1983; Weingrod 1966) among Jews. The anthropological literature on Palestinian Arabs typically treats Bedouins separately from Arabs (from north of the Negev). Ethnographies about Bedouins often focus on tribal structures (Ginat 1987; Kressel 1996; Marx 1967), gender roles (Dinero 2006; Fenster 1999), and nomadism and troubled encounters with modernity (Marx and Shmueli 1984; Meir 1998; Abu-Rabia 2001; Abu-Rabia-Queder 2006; Abu-Saad, Horowitz, and Abu-Saad 2007).

25. Dan Rabinowitz (1997) and Susan Slyomovics (1998) examine uneasy Palestinian and Jewish neighbors in sites in northern Israel. Cédric Parizot (2009) discusses Jewish Israeli and Palestinian interactions across the Separation Barrier around the West Bank. And Maia Hallward (2011) and Marcelo Svirski (2013) consider Jewish-Arab social activism ethnographically.

Chapter 1: Narrating Present Pasts

1. Agriculture never provided more jobs than the service or manufacturing sectors of the economy, nor did it lead Israel's GDP (Kellerman 1993). However, cooperative agricultural settlements established territorial claims, fostered many of Israel's military and political leaders, and provided the role models guiding Jewish Israelis during early statehood (Almog 2000).

2. Scholars debate Bedouins' historical practices of nomadism and sedentism. Compare Emanuel Marx's (1967) account of seasonal movement with Cédric Parizot's

(2001) discussion of dry farming and wage labor with the British in the early 1900s (see also Kressel, Ben David, and Abu Rabia 1991).

3. This contrast of narratives is prevalent in many colonial contexts, as colonizers and colonized vie to define the past of contested landscapes in ways that anticipate a future amenable to their cause (Cronon 1983; Lines 1991).

4. Thorough histories of Zionism from Zionist, revisionist, and post-Zionist perspectives have already been written (e.g., Attias and Benbassa 2003; Kellerman 1993; Laqueur 1989; Levensohn 1941; Piterberg 2008; Shapira 2012; Sternhell 1998).

5. Lands purchased by the JNF prior to 1948 accounted for only about 5.7% of the area of Mandate Palestine (Forman and Kedar 2004:811).

6. This symbolic power is often practiced in colonial contexts (Anderson 1991; Carter 1987; Mitchell 1994).

7. Though women performed physical labor too, the masculine New Hebrew is most emblematic, visualized in posters of brawny men farming and verbalized by Zionist poets and writers (Almog 2000; Berg 2001).

8. Israel is not unique in privileging agriculture over other land uses. American private property was based on the Jeffersonian ideal of the yeoman farmer (Krall 2002; Locke 1988), and Australia's declaration of *terra nullius* denied the land claims of Aboriginal residents in favor of colonial ranchers on similar grounds (Lines 1991; Povinelli 2002). Notably, Australia's High Court overturned the *terra nullius* designation of Aboriginal peoples' lands in 1992.

9. By numerous measures, urban development and service industries (health care, business, and finance services) employed more people and produced more income than agriculture (Kellerman 1993). Collective settlements housed comparatively small numbers and have never been financially self-sufficient, relying instead on donations and, later, on state funds (Sherman and Schwartz 1995).

10. Ben-Gurion may have been alluding to the famous slogan of the Zionist movement, "If you will it, it is no dream," originating from a statement on the title page of Herzl's (1960) *Altneuland*.

11. Ecological nationalism has been mobilized as a more liberal discourse than ethnic nationalism in many places, including South Asia (Cederlöf and Sivaramakrishnan 2006), Eastern Europe (Dawson 1996), and Western Europe (Hamilton 2002).

12. Agriculture's share of the workforce dropped from 6.5% in the 1960s to 1.8% by 2007 (Benvenisti 2000:315), and its contribution to Israel's gross national product decreased from 30% in the 1950s to 3% in the 1990s (Tal 2002:238).

13. This erasure was a common mode of denying coeval status between colonized and colonizers (Fabian 1983).

14. These forceful tactics were accompanied by conciliatory public statements asserting these groups' "determination to live with the Arab people on terms of concord and mutual respect" (as cited in Levensohn 1941:83).

15. After 1950, a majority of immigrants came from non-European countries (Shapira 2012), and more than 80% of immigrants arriving to the Negev were from the Middle East (Weingrod 1966:50).

16. In these decades, the disciplines of sociology and anthropology were taking

shape in Israel, and Jewish Israelis affiliated with state institutions (such as surveillance services) focused on "others at home" (Goodman and Loss 2009).

17. Bedouins of the Naqab, who raised fat-tailed sheep and black goats that could not travel very fast and far, had smaller circuits of movement than groups in more arid regions of Saudi Arabia, Iraq, and Jordan who raised only camels, but seasonal migration was still important for their lifestyle (Bailey 1991).

18. Arab countries of the Middle East also provide numerous examples of sedentarization, though incentives have been as common as coercive tactics (Chatty 2006; Cole 2003; Davis 2000; Abu-Lughod 1986).

19. For contrasting views about the political and ecological causes and effects of this and other herding laws in Israel, see Portnov and Safriel (2004), Olsvig-Whittaker et al. (2006), and Falah (1985).

20. This narrative also echoes common Palestinian nationalist imagery of remaining steadfast on the land and feeling deeply connected to a single place, and Naqab landrights activists have engaged this layered symbolism in creative ways (McKee 2014).

21. While such generalizations may be narrative choices to simplify and focus an account, they also mark a fading tradition in the Naqab. Storytelling and poetry recitation are no longer common, and in the absence of a written tradition recording local events and practices, many young people know only fragments of this information. Practices and material objects within the narrations help to anchor these fragments.

22. Classic anthropological literature also depicts Bedouins in a relationship of symbiotic codependence with their flocks and cites ecological models that stress equilibrium (Marx 1967; Abu-Rabia 2002).

23. Outsiders' observations of Naqab life at the time also challenge a narrative of natural harmony with reports of high rates of disease and mortality (el-Aref 1974).

24. Diana Allan (2007:253) and Sa'di and Abu-Lughod (2007:14–15) report that directly following the war, "Nakba" was not widely used among Palestinians elsewhere, either, because of its connotation of permanence. Instead, until the late 1950s, Palestinians referred to the events of 1948 as *sanat al-hujayl* (the year of escape) or *sanat al-hijra* (the year of migration), with an open connotation of possible return.

25. The British began surveying land occupation in 1920 and initiated a process of settling and recording land claims, but they accounted for only 20% of Palestine's land area by 1948 (Abu Hussein and McKay 2003:108–9).

26. Hillel Cohen (2010) also reports that of the 10% of Negev Bedouins who remained in Israel after 1948, most came from tribes whose leaders agreed to aid Zionist leaders during the war or remain neutral.

27. Israeli citizens labeled as Druze are required to serve in the military, those identified as Bedouin can volunteer, and those labeled as Palestinian are discouraged from enlisting (Kanaaneh 2009). However, Parizot reports that few Bedouins volunteer; "the stereotyped image of Bedouins as eager volunteers for military duty is more of a myth than a reality" (2001:103).

28. Because of its growing weight in international conventions and implication of solidarity with similar groups around the world, the indigenous label can be rhetorically powerful for land claims (Dove 2006). The applicability of the term for Bedouins

in Israel is hotly contested in scholarly literature (e.g., Amara, Abu-Saad, and Yiftachel 2013; Frantzman, Yahel, and Kark 2012). A few Bedouin residents discussed being "indigenous," explicitly (in English) or implicitly by comparison with Native Americans. Most residents, however, did not use this international language of indigeneity to assert their native land ties.

29. Often one individual could be called either *arab* or *bedu*, depending on the speaker's perspective. The political and social implications of each label have shifted across cultural contexts and in different historical periods (Cole 2003; Abu-Lughod 1986).

Chapter 2: Seeking Recognition

This chapter draws on some material also published in Emily McKee, 2015, "Demolitions and Amendments: Coping with Cultural Recognition and Its Denial in Southern Israel," *Nomadic Peoples* 19 (1): 95–119.

1. I use the villages' proper names here because residents are striving to gain recognition for their villages, and these struggles have already been well publicized.

2. Videos made by residents and allies appeared on YouTube (e.g., www.youtube.com/watch?v=ujx56Ky6Xes) and online news sites (e.g., www.guardian.co.uk/world/video/2010/jul/28/palestinian-territories-israel).

3. See Gordon (2010), Hartman (2010), and Sanders (2010).

4. See Abu Hussein and McKay (2003), Forman and Kedar (2004), and Kedar (2003) for discussions of relevant land law within Israel.

5. Similar conflicts over incompatible notions of ownership and land use have arisen in many colonial contexts, where the purportedly universal bases of Western property law (Rose 1994) clash with other standards (Nadasdy 2003; Williams 1986).

6. See, for example, media coverage in *Maan News*, "Israel Demolishes al-Araqib Village Buildings for 80th Time" (http://www.maannews.com/eng/ViewDetails.aspx?id=753872); and from *Inter Press Service*, "Negev Bedouin Resist Israeli Demolitions 'To Show We Exist'" (http://www.ipsnews.net/2015/02/negev-bedouin-resist-israeli-demolitions-to-show-we-exist/).

7. Commentators cite between thirty-nine and fifty unrecognized villages on the basis of differing threshold criteria for distinguishing villages from less formal settlements. In the 1990s, the figure of forty-five villages was publicized by the Regional Council for Unrecognized Villages, a newly established advocacy organization, using an Israeli governmental definition of "village" as a locale with five hundred residents or more. Beginning in 2004, this figure has become more controversial as the Israeli government has begun partially recognizing a number of Bedouin villages.

8. Nine communities that gained statutory recognition under the Abu Basma Regional Council (formed in 2005) saw few improvements such as paved roads, connection to the national electricity grid, or water access.

9. Observations are based on farm visits and interviews at five farmsteads and several published interviews with farmstead managers.

10. Knesset committee debate of NDA amendment May 27, 2010.

11. Precipitation levels are lowest in the Arava Valley of the southeast Negev (25mm annual) and highest in the northwest (200–300mm annual) (Hillel 1982:74).

12. Dayan, *Ha'aretz* interview, July 31, 1963.

13. Since statehood, the Negev region has been divided into regional councils. Until 2003, there were eleven regional councils, all of which governed Jewish communities. Appointed state agencies have administered to Bedouins' affairs, including the provision of health and education services, water infrastructure, and land-use regulations.

14. Scholarly commentators and community activists alike note parallels between the bureaucratic treatment of Bedouin Arabs in Israel and that of indigenous and minority groups elsewhere (Dinero 2010; Abu-Saad 2008; Swirski and Hasson 2006). Bedouin rights advocates often spoke of Native Americans, highlighting the fact that consolidation of Bedouin affairs under separate governmental bodies does not accompany any recognition of sovereignty or treaty rights, as is the case for the Bureau of Indian Affairs in the United States.

15. These include a 1989 proposal by twenty-five sheiks that accepted the general terms of previous government plans but called for higher compensation (Swirski and Hasson 2006), and several plans proposed in recent years by teams of Bedouin Arab residents and urban planners to formalize boundaries and improve infrastructure for individual villages (Meir 2005).

16. Commissions and resolutions from executive, legislative, and judicial branches of government, including an interministerial committee in 1962, the Albeck Commission in 1975, the Negev Land Acquisition Law (Peace Treaty with Egypt) in 1980, the Supreme Court ruling in 1984 on the el-Hawashla case, and the "Land Settlement and Compensation Plan for the Evacuees in the Bedouin Diaspora in the Negev" Cabinet Resolution of 1997, have all resulted in similar stances and recommendations, though with some variation in the level of compensation offered (Swirski and Hasson 2006:200).

17. The initial governmental decision (number 881) to establish the council was made in 2003, but a budget was not assigned until 2005 (Government Secretariat 2005).

18. Bedouin Arabs report widespread employment discrimination from individual employers, and they face structural disadvantages in the frequent requirement of past military service for many stable and well-paid jobs (Swirski and Hasson 2006).

19. On "insurgent planning," see Yiftachel (2009) and Meir (2005) in the context of the Negev, and Sandercock (1999) and Sweet (2010) in other contexts.

20. The Recognition Forum is a coalition of organizations seeking coexistence among Israeli Jews and Arabs and resolution of land conflict in the Negev. Their members include Bustan, Gush Shalom, the Israeli Committee Against House Demolitions, the Negev Coexistence Forum for Civil Equality, and Rabbis for Human Rights, among other groups.

21. This account is based on several interviews, my own attendance at one hearing, and the detailed notes of another hearing published online by a member of Gush Shalom (Keller 2009).

22. However, unlike some multicultural settings, Israel has no provisions for recognizing title on tribal, "aboriginal," or cultural terms (Levine 2010; cf. Nadasdy 2002; Povinelli 2002).

23. JNF. 2008. "Individual Farmsteads in the Negev." http://www.kkl.org.il.

24. The slogan refers to Ben-Gurion's quote celebrating the Negev as a Zionist frontier:

"In the Negev shall be tested the capacity of the people of Israel for science and research" (Ba-negev yvachen kosher ha-maedah v-ha-machkar shel ha-am b-yisrael).

25. Analysis of these Knesset debates of the NDA law is based on transcripts from October 26, 2009; March 16, 2010; and May 27, 2010.

26. Knesset proceedings, October 26, 2009.

27. Ibid.

28. Paul Nadasdy (2003) and Elizabeth Povinelli (2002) offer useful comparative ethnographic accounts of property law in Canada and Australia.

29. A robust literature debates the status of citizenship and democracy in Israel, particularly since the late 1990s (see also Abu Hussein and McKay 2003; Dowty 1999; Ghanem, Rouhana, and Yiftachel 1998; Kook 2000; Rabinowitz 2001).

Bridge: Distant Neighbors

1. During my last month of fieldwork in 2009, the long-promised plans for bus service to Bedouin Arab towns were finally initiated. This system was still separated from the main national routes, with Rahat serving as the hub and providing bus service into Beersheba and several of the recognized Bedouin Arab towns (though none of the unrecognized villages). Over the intervening years, bus connections between Beersheba and the Bedouin Arab towns have been growing too.

2. Such meeting spaces and buffer zones in the Negev receive far too little analytic attention. However, some ethnographic studies address meeting areas outside the Negev, including Rabinowitz's (1997) ethnography of Natzerat Illit, Slyomovic's (1998) examination of Ein Hod/Ayn Hawd, Kanaaneh's (2009) account of Palestinian soldiers in the Israeli military, Parizot's (2009) study of social and economic practices around the West Bank Separation Barrier, and Svirsky's (2013) consideration of Arab-Jewish activism in Israel-Palestine.

Chapter 3: Coping with Lost Land

1. Like the "multiresource economy" (Salzman 1980) identified among Bedouin Arab groups across the Middle East (Marx 1984), this urban adaptation was part of a diversified strategy that relied on family cooperation (Kressel 1984; Marx 1980; Rowe 1999).

2. Often translated as "sanctity" or "sanctuary" from formal Arabic, I generally heard the term *hurma* used colloquially to refer to the women of a family.

3. However, Marx (1980) finds simultaneous individualization and continued economic cooperation within Bedouin lineages.

4. Permaculture is an approach to sustainable land-use design that attempts to mimic relationships found in natural ecologies. It is now a global school of thought and figures prominently in social and environmental activism.

5. Such symbolic marketing of "the past" and Bedouin hospitality has been big business in other Middle East contexts too (Shryock 2004b).

6. This reliance on family for the capital to start a business enterprise, creating a "family firm," is common among Negev Bedouin entrepreneurs (Jakubowska 2000).

7. Similar ventures in the Negev include a cooperative of Bedouin Arab shep-

herds producing organic milk and meat and organizations of women weaving rugs and embroidering.

8. Amna used the Arabic word *thaqaafa* (culture, education, and cultivation) rather than *hadaara* (culture, civilization).

9. This follows a wider trend in which arguments about the need to civilize local residents and prevent environmental degradation are used as justification for colonial and neocolonial interventions (Argyrou 1997; Davis 2005).

Chapter 4: Reforming Community

1. The group generally referred to as "Cochini Jews" actually moved to Israel from five cities in Kerala: Cochin, Ernakulam, Mala, Parur, and Chennamangalum.

2. The Cochin area has been a hub of international trade for centuries, situated along trade routes between Asia, Africa, and the Middle East. Jewish traders were major figures in this trade, which interwove the lives—business and intimate—of Jews, Muslims, and Hindus (Ghosh 1993).

3. Likewise, researchers of the Jewish community in Cochin report that although Jews lived in "voluntary ghettoes" in Indian cities, there were "harmonious relations between the Cochin Jews and all other Malayali-speaking residents" (see also Katz and Goldberg 2005; Koder 1974; Mandelbaum 1975:75).

4. Though the issue of "caste" divisions among Cochini Jews between "white" or Paradesi Jews and dark-skinned individuals whose Jewish heritage was questioned has preoccupied researchers of Indian Jewry (Katz and Goldberg 2005; Mandelbaum 1975), and some memoirists (Daniel and Johnson 1995), these intra-Jewish divisions were absent from Dganim narratives and did not seem important for *moshav* social life.

5. *Edot* translates broadly to "ethnic groups" but is generally used to distinguish only between Jewish ethnic groups.

6. Members of other immigrant groups also identify more strongly with a particular *eda* than with one side of the Mizrahi-Ashkenazi divide (Leichtman 2001). For more on *edot*, see Anteby-Yemini (2004) and Domínguez (1989).

7. *l-hafeakh*, literally, "to turn over," indicates both "to plow" and "to transform."

8. Chaim's and other residents' references to sacrifice as a collective generational task recall a Talmudic text they often cited in brief: "Let all who work for the community do so from a spiritual motive, for then the merit of their fathers will sustain them, and their righteousness will endure forever" (Avot, "Ethics of the Fathers" 2:2).

9. Though all these elderly residents understood Hebrew, their fluency varied. Few younger *moshav* members spoke Malayalam well, but many understood it.

10. This temporary permission is called *shimush horeg*, or "nonconforming use."

Chapter 5: Challenging Boundaries

1. Devorah reported these death threats during an interview, but did not specify their source. As far as I can learn, no physical harm came to anyone involved.

2. As Maia Hallward (2011) notes, this type of "reconfiguration" work became more common among Palestinian-Israeli peace-building groups after 2008 in the midst of increasing unilateralism in Palestinian-Israeli political relations.

3. In land struggles elsewhere, indigenous rights activists reify the identity expectations that marginalized them in the first place (Nadasdy 2003; Sylvain 2005), and both governmental and nongovernmental actors embroiled in conflict over plans for a massive development project may rely on nationalist ideology (Doane 2005).

4. Bustan's annual budget was also small compared to other Israeli NGOs. As a condition of my participation in planning meetings, I agreed not to disclose specific financial figures.

5. bustan.org, 2008.

6. The SPNI derives 40–60% of its budget from the state government in the form of subsidies for school trips (Selwyn 1995).

7. H.C. 8062/05, Enass Al-Atrash, et al. vs. The Ministry of Health, et al., 2005.

8. In 2009, the centrist national government was replaced by a conservative coalition generally acknowledged to be more supportive of Judaization projects and harsher defenders against Bedouin "encroachment" on state lands. Bustan's opting out of media-focused advocacy may also have been prompted by these political developments. Public acknowledgment of Bedouin Arabs' substantive citizenship rights seemed less likely under the new government.

9. For foundational texts on the principles and practices of permaculture, see Mollison and Holmgren (1987); Mollison (1987); Bell (2004).

10. Globally circulating ideologies about the relative value of different sorts of knowledge value the engineer or scientist for the narrow specialization of *techne*, i.e., the mastery and the rigorous application of universal principles, more than the diffuse skills and "gut feeling" of *mētis* (Haraway 1988; Scott 1998). Of course, actual scientists use *mētis* as well as *techne* (Callon 1986; Latour 1987), but the improvisation of *mētis* is discouraged and contained in large-scale planning.

11. While this book was in publication, I learned that Bustan has dissolved as an NGO. The former director informed me that the Eco-Khan continued to operate, but it was no longer led by Bustan. As is common with NGOs, many former Bustan staff members have moved on to work with other environmental and social justice groups.

Conclusion

1. The neighboring villages of 'Atir and Um al-Hiran face government eviction plans in order to create a Jewish town (to be named Hiran) and forest (to be named Yatir Forest).

References

Abbink, Jon. 2000. "Tourism and Its Discontents: Suri–Tourist Encounters in Southern Ethiopia." *Social Anthropology* 8 (1): 1–17.

Abu-Bader, Suleiman, and Daniel Gottlieb. 2008. "Education, Employment and Poverty among Bedouin Arabs in Southern Israel." *HAGAR: Studies in Culture Polity and Identities* 8 (2): 121–35.

Abu Hussein, Hussein, and Fiona McKay. 2003. *Access Denied: Palestinian Land Rights in Israel.* London: Zed Books.

Abu-Lughod, Janet L. 1987. "The Islamic City: Historic Myth, Islamic Essence, and Contemporary Relevance." *International Journal of Middle East Studies* 19 (2): 155–76.

Abu-Lughod, Lila. 1986. *Veiled Sentiments: Honor and Poetry in a Bedouin Society.* Berkeley: University of California Press.

———. 1990. "The Romance of Resistance: Tracing Transformations of Power through Bedouin Women." *American Ethnologist* 17 (1): 41–55.

Abu-Rabia, Aref. 1994. *The Negev Bedouin and Livestock Rearing: Social, Economic and Political Aspects.* Oxford: Berg.

———. 2001. *A Bedouin Century: Education and Development among the Negev Tribes in the 20th Century.* New York: Berghahn Books.

———. 2002. "Negev Bedouin: Displacement, Forced Settlement and Conservation." In *Conservation and Mobile Indigenous Peoples,* edited by Dawn Chatty and Marcus Colchester, 202–11. New York: Berghahn Books.

Abu-Rabia, Safa. 2010. "Memory, Belonging, and Resistance: The Struggle over Place among the Bedouin-Arabs of the Negev." In *Remembering, Forgetting and City Builders,* edited by Tovi Fenster and Haim Yacobi, 65–84. Burlington: Ashgate.

Abu-Rabia-Queder, Sarab. 2006. "Between Tradition and Modernization: Understanding the Problem of Female Bedouin Dropouts." *Folklore* 27 (1): 3–17.

Abu-Saad, Ismael. 2005. "Forced Sedentarisation, Land Rights and Indigenous Resistance: The Palestinian Bedouin in the Negev." In *Catastrophe Remembered: Palestine, Israel and the Internal Refugees: Essays in Memory of Edward W. Said (1935–2003),* edited by Nur Masalha, 113–39. London: Zed Books.

———. 2008a. "Introduction: State Rule and Indigenous Resistance among Al Naqab Bedouin Arabs." *HAGAR: Studies in Culture Polity and Identities* 8 (2): 3–24.

———. 2008b. "Spatial Transformation and Indigenous Resistance: The Urbanization of the Palestinian Bedouin in Southern Israel." *American Behavioral Scientist* 51 (12): 1713–54.

Abu-Saad, Ismael, and Harvey Lithwick. 2000. *A Way Ahead: A Development Plan for the Bedouin Towns in the Negev*. Beersheva: Center for Bedouin Studies and Development, Ben Gurion University.

Abu-Saad, Kathleen, Tamar Horowitz, and Ismael Abu-Saad, eds. 2007. *Weaving Tradition and Modernity*. Beersheva: Center for Bedouin Studies and Development, Ben Gurion University.

Adely, Fida. 2012. *Gendered Paradoxes: Educating Jordanian Women in Nation, Faith, and Progress*. Chicago: University of Chicago Press.

Alexander, Catherine, and Joshua Reno, eds. 2012. *Economies of Recycling: The Global Transformation of Materials, Values and Social Relations*. London: Zed Books.

Aljazeera. 2014. "Israeli Court Rejects Bedouin Request for Bomb Shelter." *The Stream*, July 21. http://stream.aljazeera.com/story/201407212248-0023949.

Allan, Diana K. 2007. "The Politics of Witness: Remembering and Forgetting 1948 in Shatila Camp." In *Nakba: Palestine, 1948, and the Claims of Memory*, edited by Ahmad H. Sa'di and Lila Abu-Lughod, 253–84. New York: Columbia University Press.

Almadar, Staff. 2008. "Some Homes in the Bedouin Unrecognized Villages Have Electricity." *Almadar*. http://almadar.co.il.

Almi, Orly. 2003. *No Man's Land: Health in the Unrecognized Villages in the Negev*. Tel Aviv: Physicians for Human Rights and the Regional Council of Unrecognized Villages of the Negev. http://www.phr.org.il.

Almog, Oz. 2000. *The Sabra: The Creation of the New Jew*. Berkeley: University of California Press.

Amara, Ahmad, Ismael Abu-Saad, and Oren Yiftachel, eds. 2013. *Indigenous (In)Justice: Human Rights Law and Bedouin Arabs in the Naqab/Negev*. Cambridge: Harvard University Press.

Anderson, Benedict. 1991. *Imagined Communities: Reflections on the Origin and Spread of Nationalism*. London: Verso.

Appadurai, Arjun. 1996. *Modernity at Large: Cultural Dimensions of Globalization*. Minneapolis: University of Minnesota Press.

Ardener, Edwin. 1989. "'Remote Areas': Some Theoretical Considerations." In *The Voice of Prophecy and Other Essays*, edited by Malcolm Chapman, 211–23. New York: Blackwell.

Argyrou, Vassos. 1997. "'Keep Cyprus Clean': Littering, Pollution, and Otherness." *Cultural Anthropology* 12 (2): 159–78.

Ashkenazi, Michael, and Alex Weingrod. 1987. *Ethiopian Jews and Israel*. New Brunswick: Transaction.

Attias, Jean-Christophe, and Esther Benbassa. 2003. *Israel, the Impossible Land*. Stanford: Stanford University Press.

Bahloul, Joelle. 1993. "Remembering the Domestic Space: A Symbolic Return of Sephardic Jews." In *Going Home*, edited by Jack Kugelmass, 133–50. Evanston: Northwestern University Press.

———. 1999. "On 'Cabbages and Kings': The Politics of Jewish Identity in Post-Colonial French Society and Cuisine." In *Food in Global History*, edited by Raymond Grew, 92–106. Global History Series. Boulder: Westview Press.

Bailey, Clinton. 1991. *Bedouin Poetry from Sinai and the Negev: Mirror of a Culture*. Oxford: Oxford University Press.

———. 2009. *Bedouin Law from Sinai and the Negev: Justice without Government*. New Haven: Yale University Press.

Baldwin, Elaine. 1972. *Differentiation and Co-Operation in an Israeli Veteran Moshav*. Manchester: Manchester University Press.

Bardenstein, Carol. 1998. "Threads of Memory and Discourses of Rootedness: Of Trees, Oranges and Prickly-Pear Cactus in Israel/Palestine." *Edebiyat* 8: 1–36.

Barzilai, Amnon. 2004. "The Bedouin Intifada: It's Not If, but When." *Haaretz*, May 25. Online edition. http://www.haaretz.com.

Begin, Ze'ev B. 2013. *Regulating Settlement of the Negev Bedouin [hasdarat hityashvut bedouim b'negev]*. State of Israel. http://www.pmo.gov.il.

Bell, Michael. 2004. *Farming for Us All: Practical Agriculture and the Cultivation of Sustainability*. University Park: Pennsylvania State University Press.

Ben-David, Orit. 1997. "Tiyul (Hike) as an Act of Consecration of Space." In *Grasping Land: Space and Place in Contemporary Israeli Discourse and Experience*, edited by Eyal Ben-Ari and Yoram Bilu, 129–46. Albany: SUNY Press.

Ben-Porat, Guy, and Bryan S. Turner. 2011. *The Contradictions of Israeli Citizenship: Land, Religion and State*. New York: Routledge.

Ben-Rafael, Eliezer. 2007. "Mizrahi and Russian Challenges to Israel's Dominant Culture: Divergences and Convergences." *Israel Studies* 12 (3): 68–91.

Benstein, Jeremy. 2005. "Between Earth Day and Land Day: Palestinian and Jewish Environmentalisms in Israel." In *Palestinian and Israeli Environmental Narratives*, edited by Stuart Schoenfeld, 51–74. Toronto: Centre for International and Security Studies, York University.

Benvenisti, Meron. 2000. *Sacred Landscape: The Buried History of the Holy Land since 1948*, translated by Maxine Kaufman-Lacusta. Berkeley: University of California Press.

Berg, Gerry. 2001. "Zionism's Gender: Hannah Meisel and the Founding of the Agricultural Schools for Young Women." *Israel Studies* 6 (3): 135–65.

Biale, David. 1992. "Zionism as an Erotic Revolution." In *People of the Body*, edited by Howard Eilberg-Schwartz, 283–308. Albany: SUNY Press.

Biersack, Aletta, and James B. Greenberg. 2006. *Reimagining Political Ecology*. Durham: Duke University Press.

Biggs, Bruce. 1989. "Humpty-Dumpty and the Treaty of Waitangi." In *Waitangi: Maori and Pakeha Perspectives of the Treaty of Waitangi*, edited by Ian Hugh Kawharu, 300–312. Auckland: Oxford University Press.

Bishara, Amahl. 2003. "House and Homeland: Examining Sentiments about and Claims to Jerusalem and Its Houses." *Social Text* 21 (2): 141–62.

Blady, Ken. 2000. *Jewish Communities in Exotic Places.* Northvale: Jason Aronson.

Bloch, Linda-Renée. 2003. "Who's Afraid of Being a Freier? The Analysis of Communication through a Key Cultural Frame." *Communication Theory* 13 (2): 125–59.

Bloom, Etan. 2011. *Arthur Ruppin and the Production of Pre-Israeli Culture.* Studies in Jewish History and Culture. Leiden: Brill.

Bourdieu, Pierre. 1977. *Outline of a Theory of Practice.* Cambridge: Cambridge University Press.

Braverman, Irus. 2009. *Planted Flags: Trees, Land, and Law in Israel/Palestine.* Cambridge: Cambridge University Press.

Brosius, J. Peter. 1999. "Analyses and Interventions: Anthropological Engagements with Environmentalism." *Current Anthropology* 40 (3): 277–88.

Brous, Devorah. 2007. *Israeli Government Destroys Bedouin Crops.* Israeli Coalition Against House Demolitions. http://www.icahd.org.

Brubaker, Rogers. 1996. *Nationalism Reframed: Nationhood and the National Question in the New Europe.* Cambridge: Cambridge University Press.

———. 2004. *Ethnicity without Groups.* Cambridge: Harvard University Press.

Bryant, Rebecca. 2008. "Writing the Catastrophe: Nostalgia and Its Histories in Cyprus." *Journal of Modern Greek Studies* 26 (2): 399–422.

Bullard, Robert Doyle. 1994. *Unequal Protection: Environmental Justice and Communities of Color.* San Francisco: Sierra Club Books.

Bunten, Alexis Celeste. 2008. "Sharing Culture or Selling Out? Developing the Commodified Persona in the Heritage Industry." *American Ethnologist* 35 (3): 380–95.

Burdick, John. 1995. "Uniting Theory and Practice in the Ethnography of Social Movements: Notes toward a Hopeful Realism." *Dialectical Anthropology* 20: 361–85.

Butler, Judith. 1993. *Bodies That Matter: On the Discursive Limits of "Sex."* New York: Routledge.

Callon, Michel. 1986. "Some Elements of a Sociology of Translation: Domestication of the Scallops and the Fishermen of St Brieuc Bay." In *Power, Action, and Belief: A New Sociology of Knowledge,* edited by John Law, 196–233. London: Routledge.

Campbell, Ben. 2005. "Changing Protection Policies and Ethnographies of Environmental Engagement." *Conservation and Society* 3 (2): 280–322.

Caplan, Neil. 1978. *Palestine Jewry and the Arab Question, 1917–1925.* New York: Routledge.

Carsten, Janet. 1997. *The Heat of the Hearth: The Process of Kinship in a Malay Fishing Community.* Oxford: Clarendon Press.

Carter, Paul. 1987. *The Road to Botany Bay: An Exploration of Landscape and History.* Minneapolis: University of Minnesota Press.

Casey, Edward S. 1996. "How to Get from Space to Place in a Fairly Short Stretch of Time." In *Senses of Place,* edited by Steven Feld and Keith H. Basso, 13–52. Santa Fe: School of American Research Press.

Cederlöf, Gunnel, and K. Sivaramakrishnan. 2006. *Ecological Nationalisms: Nature, Livelihoods, and Identities in South Asia.* Seattle: University of Washington Press.

Chafets, Ze'ev. 1986. *Heroes and Hustlers, Hard Hats and Holy Men: Inside the New Israel.* New York: William Morrow.

Chapin, Jessica. 2003. "Reflections from the Bridge." In *Ethnography at the Border*, edited by Pablo Vila, 1–22. Minneapolis: University of Minnesota Press.

Chatty, Dawn. 2006. *Nomadic Societies in the Middle East and North Africa*. Leiden: Brill.

Checker, Melissa. 2005. *Polluted Promises: Environmental Racism and the Search for Justice in a Southern Town*. New York: NYU Press.

Chetrit, Sami Shalom. 2000. "Mizrahi Politics in Israel: Between Integration and Alternative." *Journal of Palestine Studies* 29 (4): 51–65.

Choy, Timothy K. 2005. "Articulated Knowledges: Environmental Forms after Universality's Demise." *American Anthropologist* 107 (1): 5–18.

Cohen, Hillel. 2010. *Good Arabs*, translated by Haim Watzman. Berkeley: University of California Press.

Cohen, Robin. 1997. *Global Diasporas: An Introduction*. Seattle: University of Washington Press.

Cohen, Shaul. 1993. *The Politics of Planting: Israeli-Palestinian Competition for Control of Land in the Jerusalem Periphery*. Chicago: University of Chicago Press.

———. 2011. "Environmentalism Deferred: Nationalisms and Israeli/Palestinian Imaginaries." In *Environmental Imaginaries of the Middle East and North Africa*, edited by Diana K. Davis and Edmund Burke, 246–64. Athens: Ohio University Press.

Cole, Donald P. 2003. "Where Have the Bedouin Gone?" *Anthropological Quarterly* 76 (2): 235–67.

Cooley, Alexander, and James Ron. 2002. "The NGO Scramble: Organizational Insecurity and the Political Economy of Transnational Action." *International Security* 27 (1): 5–39.

Cooper, Frederick, and Anne Stoler, eds. 1997. *Tensions of Empire: Colonial Cultures in a Bourgeois World*. Berkeley: University of California Press.

Coutin, Susan Bibler. 2003. "Illegality, Borderlands, and the Space of Nonexistence." In *Globalization under Construction: Governmentality, Law, and Identity*, edited by Richard Warren Perry and Bill Maurer, 171–202. Minneapolis: University of Minnesota Press.

Cronon, William. 1983. *Changes in the Land: Indians, Colonists, and the Ecology of New England*. New York: Hill and Wang.

———. 1991. *Nature's Metropolis: Chicago and the Great West*. New York: W. W. Norton.

Daniel, Ruby, and Barbara C. Johnson. 1995. *Ruby of Cochin: An Indian Jewish Woman Remembers*. Philadelphia: Jewish Publication Society.

Davis, Diana. 2000. "Environmentalism as Social Control? An Exploration of the Transformation of Pastoral Nomadic Societies in French Colonial North Africa." *Arab World Geographer* 3 (3): 182–98.

———. 2005. "Potential Forests: Degradation Narratives, Science, and Environmental Policy in Protectorate Morocco, 1912–1956." *Environmental History* 10 (2): 211–38.

Davis, Diana, and Edmund Burke, eds. 2011. *Environmental Imaginaries of the Middle East and North Africa*. Athens: Ohio University Press.

Dawson, Jane I. 1996. *Eco-Nationalism: Anti-Nuclear Activism and National Identity in Russia, Lithuania, and Ukraine*. Durham: Duke University Press.

De Certeau, Michel. 1984. *The Practice of Everyday Life*. Berkeley: University of California Press.

De Cesari, Chiara. 2010. "Creative Heritage: Palestinian Heritage NGOs and Defiant Arts of Government." *American Anthropologist* 112 (4): 625–37.

Degen, A. Allan. 2003. "Roles of Urbanised Negev Bedouin Women within Their Households." *Nomadic Peoples* 7 (December): 108–16.

Della Porta, Donatella, Massimiliana Andretta, Lorenzo Mosca, and Herbert Reiter. 2006. *Globalization from Below: Transnational Activists and Protest Networks*. Minneapolis: University of Minnesota Press.

Dennison, Jean. 2014. "Whitewashing Indigenous Oklahoma and Chicano Arizona: 21st-Century Legal Mechanisms of Settlement." *PoLAR* 37 (1): 162–80.

de-Shalit, Avner. 1995. "From the Political to the Objective: The Dialectics of Zionism and the Environment." *Environmental Politics* 4 (1): 70–87.

Deshen, Shlomo A., and Moshe Shokeid. 1974. *The Predicament of Homecoming*. Ithaca: Cornell University Press.

Dinero, Steven C. 2002. "Image Is Everything: The Development of the Negev Bedouin as a Tourist Attraction." *Nomadic Peoples* 6 (1): 69–94.

———. 2006. "Women's Roles, Polygyny and Cultural Transformation in Negev Bedouin Townships: A Gendered Landscape of National Resistance to Post-Colonial Conquest and Control." In *Nomadic Societies in the Middle East and North Africa: Entering the 21st Century*. Leiden: Brill.

———. 2010. *Settling for Less: The Planned Resettlement of Israel's Negev Bedouin*. New York: Berghahn Books.

Doane, Molly. 2005. "The Resilience of Nationalism in a Global Era: Megaprojects in Mexico's South." In *Social Movements: An Anthropological Reader*, edited by June C. Nash, 187–202. Malden: Wiley-Blackwell.

Doleve-Gandelman, Tsili. 1987. "The Symbolic Inscription of Zionist Ideology in the Space of Eretz Yisrel: Why the Native Israeli Is Called *Tsabar*." In *Judaism Viewed from Within and from Without: Anthropological Studies*, edited by Harvey E. Goldberg, 257–84. Albany: SUNY Press.

Domínguez, Virginia R. 1989. *People as Subject, People as Object: Selfhood and Peoplehood in Contemporary Israel*. Madison: University of Wisconsin Press.

Dove, Michael R. 2006. "Indigenous People and Environmental Politics." *Annual Review of Anthropology* 35 (1): 191–208.

Dowty, A. 1999. "Is Israel Democratic? Substance and Semantics in the 'Ethnic Democracy' Debate." *Israel Studies* 4 (2): 1–15.

Drori, Israel. 2009. *Foreign Workers in Israel: Global Perspectives*. Albany: SUNY Press.

Ein-Gil, Ehud. 2009. "Zionism and Oriental Jews: A Dialectic of Exploitation and Co-optation." *Race and Class* 50 (3): 62–76.

el-Aref, Aref. 1974. *Bedouin Love, Law, and Legend: Dealing Exclusively with the Badu of Beersheba*. New York: AMS Press.

Elon, Amos. 1971. *The Israelis: Founders and Sons*, 1st ed. New York: Holt, Rinehart and Winston.

Escobar, Arturo. 2001. "Culture Sits in Places: Reflections on Globalism and Subaltern Strategies of Localization." *Political Geography* 20 (2): 139–74.

———. 2008. *Territories of Difference: Place, Movements, Life*, Redes. Durham: Duke University Press.

Fabian, Johannes. 1983. *Time and the Other: How Anthropology Makes Its Object*. New York: Columbia University Press.

Falah, Ghazi. 1983. "The Development of the 'Planned Bedouin Settlement' in Israel 1964–1982: Evaluation and Characteristics." *Geoforum* 14 (3): 311–23.

———. 1985a. "How Israel Controls the Bedouin in Israel." *Journal of Palestine Studies* 14 (2): 35–51.

———. 1985b. "The Spatial Pattern of Bedouin Sedentarization in Israel." *GeoJournal* 11 (4): 361–68.

Falah, Ghazi-Walid, and Caroline Nagel, eds. 2005. *Geographies of Muslim Women: Gender, Religion, and Space*. New York: Guilford Press.

Feld, Steven, and Keith H. Basso, eds. 1996. *Senses of Place*. Santa Fe: School of American Research Press.

Feldman, Ilana. 2007. "The Quaker Way: Ethical Labor and Humanitarian Relief." *American Ethnologist* 34 (4): 689–705.

Fenichel, Deborah. 2005. "Exhibiting Ourselves as Others: Jewish Museums in Israel." Doctoral diss., Indiana University.

Fenster, Tovi. 1999. "Space for Gender: Cultural Roles of the Forbidden and the Permitted." *Environment and Planning D: Society and Space* 17 (2): 227–46.

Fisher, William F. 1997. "Doing Good? The Politics and Antipolitics of NGO Practices." *Annual Review of Anthropology* 26: 439–64.

Forman, Geremy, and Alexandre Kedar. 2004. "From Arab Land to 'Israel Lands': The Legal Dispossession of the Palestinians Displaced by Israel in the Wake of 1948." *Environment and Planning D: Society and Space* 22: 809–30.

Fortun, Kim. 2001. *Advocacy after Bhopal: Environmentalism, Disaster, New Global Orders*. Chicago: University of Chicago Press.

Foucault, Michel. 1977. *Discipline and Punish: The Birth of the Prison*. New York: Pantheon Books.

———. 1990. *The History of Sexuality*. New York: Vintage Books.

Frantzman, Seth J., Havatzelet Yahel, and Ruth Kark. 2012. "Contested Indigeneity: The Development of an Indigenous Discourse on the Bedouin of the Negev, Israel." *Israel Studies* 17 (1): 78–104.

Furani, Khaled, and Dan Rabinowitz. 2011. "The Ethnographic Arriving of Palestine." *Annual Review of Anthropology* 40 (1): 475–91.

Gal, Susan. 1995. "Lost in a Slavic Sea: Linguistic Theories and National Images in 19th Century Hungary." *Pragmatics* 5 (2): 155–66.

Ganim, As'ad, Nadim Rouhana, and Oren Yiftachel. 1998. "Questioning 'Ethnic Democracy': A Response to Sammy Smooha." *Israel Studies* 3 (2): 253–67.

Gardner, Andrew. 2005. "The New Calculus of Bedouin Pastoralism in the Kingdom of Saudi Arabia." In *Political Ecology Across Spaces, Scales, and Social Groups*, edited by Susan Paulson and Lisa L. Gezon, 76–93. New Brunswick: Rutgers University Press.

Geschiere, Peter, and Stephen Jackson. 2006. "Autochthony and the Crisis of Citizenship:

Democratization, Decentralization, and the Politics of Belonging." *African Studies Review* 49 (2): 1–7.

Ghosh, Amitav. 1993. *In an Antique Land*. New York: A.A. Knopf.

Gibson-Graham, J. K. 2006. *A Postcapitalist Politics*. Minneapolis: University of Minnesota Press.

Ginat, Joseph. 1987. *Blood Disputes among Bedouin and Rural Arabs in Israel*. Pittsburgh: University of Pittsburgh Press.

———. 1997. *Blood Revenge: Family Honor, Mediation and Outcasting*. Brighton: Sussex Academic Press.

Ginat, Joseph, and Anatoly M. Khazanov. 1998. *Changing Nomads in a Changing World*. Brighton: Sussex Academic Press.

Glazer, Penina M., and Myron Glazer. 1998. *The Environmental Crusaders: Confronting Disaster and Mobilizing Community*. University Park: Pennsylvania State University Press.

Golan, Avirama. 2008. "Texas-Style Pioneers." *Haaretz*, April 23. http://www.haaretz.com.

Goldberg, Eliezer, Yoram Bar Sela, Bilha Givon, Yossi Shai, Dudu Cohen, Sharon Gamsho, Faisal el-Huzayel, and Ahmad el-Asad. 2008. *Report of the Goldberg Commission*. http://www.pmo.gov.il.

Goldberg, Harvey E. 1972. *Cave Dwellers and Citrus Growers: A Jewish Community in Libya and Israel*. Cambridge: Cambridge University Press.

Goodman, Yehuda, and Joseph Loss. 2009. "The Other as Brother: Nation Building and Ethnic Ambivalence in Early Jewish-Israeli Anthropology." *Anthropological Quarterly* 82 (2): 477–508.

Gordon, Neve. 2010. "Ethnic Cleansing in the Israeli Negev." *Guardian*, July 28. Online edition. http://www.guardian.co.uk.

Gordon, Neve, and Erez Tzfadia. 2008. "Outsourcing Zionism." *In These Times*, February 7. www.inthesetimes.com.

Gottlieb, Nora. 2008. "Reconstruction: The Voices of Bedouin-Arab Women on the Demolition of Their Homes in the Unrecognized Villages of the Negev." *HAGAR: Studies in Culture Polity and Identities* 8 (2): 47–62.

Government Secretariat. 2005. "Completion of the Budget for the Abu Basma Regional Council (no. 3956)." http://www.pmo.gov.il.

Graeber, David. 2012. "Afterword: The Apocalypse of Objects—Degradation, Redemption and Transcendence in the World of Consumer Goods." In *Economies of Recycling: The Global Transformation of Materials, Values and Social Relations*, edited by Catherine Alexander and Joshua Reno, 277–90. London: Zed Books.

Gray, John. 1999. "Open Spaces and Dwelling Places: Being at Home on Hill Farms in the Scottish Borders." *American Ethnologist* 26 (2): 440–60.

Grossman, Ronit. 2004. "Tourism and Change in a Galilee Kibbutz: An Ethnography." In *Consumption and Market Society in Israel*, edited by Yoram S. Carmeli and Kalman Applbaum, 61–70. Oxford: Berg.

Grove, Richard H. 1995. *Green Imperialism: Colonial Expansion, Tropical Island Edens, and the Origins of Environmentalism, 1600–1860*. Cambridge: Cambridge University Press.

Guha, Ramachandra, and Juan Martinez-Alier. 1997. *Varieties of Environmentalism: Essays North and South.* New York: Earthscan.

Hallward, Maia Carter. 2011. *Struggling for a Just Peace: Israeli and Palestinian Activism in the Second Intifada.* Gainesville: University Press of Florida.

Hamilton, Paul. 2002. "The Greening of Nationalism: Nationalising Nature in Europe." *Environmental Politics* 11 (2): 27–48.

Hananel, Ravit. 2012. "The End of Agricultural Supremacy: The 2009 Reform of Israel's National Land Policy." *Israel Studies Review* 27 (2): 143–65.

Haraway, Donna J. 1988. "Situated Knowledges: The Science Question in Feminism and the Privilege of Partial Perspective." *Feminist Studies* 14 (3): 575–99.

Harel, Israel. 2010. "Green Extremism Threatens Israel's Future in the Negev." *Haaretz,* November 11, sec. Opinion. http://www.haaretz.com.

Harman, Zena. 1951. "The Assimilation of Immigrants into Israel." *Middle East Journal* 5 (3): 303–18.

Hartman, Ben. 2010. "ILA Razes Dozens of Homes in Unrecognized Beduin Village." *Jerusalem Post,* July 28. http://www.jpost.com.

Harvey, David. 1996. *Justice, Nature and the Geography of Difference.* Cambridge: Blackwell.

Heatherington, Tracey. 2010. *Wild Sardinia: Indigeneity and the Global Dreamtimes of Environmentalism.* Seattle: University of Washington Press.

Herder, Johann Gottfried. 1803. *Outlines of a Philosophy of the History of Man,* translated by T. Churchill. London: Luke Hansard.

Herzl, Theodor. 1960. *Altneuland,* 2nd ed. New York: Bloch.

Hewstone, Miles, Mark Rubin, and Hazel Willis. 2002. "Intergroup Bias." *Annual Review of Psychology* 53 (1): 575–604.

Hillel, Daniel. 1982. *Negev: Land, Water, and Life in a Desert Environment.* New York: Praeger.

Hirsch, Eric, and Michael O'Hanlon, eds. 1995. *The Anthropology of Landscape: Perspectives on Place and Space.* Oxford Studies in Social and Cultural Anthropology. Oxford: Oxford University Press.

Holston, James. 2008. *Insurgent Citizenship: Disjunctions of Democracy and Modernity in Brazil.* Princeton: Princeton University Press.

Hopkins, Nicholas S., ed. 2003. *The New Arab Family.* Cairo: American University in Cairo Press.

Horner, Deborah Frenkel. 1982. "Planning for Bedouin: The Case of Tel Sheva." *Third World Planning Review* 4 (2): 159–76.

Hoskins, Janet. 2002. "Predatory Voyeurs: Tourists and 'Tribal Violence' in Remote Indonesia." *American Ethnologist* 29 (4): 797–828.

Ingold, Tim. 2000. *The Perception of the Environment: Essays on Livelihood Dwelling and Skill.* London: Routledge.

———. 2005. "Epilogue: Towards a Politics of Dwelling." *Conservation and Society* 3 (2): 501–8.

Jakubowska, Longina. 2000. "Finding Ways to Make a Living: Employment among the Negev Bedouin." *Nomadic Peoples* 4 (2): 94–105.

Johal, Am. 2008. "The Bedouin Face Dispossession in the Desert." *Rabble.ca*, January. http://www.rabble.ca/.

Jolly, Margaret. 1992. "Banana Leaf Bundles and Skirts: A Pacific Penelope's Web." In *History and Tradition in Melanesian Anthropology*, edited by James G. Carrier, 38–63. Berkeley: University of California Press.

Joseph, Suad. 1999. *Intimate Selving in Arab Families: Gender, Self, and Identity*. Gender, Culture, and Politics in the Middle East. Syracuse: Syracuse University Press.

JTA Wire Service. 2010. "Bedouin Village Reportedly Razed." *Baltimore Jewish Times*, July 28. http://www.jewishtimes.com.

Kabha, Mustafa. 2007. "The Hebrew Online Media's Treatment of Arab Citizens in the Negev." *HAGAR: Studies in Culture Polity and Identities* 7: 159–72.

Kanaaneh, Rhoda. 2002. *Birthing the Nation: Strategies of Palestinian Women in Israel*. Berkeley: University of California Press.

———. 2009. *Surrounded: Palestinian Soldiers in the Israeli Military*. Stanford: Stanford University Press.

Katz, Nathan, and Ellen S. Goldberg. 2005. *Kashrut, Caste, and Kabbalah: The Religious Life of the Jews of Cochin*. New Delhi: Manohar.

Keck, Margaret E., and Kathryn Sikkink. 1998. *Activists Beyond Borders: Advocacy Networks in International Politics*. New York: Cornell University Press.

Kedar, Alexandre. 2001. "The Legal Transformation of Ethnic Geography: Israeli Law and the Palestinian Landholder 1948–1967." *NYU Journal of International Law and Politics* 33: 923–1179.

———. 2003. "On the Legal Geography of Ethnocratic Settler States: Notes towards a Research Agenda." In *Law and Geography*, edited by Jane Holder and Carolyn Harrison, 401–41. Oxford: Oxford University Press.

Kedar, Alexandre, and Oren Yiftachel. 2006. "Land Regime and Social Relations in Israel," edited by Hernando de Soto and Francis Cheneval. *Swiss Human Rights Book 1*, 127–50.

Keller, Adam, trans. 2009. "Nuri el-Okbi's Day in Court." December 12. http://toibill board.info/Okbi_eng.htm.

Kellerman, Aharon. 1993. *Society and Settlement: Jewish Land of Israel in the Twentieth Century*. Albany: SUNY Press.

———. 1996. "Settlement Myth and Settlement Activity: Interrelationships in the Zionist Land of Israel." *Transactions of the Institute of British Geographers* 21 (2): 363–78.

Kelner, Shaul. 2010. *Tours That Bind: Diaspora, Pilgrimage, and Israeli Birthright Tourism*. New York: NYU Press.

Kemp, Adriana, David Newman, Uri Ram, and Oren Yiftachel, eds. 2004. *Israelis in Conflict: Hegemonies, Identities and Challenges*. Brighton: Sussex Academic Press.

Kestler-D'Amours, Jillian. 2013. "Peddling the Myth of the Bedouin 'Take-Over.'" *Haaretz*, July 1. http://www.haaretz.com/opinion/.premium-1.533095.

Kimmerling, Baruch. 1983. *Zionism and Territory: The Socio-Territorial Dimensions of Zionist Politics*. Berkeley: Institute of International Studies, University of California.

Kirsch, Stuart. 2014. *Mining Capitalism: The Relationship between Corporations and Their Critics*. Berkeley: University of California Press.

Kirshenblatt-Gimblett, Barbara. 1998. *Destination Culture: Tourism, Museums, and Heritage*. Berkeley: University of California Press.

———. 2002. "Learning from Ethnography: Reflections on the Nature and Efficacy of Youth Tours to Israel." In *The Israel Experience: Studies in Youth Travel and Jewish Identity*, edited by Harvey Goldberg, Samuel Heilman, and Barbara Kirshenblatt-Gimblett, 267–331. Jerusalem: Melton Centre for Jewish Education.

Knesset. 1992. *Negev Development Authority Law*. http://www.negev.co.il/hok.html.

Knesset Economics Committee. 2009. *Knesset Proceedings: First Reading of the Negev Development Authority Bill (Amendment)*. Jerusalem.

Koder, S. S. 1974. *History of the Jews of Kerala*. Cochin: Chandralekha Printers.

Kook, Rebecca. 2000. "Citizenship and Its Discontents: Palestinians in Israel." In *Citizenship and the State in the Middle East: Approaches and Applications*, edited by Nils A. Butenschøn, Uri Davis, and Manuel Hassassian, 263–87. Syracuse: Syracuse University Press.

Kornberg, Jacques. 1993. *Theodor Herzl: From Assimilation to Zionism*. Bloomington: Indiana University Press.

Kosek, Jake. 2006. *Understories: The Political Life of Forests in Northern New Mexico*. Durham: Duke University Press.

Krall, Lisi. 2002. "Thomas Jefferson's Agrarian Vision and the Changing Nature of Property." *Journal of Economic Issues* 36 (1): 131–50.

Kressel, Gideon M. 1984. "Changes in Employment and Social Accommodations of Bedouin Settling in an Israeli Town." In *The Changing Bedouin*, edited by Emanuel Marx and Avshalom Shmueli, 125–55. New Brunswick: Transaction Books.

———. 1991. "Continuity and Endurance of Patrilineage in Towns." *Middle Eastern Studies* 27 (1): 79–93.

———. 1995. "'He Who Stays in Agriculture Is Not a "Freier"': The Spirit of Competition among Members of the Moshav Is Eroded When Unskilled Arab Labor Enters the Scene." In *Rural Cooperatives in Socialist Utopia: Thirty Years of Moshav Development in Israel*, edited by Moshe Schwartz, Susan H. Lees, and Gideon M. Kressel, 155–83. Westport: Praeger.

———. 1996. *Ascendancy through Aggression: The Anatomy of a Blood Feud among Urbanized Bedouins*. Wiesbaden: Harrassowitz Verlag.

———. 2003. *Let Shepherding Endure: Applied Anthropology and the Preservation of a Cultural Tradition in Israel and the Middle East*. Albany: SUNY Press.

Kressel, Gideon M., Joseph Ben David, and Khalil Abu Rabia. 1991. "Changes in Land Usage in the Negev since the Mid-Nineteenth Century." *Nomadic Peoples* 28: 28–55.

Kushner, Gilbert. 1973. *Immigrants from India in Israel: Planned Change in an Administered Community*. Tucson: University of Arizona Press.

Kymlicka, Will, and Keith G. Banting. 2006. *Multiculturalism and the Welfare State: Recognition and Redistribution in Contemporary Democracies*. Oxford: Oxford University Press.

Lambek, Michael. 2011. "Catching the Local." *Anthropological Theory* 11 (2): 197–221.

Laqueur, Walter. 1989. *A History of Zionism*. New York: Holt, Rinehart and Winston.

Latour, Bruno. 1987. *Science in Action: How to Follow Scientists and Engineers through Society*. Cambridge: Harvard University Press.

Lehn, Walter, and Uri Davis. 1988. *The Jewish National Fund*. London: Kegan Paul International.

Leibovitz-Dar, Sarah. 2006. "Poisoned Land." *Maariv*, November 10. http://www.nrg.co.il.

Leichtman, Mara. 2001. "The Differential Construction of Ethnicity: The Case of Egyptian and Moroccan Immigrants in Israel." *Identity* 1 (3): 247–72.

Levensohn, Lotta. 1941. *Outline of Zionist History*. New York: Scopus.

Levine, Hal B. 2010. "Claiming Indigenous Rights to Culture, Flora, and Fauna: A Contemporary Case from New Zealand." *PoLAR* 33 (May): 36–56.

Lévi-Strauss, Claude. 1966. *The Savage Mind*. Chicago: University of Chicago Press.

Li, Tania Murray. 2000. "Articulating Indigenous Identity in Indonesia: Resource Politics and the Tribal Slot." *Comparative Studies in Society and History* 42 (1): 149–79.

———. 2005. "Beyond 'the State' and Failed Schemes." *American Anthropologist* 107 (3): 383–94.

———. 2007. *The Will to Improve*. Durham: Duke University Press.

Lines, William J. 1991. *Taming the Great South Land: A History of the Conquest of Nature in Australia*. Berkeley: University of California Press.

Lipchin, Clive. 2007. "Water, Agriculture and Zionism: Exploring the Interface Between Policy and Ideology." In *Integrated Water Resources Management and Security in the Middle East*, edited by Clive Lipchin, Eric Pallant, Danielle Saranga, and Allyson Amster, 251–67. Dordrecht: Springer.

Lithwick, Harvey, Yehuda Gradus, and Irwin Lithwick. 1996. "From Frontier to Periphery: The Development of Israel's Negev." In *Frontiers in Regional Development*, edited by Yehuda Gradus and Harvey Lithwick, 143–70. Lanham: Rowman & Littlefield.

Locke, John. 1988. *Two Treatises of Government*, edited by Peter Laslett. Cambridge: Cambridge University Press.

Lockman, Zachary. 1996. *Comrades and Enemies*. Berkeley: University of California Press.

Luong, Pauline Jones, and Erika Weinthal. 1999. "The NGO Paradox: Democratic Goals and Non-Democratic Outcomes in Kazakhstan." *Europe-Asia Studies* 51 (7): 1267–84.

Lynch, Kevin. 1960. *The Image of the City*. Cambridge: Technology Press.

Maan News Agency. 2014. "Israeli Killed, 3 Injured as Rocket Falls near Dimona," July 19. http://www.maannews.net/eng/ViewDetails.aspx?ID=714395.

Mahmood, Saba. 2005. *Politics of Piety: The Islamic Revival and the Feminist Subject*. Princeton: Princeton University Press.

Malkki, Liisa. 1992. "National Geographic: The Rooting of Peoples and the Territorialization of National Identity among Scholars and Refugees." *Cultural Anthropology* 7 (1): 24–44.

Mandelbaum, David G. 1975. "Social Stratification among the Jews of Cochin in India and in Israel." *Jewish Journal of Sociology* 17 (2): 165–210.

Manski, Rebecca. 2006. "Bedouin Vilified among Top 10 Environmental Hazards in Israel." *News from Within*. http://www.alternativenews.org.

Markowitz, Fran. 2006. "Blood, Soul, Race, and Suffering: Full-Bodied Ethnography and Expressions of Jewish Belonging." *Anthropology and Humanism* 31 (1): 41–56.

Mars, Leonard. 1980. *The Village and the State: Administration Ethnicity and Politics in an Israeli Cooperative Village.* Surrey: Gower.

Marx, Emanuel. 1967. *Bedouin of the Negev.* Manchester: Manchester University Press.

———. 1980. "Wage Labor and Tribal Economy of the Bedouin in South Sinai." In *When Nomads Settle: Processes of Sedentarization as Adaptation and Response*, edited by Philip Carl Salzman and Edward Sadala, 111–23. New York: Bergin.

———. 1984. "Economic Change among Pastoral Nomads in the Middle East." In *The Changing Bedouin*, edited by Emanuel Marx and Avshalom Shmueli, 1–15. New Brunswick: Transaction Books.

Marx, Emanuel, and Avshalom Shmueli, eds. 1984. *The Changing Bedouin.* New Brunswick: Transaction Books.

Masalha, Nur. 2007. *The Bible and Zionism: Invented Traditions, Archaeology and Post-Colonialism in Palestine-Israel.* London: Zed Books.

McAdam, Doug, Sidney G. Tarrow, and Charles. Tilly. 2001. *Dynamics of Contention.* Cambridge Studies in Contentious Politics. New York: Cambridge University Press.

McKee, Emily. 2010. "Of Camels and 'Ca-Mail': Engaging Complex Representations of Bedouins in Activism." *Collaborative Anthropologies* 3: 81–92.

———. 2013. "Traveling between Reluctant Neighbors: Researching with Jews and Bedouin Arabs in the Northern Negev." In *Ethnographic Encounters in Israel*, edited by Fran Markowitz, 137–55. Bloomington: Indiana University Press.

———. 2014. "Performing Rootedness in the Negev/Naqab: Possibilities and Perils of Competitive Planting." *Antipode* 46 (5): 1172–89.

———. 2015, "Demolitions and Amendments: Coping with Cultural Recognition and Its Denial in Southern Israel," *Nomadic Peoples* 19 (1): 95–119.

———. 2015. "Trash Talk: Interpreting Morality and Disorder in Negev/Naqab Landscapes." *Current Anthropology* 56: 5: 733–52.

Meir, Avinoam. 1998. *As Nomadism Ends: The Israeli Bedouin of the Negev.* Boulder: Westview Press.

———. 2005. "Bedouin, the Israeli State and Insurgent Planning: Globalization, Localization or Glocalization?" *Cities* 22 (3): 201–15.

Melly, Caroline. 2010. "Inside-Out Houses: Urban Belonging and Imagined Futures in Dakar, Senegal." *Comparative Studies in Society and History* 52 (1): 37–65.

Merlan, Francesca. 1998. *Caging the Rainbow: Places, Politics, and Aborigines in a North Australian Town.* Honolulu: University of Hawai'i Press.

Mitchell, Timothy. 1990. "Everyday Metaphors of Power." *Theory and Society* 19 (5): 545–77.

Mitchell, W.J.T. 1994. *Landscape and Power.* Chicago: University of Chicago Press.

Mizrachi, Nissim, and Hanna Herzog. 2012. "Participatory Destigmatization Strategies among Palestinian Citizens, Ethiopian Jews and Mizrahi Jews in Israel." *Ethnic and Racial Studies* 35 (3): 418–35.

Modan, Gabriella Gahlia. 2007. *Turf Wars: Discourse, Diversity, and the Politics of Place.* Malden: Blackwell.

Mollison, Bill. 1987. *Permaculture Two: Practical Design for Town and Country in Permanent Agriculture*. Tyalgum: Tagari.

Mollison, Bill, and David Holmgren. 1987. *Permaculture One: A Perennial Agriculture for Human Settlements*. Tyalgum: Tagari.

Moore, Donald S. 2005. *Suffering for Territory: Race, Place, and Power in Zimbabwe*. Durham: Duke University Press.

Moore, Donald S., Jake Kosek, and Anand Pandian, eds. 2003. *Race, Nature, and the Politics of Difference*. Durham: Duke University Press.

Morris, Benny. 1999. *Righteous Victims: A History of the Zionist-Arab Conflict, 1881–1999*. New York: Knopf.

Moskowitz, Yaakov. 2007. Interview with Yaakov Moskowitz. Recording 1029, File 1119-16. David Tuviyahu Archives of the Negev.

Mosse, George L. 1985. *Nationalism and Sexuality: Respectability and Abnormal Sexuality in Modern Europe*. New York: H. Fertig.

Nadasdy, Paul. 2002. "'Property' and Aboriginal Land Claims in the Canadian Subarctic: Some Theoretical Considerations." *American Anthropologist* 104 (1): 247–61.

———. 2003. *Hunters and Bureaucrats: Power, Knowledge, and Aboriginal-State Relations in the Southwest Yukon*. Vancouver: UBC Press.

Negev Coexistence Forum. 2006. *The Arab-Bedouins of the Naqab-Negev Desert in Israel*. UN Committee on the Elimination of Racial Discrimination (CERD). http://www.internal-displacement.org.

Nelson, Cynthia, ed. 1973. *Desert and the Sown: Nomads in the Wider Society*. Berkeley: University of California Institute of International Studies.

Nonini, Donald M. 2013. "The Local-Food Movement and the Anthropology of Global Systems." *American Ethnologist* 40 (2): 267–75.

Nordstrom, Carolyn. 1997. *A Different Kind of War Story*. Philadelphia: University of Pennsylvania Press.

Ogden, Laura A. 2011. *Swamplife: People, Gators, and Mangroves Entangled in the Everglades*. Minneapolis: University of Minnesota Press.

Olsvig-Whittaker, Linda, Eliezer Frankenberg, Avi Perevolotsky, and Eugene D. Unga. 2006. "Grazing, Overgrazing and Conservation: Changing Concepts and Practices in the Negev Rangelands." *Science et Changements planétaires/Sécheresse* 17 (1): 195–99.

Ong, Aihwa. 2003. *Buddha Is Hiding: Refugees, Citizenship, the New America*. Berkeley: University of California Press.

———. 2006. *Neoliberalism as Exception: Mutations in Citizenship and Sovereignty*. Durham: Duke University Press.

Oren, Amiram. 2007. "Shadow Lands: The Use of Land Resources for Security Needs in Israel." *Israel Studies* 12 (1): 149–70.

Orenstein, Daniel E., Alon Tal, and Char Miller, eds. 2013. *Between Ruin and Restoration: An Environmental History of Israel*. Pittsburgh: University of Pittsburgh Press.

Pappé, Ilan. 2004. *A History of Modern Palestine?: One Land, Two Peoples*. Cambridge: Cambridge University Press.

Parizot, Cédric. 2001. "Gaza, Beer Sheva, Dhahriyya: Another Approach to the Negev

Bedouins in the Israeli-Palestinian Space." *Bulletin du Centre de Recherche Français de Jérusalem* 9: 98–110.

———. 2009. "Hardening Closure, Securing Disorder: Israeli Closure Policies and the Informal Border Economy between the West Bank and the Northern Negev (2000–2006)." In *Mediterranean Frontiers: Borders, Conflict and Memory in a Transnational World*, edited by Dimitar Bechev and Kalypso Nicholaidis, 177–94. London: Tauris.

Partridge, Damani James. 2008. "We Were Dancing in the Club, Not on the Berlin Wall: Black Bodies, Street Bureaucrats, and Exclusionary Incorporation into the New Europe." *Cultural Anthropology* 23 (4): 660–87.

Peled, Yoav. 2011. "The Viability of Ethnic Democracy: Jewish Citizens in Inter-War Poland and Palestinian Citizens in Israel." *Ethnic and Racial Studies* 34 (1): 83–102.

Peteet, Julie M. 1991. *Gender in Crisis: Women and the Palestinian Resistance Movement.* New York: Columbia University Press.

Peters, Michael, Shane Fudge, and Tim Jackson, eds. 2010. *Low Carbon Communities: Imaginative Approaches to Combating Climate Change Locally.* Cheltenham: Edward Elgar.

Peutz, Nathalie. 2011. "Bedouin 'Abjection': World Heritage, Worldliness, and Worthiness at the Margins of Arabia." *American Ethnologist* 38 (2): 338–60.

Piterberg, Gabriel. 2008. *The Returns of Zionism: Myths, Politics and Scholarship in Israel.* London: Verso.

Portnov, B. A., and U. N. Safriel. 2004. "Combating Desertification in the Negev: Dryland Agriculture vs. Dryland Urbanization." *Journal of Arid Environments* 56 (4): 659–80.

Povinelli, Elizabeth A. 2002. *The Cunning of Recognition: Indigenous Alterities and the Making of Australian Multiculturalism.* Durham: Duke University Press.

Qupty, Maha. 2004. *Bedouin Unrecognized Villages of the Negev.* Habitat International Coalition. http://www.hic-net.org.

Rabinow, Paul. 2002. "Midst Anthropology's Problems." *Cultural Anthropology* 17 (2): 135–49.

Rabinowitz, Dan. 1997. *Overlooking Nazareth: The Ethnography of Exclusion in Galilee.* Cambridge: Cambridge University Press.

———. 2001. "The Palestinian Citizens of Israel, the Concept of Trapped Minority and the Discourse of Transnationalism in Anthropology." *Ethnic and Racial Studies* 24 (1): 64.

———. 2002a. "Borderline Collective Consciousness: Israeli Identity, 'Arabness' and the Green Line." *Palestine-Israel Journal of Politics, Economics, and Culture* 8 (4): 38.

———. 2002b. "Oriental Othering and National Identity: A Review of Early Israeli Anthropological Studies of Palestinians." *Identities: Global Studies in Culture and Power* 9 (3): 305–25.

Rabinowitz, Dan, and Khawla Abu Baker. 2005. *Coffins on Our Shoulders: The Experience of the Palestinian Citizens of Israel.* Berkeley: University of California Press.

Ramos, Alcida Rita. 1998. *Indigenism: Ethnic Politics in Brazil.* Madison: University of Wisconsin Press.

Robbins, Paul. 2012. *Political Ecology: A Critical Introduction,* 2nd ed. Chichester: Wiley-Blackwell.

Rome, Adam. 2008. "Nature Wars, Culture Wars: Immigration and Environmental Reform in the Progressive Era." *Environmental History* 13 (3): 432–53.

Rosaldo, Renato. 1988. "Ideology, Place, and People without Culture." *Cultural Anthropology* 3 (1): 77–87.

Rose, Carol M. 1994. *Property and Persuasion: Essays on the History, Theory, and Rhetoric of Ownership.* Boulder: Westview Press.

Rosen, Steven A. 2008. "Desert Pastoral Nomadism in the Longue Duree: A Case Study from the Negev and the Southern Levantine Deserts." In *The Archaeology of Mobility*, edited by Hans Barnard and Willeke Wendrich, 115–40. Los Angeles: Cotsen Institute of Archaeology, University of California.

Rosen-Zvi, Issachar. 2004. *Taking Space Seriously: Law, Space, and Society in Contemporary Israel.* Burlington: Ashgate.

Rowe, Alan G. 1999. "The Exploitation of an Arid Landscape by a Pastoral Society: The Contemporary Eastern Badia of Jordan." *Applied Geography* 19: 345–61.

Rubin-Dorsky, Jeffrey, and Shelley Fisher Fishkin, eds. 1996. *People of the Book: Thirty Scholars Reflect on Their Jewish Identity.* Madison: University of Wisconsin Press.

Sa'di, Ahmad H., and Lila Abu-Lughod. 2007. *Nakba: Palestine, 1948, and the Claims of Memory.* New York: Columbia University Press.

Said, Edward W. 1978. *Orientalism.* New York: Vintage Books.

Salzman, Philip Carl. 1980. "Processes of Sedentarization among the Nomads of Baluchistan." In *When Nomads Settle: Processes of Sedentarization as Adaptation and Response*, edited by Philip Carl Salzman and Edward Sadala, 95–110. New York: Bergin.

Sandercock, Leonie. 1999. "Translations: From Insurgent Planning to Radical Planning Discourses." *Plurimondi* 1: 37–46.

Sanders, Edmund. 2010. "Israel Razes Homes in Bedouin Village." *Los Angeles Times*, July 28. www.latimes.com.

Schechla, Joseph. 2001. "The Invisible People Come to Light: Israel's 'Internally Displaced' and the 'Unrecognized Villages.'" *Journal of Palestine Studies* 31 (1): 20–31.

Scheper-Hughes, Nancy. 1993. *Death without Weeping: The Violence of Everyday Life in Brazil.* Berkeley: University of California Press.

Schmink, Marianne C., and Charles H. Wood. 1992. *Contested Frontiers in Amazonia.* New York: Columbia University Press.

Schoenfeld, Stuart. 2005. "Palestinian and Israeli Environmental Narratives: Proceedings of a Conference Held in Association with the Middle East Environmental Futures Project." Toronto: Centre for International and Security Studies, York University.

Schwartz, Katrina. 2006. *Nature and National Identity after Communism: Globalizing the Ethnoscape.* Pittsburgh: University of Pittsburgh Press.

Schwartz, Moshe, Susan H. Lees, and Gideon M. Kressel, eds. 1995. *Rural Cooperatives in Socialist Utopia: Thirty Years of Moshav Development in Israel.* Westport: Praeger.

Scoones, I. 1999. "New Ecology and the Social Sciences: What Prospects for a Fruitful Engagement?" *Annual Review of Anthropology* 28: 479–507.

Scott, James C. 1985. *Weapons of the Weak: Everyday Forms of Peasant Resistance.* New Haven: Yale University Press.

————. 1998. *Seeing Like a State: How Certain Schemes to Improve the Human Condition Have Failed.* New Haven: Yale University Press.

Segal, J. B. 1993. *A History of the Jews of Cochin.* London: Vallentine Mitchell.

Segev, Tom. 2000. *One Palestine, Complete: Jews and Arabs under the British Mandate.* London: Little Brown.

Selwyn, Tom. 1995. "Landscapes of Liberation and Imprisonment: Towards an Anthropology of the Israeli Landscape." In *The Anthropology of Landscape: Perspectives on Place and Space,* edited by Eric Hirsch and Michael O'Hanlon. New York: Clarendon Press.

Sened, Yonat, and Alexander Sened. 2009. "The First Days of Kibbutz Revivim." In *The Desert Experience in Israel: Communities, Arts, Science, and Education in the Negev,* edited by A. Paul Hare and Gideon M. Kressel, 13–18. Lanham: University Press of America.

Shafir, Gershon. 1996. *Land, Labor, and the Origins of the Israeli-Palestinian Conflict, 1882–1914.* Cambridge: Cambridge University Press.

Shafir, Gershon, and Yoav Peled. 2002. *Being Israeli: The Dynamics of Multiple Citizenship.* Cambridge: Cambridge University Press.

Shahar, Eitan. 2008. "A Prayer: Gates of Will—From Cochin, India toward Moshav Nevatim, Southern of Israel: The Story of Adaptation from a Multigenerational Perspective." Doctoral diss., Ben Gurion University.

Shamir, Ronen. 1996. "Suspended in Space: Bedouins under the Law of Israel." *Law and Society Review* 30 (2): 231–57.

Shapira, Anita. 2012. *Israel: A History.* Lebanon: Brandeis.

Sheffer, Gabriel, and Oren Barak, eds. 2010. *Militarism and Israeli Society.* Bloomington: Indiana University Press.

Shepher, Israel. 1983. *The Kibbutz: An Anthropological Study.* Norwood: Norwood Editions.

Sherman, Neal, and Moshe Schwartz. 1995. "The Effects of Public Financial Assistance on the Management of Moshav Economic Affairs." In *Rural Cooperatives in Socialist Utopia: Thirty Years of Moshav Development in Israel,* edited by Moshe Schwartz, Susan H. Lees, and Gideon M. Kressel, 31–54. Westport: Praeger.

Shlaim, Avi. 1995. "The Debate about 1948." *International Journal of Middle East Studies* 27 (3): 287–304.

————. 2000. *The Iron Wall: Israel and the Arab World.* New York: W.W. Norton.

Shohat, Ella. 1988. "Sephardim in Israel: Zionism from the Standpoint of Its Jewish Victims." *Social Text,* no. 19/20: 1–35.

————. 1999. "The Invention of the Mizrahim." *Journal of Palestine Studies* 29 (1): 5–20.

Shryock, Andrew. 1997. *Nationalism and the Genealogical Imagination: Oral History and Textual Authority in Tribal Jordan.* Berkeley: University of California Press.

————. 2004a. "In the Double Remoteness of Arab Detroit: Reflections on Ethnography, Culture Work, and the Intimate Disciplines of Americanization." In *Off Stage/ On Display,* edited by Andrew Shryock, 279–314. Stanford: Stanford University Press.

————. 2004b. "The New Jordanian Hospitality: House, Host, and Guest in the Culture of Public Display." *Comparative Studies in Society and History* 46 (1): 35–62.

Shuval, Hillel. 2013. "The Agricultural Roots of Israel's Water Crisis." In *Between Ruin and Restoration: An Environmental History of Israel*, edited by Daniel E. Orenstein, Alon Tal, and Char Miller, 129–45. Pittsburgh: University of Pittsburgh Press.

Silverstein, Michael, and Greg Urban. 1996. *Natural Histories of Discourse*. Chicago: University of Chicago Press.

Silverstein, Paul A. 2013. "The Pitfalls of Transnational Consciousness: Amazigh Activism as a Scalar Dilemma." *Journal of North African Studies* 18 (5): 768–78.

Slyomovics, Susan. 1998. *The Object of Memory: Arab and Jew Narrate the Palestinian Village*. Philadelphia: University of Pennsylvania Press.

Smith, A. D. 1987. *The Ethnic Origins of Nations*. Oxford: B. Blackwell.

Smooha, Sammy. 2002. "The Model of Ethnic Democracy: Israel as a Jewish and Democratic State." *Nations and Nationalism* 8 (4): 475–503.

———. 2004. "Arab-Jewish Relations in Israel as a Deeply Divided Society." In *Israeli Identity in Transition*, edited by Anita Shapira, 31–67. New York: Praeger.

Stein, Rebecca. 2008. *Itineraries in Conflict*. Durham: Duke University Press.

Sternhell, Zeev. 1998. *The Founding Myths of Israel: Nationalism, Socialism, and the Making of the Jewish State*. Princeton: Princeton University Press.

Stoller, Paul. 1982. "Signs in the Social Order: Riding a Songhay Bush Taxi." *American Ethnologist* 9 (4): 750–62.

Strathern, Marilyn. 1996. "Cutting the Network." *Journal of the Royal Anthropological Institute* 2 (3): 517–35.

Sufian, Sandra M., and Mark LeVine, eds. 2007. *Reapproaching Borders: New Perspectives on the Study of Israel-Palestine*. Lanham: Rowman & Littlefield.

Svirsky, Marcelo. 2013. *Arab-Jewish Activism in Israel-Palestine*. Ashgate.

Swedenburg, Ted. 1990. "The Palestinian Peasant as National Signifier." *Anthropological Quarterly* 63: 18–30.

———. 1995a. *Memories of Revolt: The 1936–1939 Rebellion and the Palestinian National Past*. Minneapolis: University of Minnesota Press.

———. 1995b. "With Genet in the Palestinian Field." In *Fieldwork under Fire: Contemporary Studies of Violence and Survival*, edited by Carolyn Nordstrom and Antonius C.G.M. Robben, 24–40. Berkeley: University of California Press.

Sweet, Elizabeth L. 2010. "Identity, Culture, Land, and Language: Stories of Insurgent Planning in the Republic of Buryatia, Russia." *Journal of Planning Education and Research* 30 (2): 198–209.

Swirski, Shlomo, and Yael Hasson. 2006. *Invisible Citizens*. Beersheva: Center for Bedouin Studies and Development.

Swyngedouw, Erik, and Nikolas C Heynen. 2003. "Urban Political Ecology, Justice and the Politics of Scale." *Antipode* 35 (5): 898–918.

Sylvain, Renée. 2005. "'Land, Water, and Truth': San Identity and Global Indigenism." In *Social Movements: An Anthropological Reader*, edited by June C. Nash, 216–33. Malden: Wiley-Blackwell.

Szepesi, Stefan. 2012. *Walking Palestine: 25 Journeys into the West Bank*. Northampton: Interlink.

Tal, Alon. 2002. *Pollution in a Promised Land: An Environmental History of Israel.* Berkeley: University of California Press.

Talmon, Yonina. 1972. *Family and Community in the Kibbutz.* Cambridge: Harvard University Press.

Tarrow, Sidney G. 1998. *Power in Movement: Social Movements and Contentious Politics.* Cambridge: Cambridge University Press.

Taylor, Charles, and Amy Gutmann. 1992. *Multiculturalism and the Politics of Recognition: An Essay.* Princeton: Princeton University Press.

Teschner, Naʿama. 2007. "Planning the Development of the Southern Region of Israel: Ideological, Political and Environmental Consequences." MA thesis. Institute of Desert Research, Ben-Gurion University, Sde Boker.

Teschner, Naʿama, Yaakov Garb, and Alon Tal. 2010. "The Environment in Successive Regional Development Plans for Israel's Periphery." *International Planning Studies* 15 (2): 79–97.

Tessler, Mark A. 1994. *A History of the Israeli-Palestinian Conflict.* Bloomington: Indiana University Press.

Ticktin, Miriam. 2006. "Where Ethics and Politics Meet: The Violence of Humanitarianism in France." *American Ethnologist* 33 (1): 33–49.

Trouillot, Michel-Rolph. 1991. "Anthropology and the Savage Slot: The Poetics and Politics of Otherness." In *Recapturing Anthropology: Working in the Present,* edited by Richard Gabriel Fox, 17–44. Santa Fe: School of American Research Press.

Tsing, Anna Lowenhaupt. 2005. *Friction: An Ethnography of Global Connection.* Princeton: Princeton University Press.

Turner, Victor Witter. 1957. *Schism and Continuity in an African Society: A Study of Ndembu Village Life.* Manchester: Manchester University Press.

Tzfadia, Erez. 2000. "Immigrant Dispersal in Settler Societies: Mizrahim and Russians in Israel under the Press of Hegemony." *Geography Research Forum* 20: 52–69.

———. 2008a. "Abusing Multiculturalism: The Politics of Recognition and Land Allocation in Israel." *Environment and Planning D: Society and Space* 26 (6): 1115–30.

———. 2008b. "In the Name of Zionism." *Haaretz,* September 19. www.haaretz.com.

Tzfadia, Erez, and Haim Yacobi. 2011. *Rethinking Israeli Space: Periphery and Identity.* New York: Routledge.

Verdery, K. 2003. *The Vanishing Hectare: Property and Value in Postsocialist Transylvania.* Ithaca: Cornell University Press.

Vila, Pablo, ed. 2003. *Ethnography at the Border.* Minneapolis: University of Minnesota Press.

Waldoks, Ehud Zion. 2008. "Harnessing the Sun, Empowering Beduin Equality." *Jerusalem Post,* March 18. Online edition. www.jpost.com.

Weil, Shalva. 1986. "An Overview of Research on the Bene Israel." In *Jews in India,* edited by Thomas A. Timberg, 12–27. New Delhi: Vikas.

Weingrod, Alex. 1966. *Reluctant Pioneers: Village Development in Israel.* Ithaca: Cornell University Press.

West, Paige. 2006. *Conservation Is Our Government Now: The Politics of Ecology in Papua New Guinea.* Durham: Duke University Press.

Wilk, Richard R., ed. 2006. *Fast Food/Slow Food: The Cultural Economy of the Global Food System*. Lanham: AltaMira Press.

Willen, Sarah S. 2007. "Toward a Critical Phenomenology of 'Illegality': State Power, Criminalization, and Abjectivity among Undocumented Migrant Workers in Tel Aviv, Israel." *International Migration* 45 (3): 8–38.

———. 2012. "How Is Health-Related 'Deservingness' Reckoned? Perspectives from Unauthorized Im/migrants in Tel Aviv." *Social Science and Medicine* 74 (6): 812–21.

Williams, Nancy M. 1986. *The Yolngu and Their Land: A System of Land Tenure and the Fight for Its Recognition*. Stanford: Stanford University Press.

Williams, Raymond. 1985. *Keywords: A Vocabulary of Culture and Society*. New York: Oxford University Press.

Yahav, Nir. 2008. "Bedouin Child's Illness Connected House to Electricity." *Walla News*, March 20. http://news.walla.co.il.

Yahel, Havatzelet. 2006. "Land Disputes between the Negev Bedouin and Israel." *Israel Studies* 11 (2): 1–22.

Yiftachel, Oren. 2000. "'Ethnocracy' and Its Discontents: Minorities, Protests, and the Israeli Polity." *Critical Inquiry* 26 (4): 725–56.

———. 2006. *Ethnocracy: Land and Identity Politics in Israel/Palestine*. Philadelphia: University of Pennsylvania Press.

———. 2009a. "Critical Theory and 'Gray Space': Mobilization of the Colonized." *City* 13: 246–63.

———. 2009b. "Theoretical Notes on 'Gray Cities': The Coming of Urban Apartheid?" *Planning Theory* 8 (1): 88–100.

Yiftachel, Oren, and Avinoam Meir. 1998. *Ethnic Frontiers and Peripheries: Landscapes of Development and Inequality in Israel*. Boulder: Westview Press.

Yonah, Yossi, Ismael Abu-Saad, and Avi Kaplan. 2004. "De-Arabization of the Bedouin: A Study of Inevitable Failure." In *Israelis in Conflict: Hegemonies, Identities and Challenges*, edited by Adriana Kemp, David Newman, Uri Ram, and Oren Yiftachel, 65–80. Brighton: Sussex Academic Press.

Zakim, Eric. 2006. *To Build and Be Built: Landscape, Literature, and the Construction of Zionist Identity*. Philadelphia: University of Pennsylvania Press.

Zeiderman, Austin. 2013. "Living Dangerously: Biopolitics and Urban Citizenship in Bogotá, Colombia." *American Ethnologist* 40 (1): 71–87.

Zenker, Olaf. 2011. "Autochthony, Ethnicity, Indigeneity and Nationalism: Time-Honouring and State-Oriented Modes of Rooting Individual-Territory-Group Triads in a Globalizing World." *Critique of Anthropology* 31 (1): 63–81.

Zertal, Idith. 2005. *Israel's Holocaust and the Politics of Nationhood*. Cambridge: Cambridge University Press.

Zerubavel, Yael. 1995. *Recovered Roots: Collective Memory and the Making of Israeli National Tradition*. Chicago: University of Chicago Press.

———. 1996. "The Forest as a National Icon: Literature, Politics, and the Archaeology of Memory." *Israel Studies* 1 (1): 60–99.

———. 2008a. "Desert and Settlement: Space Metaphors and Symbolic Landscapes in the Yishuv and Early Israeli Culture." In *Jewish Topographies: Visions of Space, Tradi-*

tions of Place, edited by Julia Brauch, Anna Lipphardt, and Alexandra Nocke, 201–22. Burlington: Ashgate.

———. 2008b. "Memory, the Rebirth of the Native, and the 'Hebrew Bedouin' Identity." *Social Research* 75 (1): 315–52.

Zubrzycki, Genevieve. 2001. "'We, the Polish Nation': Ethnic and Civic Visions of Nationhood in Post-Communist Constitutional Debates." *Theory and Society* 30 (5): 629.

Zusman, Pinhas. 1988. *Individual Behavior and Social Choice in a Cooperative Settlement: The Theory and Practice of the Israeli Moshav.* Jerusalem: Magnes Press.

Index